Neuroscience and the Economics of Decision Making

In the last two decades there has been a flourishing of research carried out jointly by economists, psychologists, and neuroscientists. This meltdown of barriers between competences has led toward original approaches to investigate the mental and cognitive mechanisms involved in the way the economic agent collects, processes, and uses information to make choices. This research field involves a new kind of scientist, trained in different disciplines, familiar in managing experimental data, and with the mathematical foundations of decision-making. The ultimate goal of this research is to open the black-box to understand the behavioral and neural processes through which humans set preferences and translate these behaviors into optimal choices. This volume intends to bring forward new results and fresh insights into this matter.

The topics cover a broad field dealing with the mechanisms of decision-making, moral judgments, social preferences, and the role of emotions and learning in decision-making. The collected chapters focus on issues not only specific to neuroscience and economics but also to psychology, cognitive philosophy, sociology, and marketing science. In this respect, the book deals with the interdisciplinary aspects of decision-making. Finally, all the contributions make direct or indirect explicit reference to experimental results, and this is probably the major trait d'union of the whole book.

This volume will be of great interest to students and researchers in the fields of political economy, experimental economics, and behavioral economics.

Alessandro Innocenti is Associate Professor of Economics of the Department of Political Economy, Finance and Development (DEPFID) at the University of Siena. He is also a Researcher at the Experimental Economics Laboratory LabSi, of the Research Laboratory for Behavioral Finance (BEFINLAB) and Director of the Interuniversity Center for Experimental Economics.

Angela Sirigu is currently Director of Research at the CNRS Institute des Sciences Cognitives in Lyon, France.

Routledge advances in experimental and computable economics

Edited by K. Vela Velupillai and Stefano Zambelli

University of Trento, Italy

1 **The Economics of Search**
Brian and John McCall

2 **Classical Econophysics**
Paul Cockshott, Allin F. Cottrell, Gregory John Michaelson, Ian P. Wright, and Victor Yakovenko

3 **The Social Epistemology of Experimental Economics**
Ana Cordeiro dos Santos

4 **Computable Foundations for Economics**
K. Vela Velupillai

5 **Neuroscience and the Economics of Decision Making**
Edited by Alessandro Innocenti and Angela Sirigu

Other books in the series include:

Economics Lab
An intensive course in experimental economics
Alessandra Cassar and Dan Friedman

Neuroscience and the Economics of Decision Making

Edited by Alessandro Innocenti and Angela Sirigu

Routledge
Taylor & Francis Group
LONDON AND NEW YORK

First published 2012
by Routledge
2 Park Square, Milton Park, Abingdon, Oxon OX14 4RN

Simultaneously published in the USA and Canada
by Routledge
605 Third Avenue, New York, NY 10017

Routledge is an imprint of the Taylor & Francis Group, an informa business

British Library Cataloguing in Publication Data
A catalogue record for this book is available from the British Library

Library of Congress Cataloging in Publication Data
A catalog record has been requested for this book

ISBN 13: 978-0-415-67843-8 (hbk)
ISBN 13: 978-0-203-12260-0 (ebk)

Typeset in Times New Roman
by Wearset Ltd, Boldon, Tyne and Wear

Contents

Figures

Tables

Contributors

Michela Balconi is Researcher and Assistant Professor of Neuropsychology and Cognitive Neurosciences at the Catholic University of Milan.

Francesca Benuzzi is Research Associate at the University of Modena and Reggio Emilia.

Deborah N. Black is Assistant Professor of Neurology and Psychiatry at The Health Center, Plainfield.

Jordi Brandts is Research Professor at the Department of Business Economics at the Universitat Autònoma de Barcelona and the Instituto de Análisis Económico (CSIC), Barcelona.

Seger M. Breugelmans is Assistant Professor of Social Psychology in the Department of Psychology at Tilburg University.

Alan Brothers is Senior Research Scientist at the Pacific Northwest National Laboratory.

Nicola Canessa is Assistant Professor at the Vita-Salute San Raffaele University, Milan.

Stefano F. Cappa is Professor of Cognitive Neuroscience at the Vita-Salute San Raffaele University, Milan.

Simona Conti is Research Associate at the University of Siena.

Chiara Crespi is Doctoral Student at the Vita-Salute San Raffaele University, Milan.

Angela Dalton is Staff Scientist at the Pacific Northwest National Laboratory.

Antonio Dell'Ava is Research Associate at the University of Siena.

Nicola Dimitri is Professor of Economics at the University of Siena.

Stefano Di Piazza is Research Associate at the University of Siena.

Valeria Faralla is Research Associate at the University of Siena.

Francesco Fargnoli is Neuroscience Research Associate at EVALab, University of Siena.

Susann Fiedler is Research Associate at the Max Planck Institute for Research on Collective Goods, Bonn.

Orsola Garofalo is Research Associate at the Universitat Autònoma de Barcelona.

Andreas Glöckner is Associate Professor at the Max Planck Institute for Research on Collective Goods, Bonn.

Georgios Halkias is Research Associate at the Athens University of Economics and Business.

Ilona E. de Hooge is Assistant Professor at the Department of Marketing Management at Rotterdam School of Management, Erasmus University.

Alessandro Innocenti is Associate Professor of Economics at the University of Siena.

D. William Jolley is Associate Professor, School of Business, Norwich University.

Flora Kokkinaki is Assistant Professor at the Athens University of Economics and Business.

Christoph Lumer is Associate Professor of Moral Philosophy at the University of Siena.

Paolo Nichelli is Professor of Neurology at the University of Modena and Reggio Emilia.

Andreas Nicklisch is Assistant Professor for Economics at the University of Hamburg.

Giuseppe Pantaleo is Associate Professor of Social Psychology at the Vita-Salute San Raffaele University, Milan.

Pietro Piu is Neuroscience Research Associate at the University of Siena.

Antonio Rizzo is Professor of Psychology at the University of Siena.

Alessandra Rufa is Assistant Professor of Neurosciences at EVALab, University of Siena.

Angela Sirigu is Director of Research and Director of the Neuropsychology group, Institute of Cognitive Science (ISC), Centre National de la Recherche Scientifique (CNRS), Lyon, France.

Andrea Terenzi is Research Associate at the Laboratory of Cognitive Psychology, Department of Psychology, Catholic University of Milan.

Letizia Vaccarella is Research Associate at the University of Siena.

Stephen Walsh is a Staff Scientist at Pacific Northwest National Laboratory.

Amanda White is a Staff Scientist at Pacific Northwest National Laboratory.

Paul Whitney is a Staff Scientist and Associate Division Director for Computational Mathematics at Pacific Northwest National Laboratory.

Marcel Zeelenberg is Professor of Economic Psychology, the Academic Director of Tiber, and the Head of Department of Social Psychology at Tilburg University.

Foreword

Decision-making is one of the most interdisciplinary research areas in the human and social sciences domain, employing methods and techniques from psychology, economics, philosophy, cognitive sciences and computer science. The process leading from the input (information search) to the output (final choice) involves a variety of mechanisms that need to be investigated from multiple perspectives. Researchers from very different fields are therefore asked to share concepts and methods in order to uncover and explain how individuals make complex decisions.

Among them, economists occupy a privileged position. Since the 1950s, economics has adopted a compact and self-referential theoretical framework known as rational choice theory. This view is characterized by the assumption that the decision-maker, the economic agent, follows rules of behavior that are mathematically defined and logically coherent in relation to a series of pre-determined axioms. If it is generally accepted that this paradigm represents the normative reference point of the analysis of decision-making, its validity as descriptive and predictive model is quite controversial. It is exactly this issue that motivated the foundations of behavioral economics in the 1970s. One of its leading contributors, Colin Camerer, describes the raison d'être of behavioral economics as follows:

> Because economics is the science of how resources are allocated by individuals and by collective institutions like firms and markets, the psychology of individual behavior should underlie and inform economics, much as physics informs chemistry; archaeology informs anthropology; or neuroscience informs cognitive psychology. However, economists routinely – and proudly – use models that are grossly inconsistent with findings from psychology. A recent approach, "behavioral economics," seeks to use psychology to inform economics, while maintaining the emphases on mathematical structure and explanation of field data that distinguish economics from other social sciences
>
> (Camerer 1999: 10575)

Behavioral economics is intended as a reunification of psychology and economics that would preserve the distinctive emphasis on formal models and descriptive statistics characterizing mainstream economics. According to Camerer (1999), the main object of behavioral economics is to deal with two key issues: (1) the inconsistency of the predictions of most economic models with experimental results; and (2) the rigidity of mathematical structure of those same models joined with the indefiniteness of the theoretical implications of the statistical data collected in the field.

Actually, the novelty of behavioral economics is the extensive use of experimental results from the laboratory and the field, which has progressively removed the division between formalized and empirical arguments characterizing mathematical economics since its inception. This advance has allowed the investigation of the behavioral and neural mechanisms of rational choice by abandoning the assumption of perfect rationality pervading mainstream economics.

This turning point has had a great impact on the methodological status of economics. In the last two decades research carried out jointly by economists, psychologists and neuroscientists has flourished, focusing the analysis on mental and cognitive processes involved in economic choices and decisions. This research field involves a new generation of scientists, trained in different disciplines and at ease working with experimental data and mathematical foundations of decision-making. The ultimate aim of this stream of research is to open the "black box" that contains the processes involved in the formation of preferences and choices.

This volume intends to bring forward fresh insights into this topic. It covers a wide spectrum of issues in decision-making, ranging from moral judgments to social preferences to the role of emotions and learning in decision-making, all of which are brought together in a unified framework. The chapters focus on issues not only specific to neurosciences and economics, but also to psychology, cognitive philosophy, sociology, and marketing science. In this respect, the book is an attempt to give the reader the interdisciplinary facets of decision-making studies. Finally, all the works present and/or discuss experimental results; this is probably the major *trait d'union* of the book.

The chapters, which were presented at the Labsi Conference on Neuroscience and Decision-Making held in Siena in September 2010, approach the topic of neuroscience and economic decision-making from various angles and are collected in five parts. The three chapters included in the first part (Evidence on the neuroscientific foundations of decision-making) deal with different aspects of the neuroscience of decision-making. Two of them are laboratory studies using eye-tracking technology to investigate information search. The analysis of gaze direction can indeed provide useful evidence to detect how the processes leading to decisions differentiate across individuals. Reactions to visual stimuli are mostly automatic and unconscious and their study gives important insights in how people collect and process information. For example, according to Evans' (2006) heuristic-analytic theory, heuristic processes would select the aspect of the task on which gaze direction is immediately focused and analytic processes would derive inferences from the heuristically formed representation through subsequent visual inspection. This dual account of visual attention orienting may explain the emergence of cognitive biases whenever relevant information is neglected at the heuristic stage. The chapter by Susann Fiedler, Andreas Glöckner, and Andreas Nicklisch focuses on the concept of "social value orientation," which is an indicator of the propensity to cooperate in a public-good game. Their experiment offers a clear example of how gaze direction can be used to investigate all the processes leading from information acquisition to choices. The main finding is that pro-social choices are positively correlated with the number and the duration of fixations of other players' payoffs, allowing the inference that mental processes leading to cooperation take relatively more time. Another eye-tracking study, authored by Pietro Piu, Francesco Fargnoli, and Alessandra Rufa, provides evidence in support of the dual process theory by investigating the economic model of information cascade. Their results support the hypothesis that automatic detection, as inferred from gaze direction, depends on cognitive biases. The heuristic and automatic functioning of the so-called System 1 orients attention so as to confirm rather than to eventually correct cognitive biases, while the controlled search attributable to System 2 does not necessarily modify the same biases.

The chapter written by Chiara Crespi, Giuseppe Pantaleo, Stefano F. Cappa, and Nicola Canessa offers a critical survey of the neuroscientific research on the relations between emotions and counterfactual thinking. According to decision affect theory, emotional reactions to the same outcome depend on alternative and counterfactual outcomes. For this reason, the analysis of regret plays an important role in cognitive sciences, allowing the inference that individuals anticipate emotions and are able to assess the trade-off between purely material interests and the desire to avoid future regrets. The discussion of the literature in this chapter shows clearly how insights in economic decision-making depend on combining different theoretical approaches and laboratory methods.

The chapter by Marcel Zeelenberg, Seger M. Breugelmans, and Ilona E. de Hooge opens the second part (Emotions and morality in decision-making). The authors review the literature on the effects of emotions on decision-making and discuss them in relation to the principles of behavioral economics. They conclude that emotions can be interpreted as functional programs connecting personal inclinations to individual goals. The cognitive processes leading to moral choices are experimentally investigated by Michela Balconi and Andrea Terenzi. Their analysis also aims to explain the role of automatic and unconscious processes in moral judgments. The evidence provided by adopting neuropsychological measures (event-related potentials – ERPs) and autonomic correlates confirms that not only emotions play a significant role in moral choices, but that these choices are significantly related to the activation of neural circuits which unconsciously incorporate emotional reactions in judgment. A thought-provoking philosophical digression on the topic of morality and emotional content is offered by Christoph Lumer, who discusses the theory of emotion-induced desires. He argues that the contrast between the rational theory of decision-making can be reconciled by taking into account that these desires embody the values inherent in specific satisfying emotions coupled with the present emotion.

The third part (Learning and risk attitude in decision-making) is opened by a chapter on the neuroscientific analysis of the transition from habit to addiction in gambling behavior. Pathological gambling has been the subject of extensive research for elucidating the mechanism underlying the dopaminergic reward system, which is also responsible for impulsivity proneness. By relying on an impressive amount of literature, which also includes recent findings on online gambling, William Jolley and Deborah N. Black provide experimental evidence on the Iowa Gambling Task, showing that impulsivity is a discriminating variable in developing addiction.

The experiment presented by Valeria Faralla, Francesca Benuzzi, Paolo Nichelli, and Nicola Dimitri deals with the sign effect or gain–loss asymmetry, which is a bias in intertemporal choice according to which losses are more aversive than equal gains are pleasant. In this way, the authors provide further evidence regarding the existence of a multiple-system model of intertemporal choice at a neurobiological level. Time preference is seen as the result of competition for behavioral control between limbic and paralimbic structures (medial prefrontal cortex, anterior and posterior cingulate cortex) and higher cognitive systems (lateral and dorsolateral prefrontal cortex).

The chapter of Georgios Halkias and Flora Kokkinaki, included in the fourth part (Probability and judgment in decision-making), proposes a study of marketing communication based on cognitive psychology. They focus on brand information that is incongruent with the associations tied to a specific product. This typology of messages has been considered more attractive of consumers' attention because it would increase their cognitive arousal. This perspective can provide insight in how confirmation or disconfirmation of expectations influences individual responses. Surprisingly enough, their empirical study shows that moderately incongruent brand communication performs better in terms of consumers' persuasion.

Computational modeling is an important tool in the analysis of decision-making. It allows describing and interpreting the functional organization of cognitive processes by using symbols and algorithms to simulate abstract mental functions. Angela Dalton, Alan Brothers, Stephen Walsh, Amanda White, and Paul Whitney discuss virtues and vices of four expert elicitation methods and conduct an evaluation study to assess their methodological and logistical advantages. Their work sets up a useful framework for improving organizational decision-making.

The last part of the book (Decision-making in social interaction) includes two experimental studies dealing with the role of learning in social contexts. It is a well-established fact that to acknowledge responsibility for decisions and to be obliged to report for resulting consequences has a positive impact on the quality of decision-making. The gender perspective opens new possibilities in how accountability can be obtainable. The chapter written by Jordi Brandts and Orsola Garofalo shows that gender pairings matter even in the presence of monetary incentives and women are more affected than men by the gender of the audience. Their finding contrasts with a previous experimental study of the same authors in which blood pressure and heart rate of the experimental subjects were measured. This divergence raises the methodological issue of observer bias, which is probably one of the most important in neurosciences. The final chapter, by Stefano Di Piazza, Letizia Vaccarella, Antonio Dell'Ava, Simona Conti, and Antonio Rizzo relies on Michael Tomasello's theory of shared intentionality and provides experimental evidence on social learning. Their main result is that, in place of the I-rationality proposed by economic theories, the analysis of decision-making should adopt the We-rationality based on the intentionality shared among the individuals of a given group to provide an explanation for the role played by trust and reward in social interaction.

References

Camerer, C. (1999) "Behavioral economics: reunifying psychology and economics," *Proceedings of the National Academy of Sciences of the USA*, 96: 10575–10577.

Evans, J.S.B.T. (2006) "The heuristic-analytic theory of reasoning: extension and evaluation," *Psychonomic Bulletin & Review*, 13: 378–395.

Acknowledgments

This book is based on the work presented by several contributors at the *Neuroscience and Decision Making* LabSi Conference held in Siena on September 20–21, 2010. Our thanks go to the Gruppo Monte dei Paschi (the conference main sponsor), the University of Siena (the host institution) and the Inter-university Center for Experimental Economics LabSi (the organizing institution). We want to express our special gratitude to our fellow organizer, Alessandro Santoni. We are grateful to all authors and the referees who kindly reviewed the chapters and contributed to ensure their scientific quality. Finally, we acknowledge the financial support from the Tuscany Region in the framework of PAR FAS 2007–2013 1.1.a.3 under grant ALBO project.

Part I

Evidence on the neuroscientific foundations of decision-making

Part I

1 Private and social counterfactual emotions

Behavioural and neural effects

Chiara Crespi, Giuseppe Pantaleo, Stefano F. Cappa and Nicola Canessa

Introduction

Decision-making is a multi-component and ubiquitous process prompted by the individual's needs, desires and goals. People are continuously involved in several concurrent choices, concerning both short-term and long-term purposes, in order to achieve an overall satisfactory state in line with the desired one. From a computational perspective, decision-making may be decomposed into different stages. First, the decision-maker has to realize the current state as unsatisfying. Such awareness highlights the need for the exploration of the decisional environment, i.e. the research and recognition of potentially rewarding options. Then, the evaluation of available options in terms of the cost–benefit ratios leads to select the one that might provide the better output. Choices that promote an increase of so-called 'utility', compared with those that turn out bad, are more likely to be replicated in the future. To put it differently, the valence of reinforcement (reward vs punishment) results in a positive vs negative association between the choice made and a pleasant vs unpleasant output, respectively. This association elicits subjective expectations about the reinforcing value of stimuli, and enables a learning process leading to adaptive behavioural changes. Moreover, the efforts invested to reach a well-being state are deeply rooted in a dynamic environment, where the subjective value of potential sources of reward is highly variable. Therefore, the balance between exploration and exploitation of potential sources of reward is crucial for optimal choice behaviour in an extremely complex system characterized by risk and/or uncertainty.

While such key concepts about decision-making may appear straightforward, it is by no means clear how people evaluate available options in order to choose the one that maximizes utility. Ever since the beginning of theoretical reflection and, more recently, scientific research on decision-making, this issue has been a matter of debate.

Classical economic theories of choice, locating decision-making under risk in the realm of rational cognitive processes, specify a set of normative prescriptions to describe rational economic behaviour. Within a historical framework, such prescriptions are reflected first in the notion of *expected value* (Bernoulli 1954) –

i.e. a measure of the overall *amount* of reward potentially resulting from a choice, weighted by its probability – and then in that of *expected utility* (von Neumann and Morgenstern 1944) – i.e. a measure of the *subjective* desirability of that reward, once again weighted by its probability. In particular, von Neumann and Morgenstern (1944) suggested that an individual's drive to choose a specific option under risk depends on the *desire* to maximize utility, in terms of either satisfaction or profit, and developed a set of axioms constraining the way in which people (are supposed to) represent their decisional preferences. In their view, equipped with a complete knowledge about both one's own preference-system and choice-outcomes probabilities, the rational decision-maker always goes for the alternative that maximizes expected utility. While useful for choice-quality assessment in specific settings, such a normative framework clearly appears unrealistic from the point of view of the psychological aspects of choice. To put it simply, *expected utility theory* indicates how an individual *should* choose in order to be considered rational, but is not truly informative about how real people actually decide, or why they frequently violate such normative prescriptions.

In the last decades, a renowned interest in these topics arose from cognitive psychology, and particularly from seminal studies by Amos Tversky and Daniel Kahneman leading to *prospect theory* (Kahneman and Tversky 1979), probably the most influential descriptive model of choice behaviour under risk and uncertainty. In addition, these authors describe several heuristics (i.e. simplifying strategies in cognitive demanding situations) and ensuing *cognitive biases* (i.e. systematic deviations from normative prescriptions) to account for violations of rational theories of choice (Tversky and Kahneman 1974). Within their framework, while evaluating options individuals assess their potential outcomes as gains or losses with respect to a subjective reference point, rather than in terms of their absolute value. Moreover, such evaluation entails the engagement of two distinct functions, concerning either the value or the probability of outcomes. In the first case, the traditional monotonic utility function is replaced by a *value function*, whose S-shape reflects several important properties of choice behaviour (Figure 1.1). Namely, while concavity in the gain domain reflects *risk aversion* for gains, convexity in the loss domain explains *risk seeking* for losses. The value function is steeper for losses than gains, reflecting *loss aversion*, i.e. the greater sensitivity to losses than equivalent gains (approximately twice as much). Furthermore, the status of gains and losses as related to an abstract reference point accounts for the *framing effect*, i.e. the fact that different choices (e.g. to risk or not to risk) may be elicited by different descriptions of the same decisional setting. Importantly, in *prospect theory* such a subjective value is not integrated with normatively defined probability, but rather with a psychological weight, reflecting the impact of probability on the overall value of the prospect, and mentally represented by an inverse S-shaped *weighting function*. The shape of this function represents a crucial dimension of the theory, as it reflects the individuals' tendency to overweight small probabilities and underweight medium-large ones. Both value function and weighted function share the principle

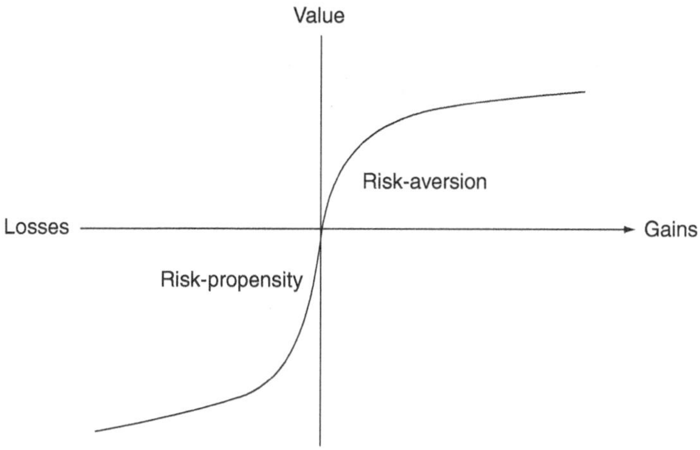

Figure 1.1 A typical value function.

of *diminishing sensitivity*, i.e. the fact that the marginal impact of a change in outcome diminishes with distance from the subjective reference point.

Since its formulation, prospect theory provided enormous theoretical and practical contributions to a descriptive approach to decision-making, i.e. how real agents make real decisions. In the meantime, other data have made it clear that decision-making cannot be conceived as a purely cognitive process, and that spontaneous facets of choice, such as loss and risk aversion, are likely to be also driven by factors other than cognition, and particularly by emotional drives (Loewenstein *et al.* 2001; Camerer 2005).

In line with this proposal, among the several theoretical approaches to emotion-based decision-making, *decision affect theory* (Mellers *et al.* 1997) suggests that choices are influenced by the anticipation of emotions that people expect to feel about the outcome. In this view, choices are strictly associated with, and can be predicted from, emotional experiences. In general, elation and disappointment arise after wins and losses, respectively. Both elation and disappointment are cognitively based emotions involving counterfactual comparisons between two *states of the world.* That is, emotional responses to the same outcome may differ, depending on alternative (counterfactual) outcomes, so that foregone outcomes work as a reference for evaluating obtained (factual) outcomes. Thus, when a counterfactual outcome is better or worse than the actual one, people experience disappointment or elation, respectively. Moreover, the *effect of surprise* associated with the outcome probability seems to modulate individuals' emotional responses, leading to an overall enhancement of emotional post-decisional experience. Namely, unexpected wins and losses are perceived as more elating and disappointing than expected ones, respectively. In sum, decision affect theory claims that maximizing subjective expected emotions is different from maximizing subjective expected utilities. In general, people select those alternatives that minimize potential negative affects. As a result, small gains may even be perceived as more pleasurable than larger ones, depending on expectations and counterfactual comparisons.

As discussed above, variables other than cognition, and precisely emotional factors, are needed to explain the decisional behaviour displayed by real decision-makers engaged in everyday-life choices. Yet, it is likely that, besides basic counterfactual feelings such as elation and disappointment, a crucial role is also played by more complex emotions arising from cognitive processing. Starting from this assumption, various attempts have been made to incorporate negative *cognitively based* feelings, such as regret, elicited by counterfactual reasoning, into a theory of choice (Bell 1982; Loomes and Sudgen 1982).

Counterfactual thinking and cognitively based emotions

Counterfactual thinking is a pervasive aspect of mental life, entailing mental simulations of alternatives to facts, events and beliefs (Epstude and Roese 2008; Roese 1997). From an ecological perspective, counterfactual thoughts play a central role in evaluating actuality, and offer tangible alternatives that contribute to regulating individuals' behaviour. Counterfactual-based evaluations of one's own experience occur spontaneously, particularly when things turn out badly. In these situations, when mental alternatives are better than reality, counterfactual thoughts are triggered by the unpleasant emotional state arising from the negative outcome. Via this mechanism, counterfactual simulations mediate, through top-down processes, more complex emotional states, such as regret/relief and envy/gloating, in the private and social domain, respectively.

Clues into the mechanisms underlying counterfactual reasoning are provided by *mental models theory* (Johnson-Laird and Byrne 1991), which encompasses counterfactual statements into a general theory of conditionals. Unlike other 'if ... then' assertions, counterfactuals make two different mental representations immediately explicit. While the first mental model is referred to actuality (i.e. the factual world), the second one is related to a possible alternative to reality (i.e. the counterfactual world). Thus, simultaneous representations of contrasting mental models elicit the experience of a wide range of complex feelings. For this reason, counterfactual thinking has been considered as a sort of *emotional amplifier* (Kahneman and Miller 1986), affecting both personal and interpersonal levels of analysis, e.g. satisfaction about the nature of reinforcement related to obtained outcomes and causal attribution mechanisms, respectively. At the personal level, the effect of counterfactuals on decision-making is well-known. Thinking counterfactually about alternative choices leads to the experience of pleasant vs unpleasant cognitively based emotions that, in turn, influence next choices. In particular, when counterfactual simulations are constructed before choice (*prefactual thinking*), the resulting emotions support the option-evaluation stage, representing a sort of emotional guide for subsequent decisional behaviours and promoting a learning process. Within the interpersonal domain, counterfactual thinking influences judgements of blame and responsibility (Alicke *et al.* 2008), as well as fairness perception (Nicklin *et al.* 2011). In both cases, counterfactual representations affect choices by means of two different cognitive mechanisms: (1) the *contrast effect*, i.e. the perceived discrepancy between reality and counterfactual alternatives; and (2) the *causal inference effect*, i.e. the recognition and dramatization of causal relationships arising from counterfactual argumentation context (Roese 1997).

Importantly, the *direction* (downward vs upward) of counterfactual comparisons accounts for the functional bases of counterfactual thinking (Epstude and Roese 2008; Roese 1997, 1999). *Downward counterfactuals* refer to representations of alternatives that are worse than reality, thus eliciting pleasant feelings, and serve an *affective function* as they may increase immediate well-being. On the contrary, *upward counterfactuals* entail alternatives that are better than reality, thus eliciting unpleasant feelings (Markman *et al.* 1993; Davis *et al.* 1995). This type of counterfactual is generated more spontaneously and frequently than downward counterfactuals (Roese and Olson 1997) and, by providing useful behavioural prescriptions, serves a *preparative function* (Landman 1993). Indeed, although such upward simulations can lead one to feel anxious and worried, as well as increase distress, they play a key role in conceptual learning, decision-making and social functioning, and promote performance improvement (Roese and Olson 1997) by facilitating behavioural intentions and enhancing motivation (Smallman and Roese 2009; Epstude and Roese 2008).

In line with this view, a cognitive model of *regulatory functions* underlying counterfactual thinking (Barbey *et al.* 2009) has been recently proposed. The framework of this model is rooted in the notion of *structured event complexes* (SECs), i.e. goal-oriented sets of events, in which elements of knowledge concerning events, such as social norms, ethical and moral rules and temporal event boundaries, are represented and organized on one's own needs, desires and motives. SEC elements constitute the basis for the evaluation of outcomes related to counterfactual alternatives. According to the model workflow, counterfactual activation occurs when a problem is encountered or anticipated, and its content is then constructed from SEC knowledge. Finally, SECs trigger behavioural intentions and motivation to sustain and maximize adaptive behaviour in order to achieve the desired goal. Therefore, the optimization of behavioural adaptations depends on many different cognitive processes, such as representation of desired goals, evaluation of possible action courses, maintenance and manipulation of task rules, response selection and execution, monitoring and comparing the actual performance with specific goals and, if needed, adjusting behaviour in order to achieve the desired outcome. Thus, the ability to generate counterfactual alternatives to reality may represent a core feature of human cognition, supporting behavioural planning and regulation. Comparing reality to *what might have been* elicits complex counterfactual-based emotions, such as regret, which play a key role in shaping decision-making (Zeelenberg *et al.* 1998) and behavioural adaptation to a dynamic environment. The motivational drive of counterfactual-based emotions in regulating adaptive behaviour can be better understood by looking at the functional role of regret. As stated above, prospect theory represents the most relevant descriptive theory of choice behaviour. Yet it does not take into account complex feelings and anticipated emotions, even though it is now largely accepted that emotions are involved in the whole decision-making process, from option evaluation to outcome realization (Zeelenberg and Breugelmans 2008). The traditional segregation of cognitive and emotional processes is overcome, to the extent that, in the approach known as 'emotion-based decision-making', regret and other complex counterfactual-based emotions emerge as the result of the *interplay* between cognitive and emotional processes. From a functional point of view, emotions fulfil an adaptive role by emphasizing specific goals and mobilizing energy in order to modulate behaviour (Bagozzi *et al.* 2003). In particular, within the *feeling-is-for-doing* approach (Zeelenberg and Pieters 2007) emotions are conceived as the primary motivational system for goal-directed behaviour, and defined by specific qualities, so that different feelings are associated with different contents, and thus may induce different courses of action. Accordingly, motivational functions appear to be emotion-specific and cannot be reduced to the overall valence of specific feelings. This entails that regret is functionally different from other negative emotions, such as disappointment, shame or guilt. In particular, as stated by so-called *theory of regret regulation*, the feeling of regret constitutes the most typical among the emotions associated with decision-making processes. Regret is defined as an aversive cognitively based emotion triggered by upward counterfactuals, i.e. the comparison between the factual outcome and the more pleasurable consequences of foregone options. Unlike the basic feeling of disappointment, which entails a counterfactual comparison across states of the world that are not under one's own control, regret is crucially characterized by a sense of responsibility for the factual outcome (Mellers *et al.* 1997). This is the reason why people are strongly motivated to minimize it, while they also aim to maximize utility in the future. The complex emotion of regret can be experienced after outcome realization (*retrospective regret*, informing people about the level of goal attainment), as well as during options evaluation (*anticipated regret*, signalling potential regrettable options). In both cases, regret holds an adaptive function. Along with behavioural prescriptions elicited by counterfactual analyses of reality, the experience of regret allows people to learn from the past and to predict the consequences of outcomes, thus crucially contributing to behavioural adaptations to the environment.

Regret and decision-making in the brain

Evidence in favour of the behaviourally adaptive role of the experience and anticipation of regret/relief has been recently provided by a series of studies, aiming to investigate the brain structures mediating these emotions, both in healthy and brain-lesioned individuals (Camille *et al.* 2004; Coricelli *et al.* 2005; Canessa *et al.* 2009, 2011). Most of these studies employed a gambling task previously developed by Barbara Mellers *et al.* (1999) to elicit in the participants the two main precursors of regret and relief: namely, knowing that 'things would have been better under a different choice' (Coricelli *et al.* 2007) and being directly *responsible* for the outcomes.

The regret gambling task

This task is composed of several consecutive trials, requiring participants to choose which, between two available gambles, they wish to play. Gambles are depicted as '*wheels-of-fortune*' in which different probabilities of variable amounts of gain or loss are graphically represented by the relative size of sectors of the wheel (Figure 1.2). Immediately after the choice the gambles are played and the results are shown.

Importantly, the studies performed so far have modulated the quality and intensity of participants' emotional reactions to the obtained outcomes by introducing experimental conditions that differ with respect to a few crucial dimensions. The first is represented by '*information*', and is manipulated through specific feedbacks provided to participants. In 'partial-feedback' conditions they are shown only the outcome of the chosen gamble, thus eliciting feelings of elation or disappointment for an outcome (gain or loss, respectively) that ultimately depends on factors that are not under their control, such as the casual rotation of a spinning-wheel. In 'complete-feedback' conditions participants are shown the outcome of both chosen and discarded gambles, thus leading them to quantify and evaluate the financial consequences of unselected alternatives, and particularly to compare what they obtained (the factual outcome) with what they *might have obtained, had they made a different choice* (the counterfactual outcome). As mentioned before, however, the complex emotions of regret and relief are elicited when one feels a personal responsibility regarding the outcome of her/his deliberate choice. Thus, the second dimension manipulated concerns the sense of responsibility for one's own outcomes, which is high when participants are asked to choose for themselves which gamble they want to play ('choose' condition), and low when a computer randomly chooses a gamble in their place ('follow' condition). It is worth remembering that the two dimensions of 'knowledge of foregone outcomes' and 'sense of responsibility' are crucial prerequisites for the experience of regret or relief, that would be otherwise

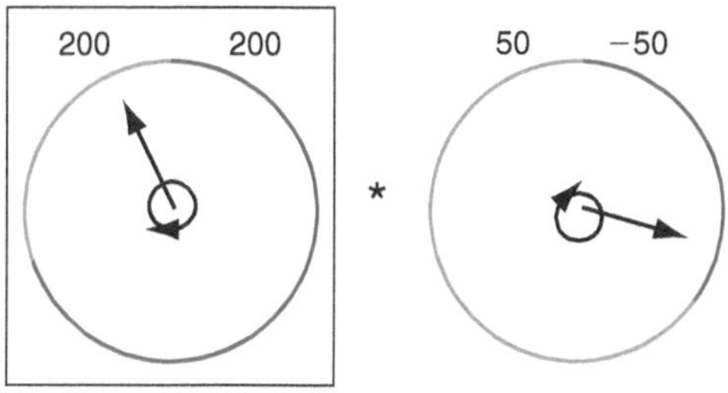

Figure 1.2 Graphical depiction of the gambling task.

replaced by the basic feelings of disappointment or elation. A third dimension that can be manipulated concerns the *intensity* of emotions elicited in the player via the size of gains or losses on a discrete continuous scale, e.g. a factual loss of 200 (arbitrary units) in the face of a counterfactual gain of 50, thus representing an overall regret of 250.

The neural bases of regret experience and regret-based behavioural change

Equipped with this task, neuropsychologists and neuroscientists have addressed the neural bases of both the experience of regret at outcome, and of regret-based adaptive behavioural learning at choice, by studying the performance of healthy and brain-injured individuals.

In this endeavour, a first step is represented by the description of impaired emotion-based decision-making following orbitofrontal cortex (OFC) damage by Camille *et al.* (2004). These authors compared three groups of subjects (15 healthy controls, five patients with OFC lesions and three control patients with lesions sparing the OFC) in terms of (1) *performance* in the task described above (i.e. the ability to learn from past choice-outcomes), with both 'complete' and 'partial' feedback conditions, and real financial outcomes; (2) *subjective* emotional reactions to outcomes, via explicit emotional ratings; (3) *objective* emotional reactions to outcomes, via skin conductance response (SCR). Not surprisingly, they observed that in healthy participants (and in control-patients) both subjective and physiological emotional reactions depend on the valence of the outcome, with gains and losses generally eliciting positive and negative reactions, respectively. Yet, such reactions also crucially depend on the foregone outcome, so that, for instance, disappointment for a loss is larger (and elation for a gain is smaller) when the non-obtained outcome of the chosen gamble is a large win. Moreover, in line with the previously described effects of counterfactual thinking, such modulation is by far stronger in complete- than partial-feedback conditions, to the extent that a loss of 50 does not elicit a negative affect when the foregone outcome is a larger loss of 200. On the contrary, positive outcomes may result in the emotion of regret if compared to an even more positive unselected outcome, thus highlighting the specificity of regret as opposed to disappointment. Importantly, a different picture seems to emerge from the analysis of OFC patients' behaviour. On the one hand, their reactions are modulated by the non-obtained outcome of the unchosen gamble, indicating preserved emotional expression and interest in monetary outcomes (i.e. elation or disappointment). Yet, in OFC patients, neither subjective nor physiological emotional reactions are influenced by the outcome of the unchosen gamble, thus highlighting impaired regret in the face of preserved disappointment. These emotional reactions to the outcomes of decision-making have then been assessed in terms of *anticipated* disappointment or regret when making a new choice, in both patients and controls. To assess the specific role of the OFC in mediating regret-based learning (i.e. the anticipation of future regret when making subsequent choices), Camille *et al.* (2004) tested a model of choice incorporating the impact of both anticipated disappointment and regret, as well as the effect of expected value predicted by 'rational' theories of choice (see above). The main result is that while controls' choices depend on both expected value and anticipated regret, only the former is considered by OFC patients. The immediate consequence is that while controls can take advantage of regret-based learning (thus earning more in the complete- than partial-feedback condition), OFC patients do not show significant performance differences between the two conditions (and generally end the task with a net loss). Interestingly, since the study is designed so that gambles with the highest expected value win less frequently than those with the lowest expected value, these patients embody the somehow paradoxical condition of 'perfectly rational' decision-makers who rely only on expected value, yet lose money because of impaired learning from the emotional value of foregone choices. In sum, unlike controls, OFC patients do not display the emotional and physiological effects of the experience of regret, nor can learn from past experience to anticipate regret at subsequent choices. Besides highlighting the adaptive behavioural role of regret experience (as distinct from mere disappointment for losses), these results also show the crucial and specific role of the OFC in generating this emotional facet of counterfactual thinking, rather than a generic negative affect elicited by losses. While consistent with anatomical, physiological and functional available data on this region (see Kringelbach and Rolls 2004), these results suggest an interpretation of the OFC's role in emotion-based decision-making that differs from Damasio's Somatic Marker hypothesis (see Bechara *et al.* 2000). The difference is subtle but crucial since, while the latter conceives the OFC as the 'neural link' between memory of past experiences and a bottom-up emotional 'hunch' marking risky choices, the data just reviewed highlight its role in terms of *top-down* emotional modulation elicited by counterfactual thinking, i.e. by cognitive processing. Whatever the interpretation of the OFC's role, the decisional impairment displayed after its damage shows that its involvement, which emotionally results in a negative feeling, is a necessary drive for appropriate behavioural adaptation.

In addition, an interpretation in terms of regret processing was supported by neuroimaging studies of human subjects playing the same gambling task, with both 'complete/partial' feedback, and 'choose/follow' (see above) conditions. Coricelli *et al.* (2005) used functional magnetic resonance imaging (*f*MRI) to investigate the brain regions involved in the experience of regret, and those associated with the effects of such experience on the anticipation of regret at subsequent choices. In line with the data by Camille *et al.* (2004), they observed that regret and disappointment are mediated by different neural structures (but see Chua *et al.* 2009 for partially different results). In particular, the experience of regret involves the medial OFC along with structures involved in cognitively induced responses to aversive and painful stimuli (anterior cingulate cortex – ACC) and in declarative memory (hippocampal regions). Instead, experiencing disappointment for losses engages other brain regions, including the brainstem periaqueductal grey matter involved in processing aversive and painful stimuli

(Peyron *et al.* 2000), as well as in inhibitory mechanisms modulating defensive behaviour (Brandao *et al.* 2008). Importantly, it is not the OFC's only role to mediate the emotional experience of regret. This region also underpins a *learning* process elicited by this complex and painful emotion, aimed to minimize its occurrence in the future. A model of choice analogous to that used with OFC patients by Camille *et al.* (2004; see above) confirmed that in the partial-feedback condition subjects' decisional behaviour is driven by both the anticipation (i.e. minimization) of potential disappointment, and by the maximization of expected value. In 'complete-feedback' conditions, in contrast, anticipated disappointment is overcome by anticipated regret, as only the latter exerts a significant behavioural influence. This finding, reflecting the higher aversiveness of regret compared with disappointment (see also SCR findings by Camille *et al.* 2004), paralleled an increase of regret aversion, rather than of risk aversion, throughout the experiment. On the neural side, the cumulative effect of regret is reflected in the reactivation, at choice, of the medial OFC, somatosensory cortex, inferior parietal lobule and amygdala. In line with data suggesting a role of the OFC while processing subjective values of appetitive/aversive stimuli (e.g. Plassmann *et al.* 2010), the authors suggested that this network provides an updated representation of the value of the gambles, based on the previous experiences of regret. This representation embodies the negative affect associated with cumulative regret, thus biasing choices towards regret aversion. In this view, the OFC defines and continuously updates the emotional value of the error given by the difference between the obtained outcome and the unselected alternatives (i.e. a 'fictive prediction-error' – Lohrenz *et al.* 2007; Chiu *et al.* 2008; see below) that, if chosen, would have produced better results. The decisional impairment observed in OFC patients (Camille *et al.* 2004) shows that this error, which emotionally results in the negative feeling of regret, is a necessary drive for behavioural adaptation.

The social side of regret and relief: empathy and envy

Highlighting the driving role of emotions on choice entails one important consequence in terms of their influence on behaviour. Emotions are shared through mechanisms of empathy (Preston and de Waal 2002) and emotional contagion (Barsade 2002) that, as shown by advancements in social neuroscience (Adolphs 2010), are neurally associated with 'resonant' brain mechanisms (Singer *et al.* 2004; Wicker *et al.* 2003). The 'core' notion of this sector of neuroscientific research is that, even though there may be several ways in which others' emotions can be understood, one such mechanism is based on the reactivation of the brain regions associated with the observer's first-person emotional experience (Gallese *et al.* 2004). In support of this view, such a neural 'mirror response' has been shown in conditions involving basic-level emotional stimuli, such as visual expressions of disgust (Wicker *et al.* 2003) or cues signalling pain (Singer *et al.* 2004), as well as with regard to tactile sensations (Keysers *et al.* 2004).Therefore, any evidence that emotions shape decision-making raises the issue of potential *social* influences on choice, possibly via the reactivation of outcome-related emotions in the observers' brains. In this regard, behavioural studies (van Harreveld *et al.* 2008) and neural-network simulations (Marchiori and Warglien 2008) show that in social decisional contexts one's own decisions and behaviours may be strongly influenced by interactive learning, i.e. learning from what other individuals experience as a result of their choices. One might then wonder how such learning occurs, and particularly whether the negative, regretful outcomes of other individuals are coded in the decision-maker's brain as pure 'cold' numerical quantities, or rather in terms of 'hot' resonant emotions. Clues into this issue come from behavioural evidence, suggesting that merely attending a negative situation occurring to another individual elicits in the observer the same mental processes as in a first-person situation (Girotto *et al.* 2007; Pighin *et al.* 2011). The latter studies examined counterfactual reasoning in social contexts by comparing reported mental simulations of actors and observers of different situations all resolving negatively. By comparing actors' and observers' counterfactuals, they showed that observers tend to mentally simulate alternative post-decisional solutions to those situations as actors themselves do. These results thus suggest that, when faced with the negative outcome of another person's choices, individuals tend to react as if they were personally involved in that situation.

Based on these convergent reports, Canessa *et al.* (2009) used the same gambling task described above to test whether a 'resonant' neural mechanism is activated both when experiencing and when attending complex, cognitively generated emotions such as regret. In their study, in different trials participants either chose one of the two gambles, resulting in real gains or losses, or observed the same sequence of events (gamble evaluations, decisions, outcome evaluations), this time experienced by another individual playing the same task in a nearby room ('choose' conditions). As a baseline, the computer randomly chose one of the gambles for the participant or for the other player ('follow' conditions). In line with predictions, in two related experiments they showed that observing the regretful outcomes of someone else's choices activates the same regions that are activated during a first-person experience of regret, i.e. the medial OFC, anterior cingulate cortex and hippocampus (Canessa *et al.* 2009). This finding suggests that the understanding of others' regret is mediated by the reactivation of the same brain regions that induce the feeling of regret in the beholder during a first-person experience. Through this mechanism, others' emotional states are mapped on the same areas that underlie one's own direct experiences, therefore allowing the automatic understanding of the cognitive/emotional states that is intrinsic to the complex emotion of regret in others. In support of this hypothesis, the reactivation of the medial OFC (the 'core' region within the regret network) was stronger in female than male participants, likely reflecting their higher empathic aptitude as assessed with a test of emotional empathy (balanced emotional empathy scale – BEES; Mehrabian and Epstein 1972; Meneghini *et al.* 2006).

In a subsequent study, the same authors addressed the issue of interactive learning in the social domain by investigating whether this resonant mechanism also underpins learning from others' previous outcomes, besides from one's own ones (Canessa *et al.* 2011). In line with previous data, on the behavioural side they observed a change in subjects' risk aptitude coherent with the outcomes of regret/relief of her/his previous decision. That is, increased risk-seeking after 'relief for a risky choice' and 'regret for a non-risky choice', and reduced risk-seeking after 'relief for a non-risky choice' and 'regret for a risky choice'. Crucially, however, a significant behavioural adaptation elicited by previous experience was observed also after the other player's previous outcomes (i.e. after both one's own and another's regret or relief). Instead, no significant behavioural change was observed after an outcome resulting from a random-choice by the computer (i.e. after disappointment or elation). This negative result indicates that the behavioural influence observed in 'choose' conditions does not merely result from the association between a given choice type and its outcome per se, but rather from the amplified emotional responses of regret/relief associated with a sense of responsibility for the obtained outcomes. This behavioural adaptation from past outcomes is reflected in cerebral regions specifically coding the effect of previously experienced regret/relief when making a new choice. Activity in the subgenual cortex and caudate nucleus tracked the outcomes that increased risk seeking (relief for a risky choice and regret for a non-risky choice). These regions were also more strongly activated by final risky, compared with non-risky, decisions, and their conjoint activity is likely to reflect the motivational drive arising from previous outcomes that highlighted the reward value of risky options (Daw and Doya 2006). Instead, activity in the medial OFC, amygdala and periaqueductal grey matter reflected the outcomes reducing risk seeking (relief for a non-risky choice and regret for a risky choice). All these regions, along with the anterior insula, were also more strongly activated while making non-risky vs risky choices. Based also on previous proposals (see above), these data suggest that the medial OFC reflects adaptive learning from past emotional experiences reducing risk seeking and, via connections with the amygdala, insula and periaqueductal grey matter (Augustine 1996; Reynolds and Zahm 2005) activates the negative feeling associated with regret and its anticipation.

Crucially, a subset of these regions reflected both first- and third-person previous outcomes when making new choices. This finding, that fits with the influence from others' outcomes highlighted by behavioural data, extended for the first time the concept of emotional resonance to the decisional domain, where such a shared response might act as one of the neural mechanisms underlying social learning. Paralleling the behavioural effects of learning from others' emotions, this mechanism would entail the mapping of the emotional consequences of others' choices on the same emotional states that are experienced as a first-person, through the reactivation of the same cerebral regions that are involved in their direct experience. Importantly, however, different neural mechanisms seem to underpin social influences towards oppositely directed behavioural changes (risk seeking increase vs decrease). Namely, only the outcomes that reduce risk seeking undergo a genuine resonance mechanism involving emotion-related regions such as the medial OFC, somatosensory cortex and periaqueductal grey matter. Those increasing risk seeking, instead, exert their effect through the dorsal striatum and the inferior parietal cortex, involved in coding expected value (Platt and Glimcher 1999). In support of this functional segregation, only activity in the medial OFC reflecting the attended outcomes that reduce risk seeking was significantly correlated with individual empathy scores. Moreover, this was the only region showing a significant gender effect. Namely, its activity was stronger in females than males, a result that is in agreement both with previously reported gender effects in a resonant mechanism for regret involving the medial OFC (Canessa *et al.* 2009), as well as with behavioural data showing females to be more prone than males to an influence from the other player's outcomes, and particularly those reducing risk seeking.

It is worth noting that these results, and their interpretation, are at variance with those reported by other authors who investigated the behavioural effects of choice-related emotions in a social context. Bault *et al.* (2008) started from the assumption, widely held in social psychology theories such as so-called *social comparison theory* (Festinger 1954), that a strong determinant of human motivated behaviour is represented by social status. That is, comparisons with other individuals, leading to complex emotions such as envy and gloating, would contribute to update representation of our Self, finally resulting in behavioural changes in social contexts. Building on previously reviewed studies on counterfactual-based emotions, Bault *et al.* (2008) conceive envy and gloating as the social analogues of regret and relief, respectively, related to the (mis)fortune of others (i.e. others' choice-outcomes), rather than to private foregone outcomes. Despite the crucial difference with regret and relief in terms of their point of reference (one's own vs others' outcomes), envy and gloating still influence behaviour, by tracking changes in social status due to superior/inferior outcomes with respect to those happening to others. Based on these assumptions, these authors tested the hypotheses that (1) social contexts may amplify outcome-related emotions, and (2) that such amplification will result in social emotions influencing behaviour differently than their private counterparts. To this purpose, they modified the gambling task described above so that, in different trials, participants either played in isolation (as in the original version, thus experiencing regret or relief when knowing the actual and foregone outcomes), or played along with another individual (thus knowing her/his choice). In the latter case, they might make the same decision as the opponent (thus experiencing shared regret or shared relief when their outcomes were worse or better compared with the foregone outcome, respectively), or different choices (thus experiencing envy or gloating when their outcomes were worse or better compared with the other's ones, respectively). As a measure of emotional arousal, both skin conductance response and heart rate were recorded. They observed that emotions were stronger in the two-players than one-player condition, but only when the two players had made different choices. In other words, envy and gloating are emotionally more arousing than regret and relief, that in turn are stronger than shared regret and relief. Second, such emotional evaluation was higher for gloating than envy (and for regret than relief), thus indicating that, contrary to classical observations on private decision-making (Kahneman and Tversky 1979), 'social gains loom larger than social losses' (Bault *et al.* 2008). This result entails that, in such competitive social context, the utility associated with gloating is higher than the dis-utility associated with envy. Accordingly, the authors predict that such different effects of emotions in private and social contexts will reflect in different behavioural adaptations when subsequent choices are made with risk-seeking vs risk-averse opponents, because previous rewarding experiences of gloating will drive participants to make risky choices in the future. Indeed, their results confirmed that, throughout the task, participants became bold decision-makers when playing with a prudent (risk-averse) opponent with low average earnings, and prudent when playing with a risk-seeking (i.e. driven by expected value) opponent with relatively high earnings. Overall, these results highlight the differential effect of emotions in private contexts (where aversion to regret rules) and social contexts (where seeking for gloating rules). In particular, they highlight the competitive facet of social emotions when elicited in a competitive context like the present one.

It is important to discuss, however, that the results by Bault *et al.* (2008) do not necessarily conflict with the interpretation in terms of 'resonance' of others' emotional experiences suggested by Canessa *et al.*'s (2009, 2011) results. From the methodological standpoint, the two studies crucially differ with regard to the elicitation of social comparisons, which was emphasized in the former study and minimized (by having subjects playing in different trials) in the latter. Nonetheless, the behavioural results by Bault *et al.* (2008) highlight the dominant effect of envy and gloating over shared regret and relief in competitive social contexts. Future studies may then help to disentangle the neural bases of these different emotions on choice-related behavioural adaptations. Most importantly, however, it is worth noting that experiencing envy and gloating for another's fortunes or misfortunes is likely to require the understanding of her/his emotional state. In line with the proposed role of a mirror-like response in social cognition (Gallese *et al.* 2004), then, such a resonant mechanism for the experiential understanding of others' choice-related emotions may even represent a prerequisite upon which envy and gloating can develop, and exert their influence on decision-making in competitive social settings.

The computational side of regret

It is worth mentioning that the notion of 'counterfactual emotions', and their role in experience-based behavioural adaptations, has been acknowledged also within a computational approach to decision-making, such as the one represented by reinforcement-learning theory (see Sutton and Barto 1998). This approach is rooted in the notion of *prediction error*, a measure of the difference between predicted and actual rewards that underpins motivation and behavioural learning, associated by model-based neurophysiological studies with mesolimbic dopaminergic activity (see Schultz 2007). Interestingly, recent developments in computational neuroscience consider together both the 'computational role' of prediction error and its affective consequences elicited by *foregone* outcomes. In this extended view, the difference between factual and counterfactual outcomes, i.e. a '*fictive*' prediction error, constitutes an additional learning signal that increases the explanatory power of reinforcement learning models (Lohrenz *et al.* 2007; Chiu *et al.* 2008; see Sommer *et al.* 2009) and elicits emotional consequences. Indeed, while the processing of a fictive prediction error by the dopaminergic striatum, devoid of affective content, is in itself sufficient to account for the behavioural adaptation resulting from past experience (Sommer *et al.* 2009), the emotional consequences of evaluating alternative outcomes (Camille *et al.* 2004; Coricelli *et al.* 2005) contribute to such learning process by strengthening anticipatory regret and relief via the involvement of the medial OFC and related neural structures.

Conclusions

In conclusion, as shown by the reviewed data the social cognitive neuroscience approach enables the rigorous study of complex social emotions in the laboratory, taking advantage of multiple approaches, from classical lesion-based studies to neuroimaging investigations. Importantly, a better understanding of the neural basis of the emotions that appear to play a powerful role in modulating our everyday behaviour in real-life decision-making may have important consequences in areas that go well beyond theoretical neuroscience.

References

Adolphs, R. (2010) 'Conceptual challenges and directions for social neuroscience', *Neuron*, 65: 752–767.

Alicke, M.D., Buckingham, J., Zell, E. and Davis, T. (2008) 'Culpable control and counterfactual reasoning in the psychology of blame', *Personality & Social Psychology Bulletin*, 34: 1371–1381.

Augustine, J.R. (1996) 'Circuitry and functional aspects of the insular lobe in primates including humans', *Brain Research Reviews*, 22: 229–244.

Bagozzi, R.P., Dholakia, U.M. and Basuroy, S. (2003) 'How effortful decisions get enacted: the motivating role of decision processes, desires and anticipated emotions', *Behavioral Decision Making*, 16: 273–295.

Barbey, A.K., Krueger, F. and Grafman, J. (2009) 'Structured event complexes in the medial prefrontal cortex support counterfactual representations for future planning', *Philosophical Transactions of the Royal Society B: Biological Sciences*, 364: 1291–1300.

Barsade, S.G. (2002) 'The ripple effect: emotional contagion and its influence on group behavior', *Administrative Science Quarterly*, 47: 644–675.

Bault, N., Coricelli, G. and Rustichini, A. (2008) 'Interdependent utilities: how social ranking affects choice behavior', *PLoS One*, 3: e3477.

Bechara, A., Damasio, H. and Damasio, A.R. (2000) 'Emotion, decision making and the orbitofrontal cortex', *Cerebral Cortex*, 10: 295–307.

Bell, D.E. (1982) 'Regret in decision making under uncertainty', *Operations Research*, 30: 961–981.

Bernoulli, D. (1954) 'Exposition of a new theory on the measurement of risk'; trans. D. Bernoulli (1738) 'Specimen theoriae novae de mensura sortis', *Academiae Scientiarum Imperialis Petropolitanae, Tomus*, 5: 175–192, *Econometrica*, 22: 23–36.

Brandao, M.L., Zanoveli, J.M., Ruiz-Martinez, R.C., Oliveira, L.C. and Landeira-Fernandez, J. (2008) 'Different patterns of freezing behavior organized in the periaqueductal gray of rats: association with different types of anxiety', *Behavioural Brain Research*, 188: 1–13.

Camerer, C. (2005) 'Three cheers – psychological, theoretical, empirical – for loss aversion', *Journal of marketing research*, 42: 129–133.

Camille, N., Coricelli, G., Sallet, J., Pradat-Diehl, P., Duhamel, J.R. and Sirigu, A. (2004) 'The involvement of the orbitofrontal cortex in the experience of regret', *Science*, 304: 1167–1170.

Canessa, N., Motterlini, M., Di Dio, C., Perani, D., Scifo, P., Cappa, S.F. and Rizzolatti, G. (2009) 'Understanding others' regret: a FMRI study', *PLoS One*, 4: e7402.

Canessa, N., Motterlini, M., Alemanno, F., Perani, D. and Cappa, S.F. (2011) 'Learning from other people's experience: a neuroimaging study of decisional interactive-learning', *Neuroimage*, 55: 353–362.

Chiu, P.H., Lohrenz, T.M. and Montague, P.R. (2008) 'Smokers' brains compute, but ignore, a fictive error signal in a sequential investment task', *Nature Neuroscience*, 11: 514–520.

Chua, H.F., Gonzalez, R., Taylor, S.F., Welsh, R.C. and Liberzon, I. (2009) 'Decision-related loss: regret and disappointment', *Neuroimage*, 47: 2031–2040.

Coricelli, G., Critchley, H.D., Joffily, M., O'Doherty, J.P., Sirigu, A. and Dolan, R.J. (2005) 'Regret and its avoidance: a neuroimaging study of choice behavior', *Nature Neuroscience*, 8: 1255–1262.

Coricelli, G., Dolan, R.J. and Sirigu, A. (2007) 'Brain, emotion and decision making: the paradigmatic example of regret', *Trends in Cognitive Science*, 11: 258–265.

Davis, C.G., Lehman, D.R., Wortman, C.B., Cohen Silver, R. and Thompson, S.C. (1995) 'The undoing of traumatic life events', *Personality & Social Psychology Bulletin*, 21: 109–124.

Daw, N.D. and Doya, K. (2006) 'The computational neurobiology of learning and reward' *Current Opinion in Neurobiology*, 16: 199–204.

Epstude, K. and Roese, N.J. (2008) 'The functional theory of counterfactual thinking', *Personality and Social Psychology Review*, 12: 168–192.

Festinger, L. (1954) 'A theory of social comparison processes', *Human Relations*, 7: 117–140.

Gallese, V., Keysers, C. and Rizzolatti, G. (2004) 'A unifying view of the basis of social cognition', *Trends in Cognitive Science*, 8: 396–403.

Girotto, V., Ferrante, D., Pighin, S. and Gonzalez, M. (2007) 'Postdecisional counterfactual thinking by actors and readers', *Psychological Science*, 18: 510–515.

Johnson-Laird, P.N. and Byrne, R.M. (1991) *Deduction*, Hillsdale, NJ: Lawrence Erlbaum Associates.

Kahneman, D. and Miller, D.T. (1986) 'Norm theory: comparing reality to its alternatives', *Psychological Review*, 93: 136–153.

Kahneman, D. and Tversky, A. (1979) 'Prospect theory: an analysis of decision under risk', *Econometrica*, 47: 263–291.

Keysers, C., Wicker, B., Gazzola, V., Anton, J.L., Fogassi, L. and Gallese, V. (2004) 'A touching sight: SII/PV activation during the observation and experience of touch', *Neuron*, 42: 335–346.

Kringelbach, M.L. and Rolls, E.T. (2004) 'The functional neuroanatomy of the human orbitofrontal cortex: evidence from neuroimaging and neuropsychology', *Progress in Neurobiology*, 72: 341–372.

Landman, J. (1993) *Regret: The Persistence of the Possible*, New York, NY: Oxford University Press.

Loewenstein, G.F., Weber, E.U., Hsee, C.K. and Welch, N. (2001) 'Risk as feelings', *Psychological Bulletin*, 127: 267–286.

Lohrenz, T., McCabe, K., Camerer, C.F. and Montague, P.R. (2007) 'Neural signature of fictive learning signals in a sequential investment task', *Proceedings of the National Academy of Sciences of the USA*, 104: 9493–9498.

Loomes, G. and Sugden, R. (1982) 'Regret theory: an alternative theory of rational choice under uncertainty', *Economic Journal*, 92: 805–824.

Marchiori, D. and Warglien, M. (2008) 'Predicting human interactive learning by regret-driven neural networks', *Science*, 319: 1111–1113.

Markman, K.D., Gavanski, I., Sherman, S.J. and McMullen, M.N. (1993) 'The mental simulation of better and worse possible worlds', *Journal of Experimental Social Psychology*, 29: 87–109.

Mehrabian, A. and Epstein, N. (1972) 'A measure of emotional empathy', *Journal of Personality*, 40: 525–543.

Mellers, B.A., Schwartz, A., Ho, K. and Ritov, I. (1997) 'Decision affect theory: emotional reactions to the outcomes of risky options', *Psychological Science*, 8: 423–429.

Mellers, B.A., Schwartz, A. and Ritov, I. (1999) 'Emotion-based choice', *Journal of Experimental Psychology: General*, 128: 1–14.

Meneghini, A.M., Sartori, R. and Cunico, L. (2006) 'Adattamento e validazione su campione italiano della Balanced Emotional Empathy Scale di A. Mehrabian', *Ricerche di Psicologia*, 29: 123–152.

Nicklin, J.M., Greenbaum, R., McNail, L.A., Folger, R. and Williams, K.J. (2011) 'The importance of contextual variables when judging fairness: an examination of counterfactual thoughts and fairness theory', *Organizational Behavior and Human Decision Processes*, 114: 127–141.

Peyron, R., Laurent, B. and Garcia-Larrea, L. (2000) 'Functional imaging of brain responses to pain: a review and meta-analysis', Clinical *Neurophysiology*, 30: 263–288.

Pighin, S., Byrne, R.M., Ferrante, D., Gonzalez, M. and Girotto, V. (2011) 'Counterfactual thoughts about experienced, observed and narrated events', *Thinking and Reasoning*, 17: 197–211.

Plassmann, H., O'Doherty, J.P. and Rangel, A. (2010) 'Appetitive and aversive goal values are encoded in the medial orbitofrontal cortex at the time of decision making', *Journal of Neuroscience*, 30: 10799–10808.

Platt, M.L. and Glimcher, P.W. (1999) 'Neural correlates of decision variables in parietal cortex', *Nature*, 400: 233–238.

Preston, S.D. and de Waal, F.B. (2002) 'Empathy: its ultimate and proximate bases', *Behavioral and Brain Sciences*, 25: 1–20; discussion 20–71.

Reynolds, S.M. and Zahm, D.S. (2005) 'Specificity in the projections of prefrontal and insular cortex to ventral striatopallidum and the extended amygdala', *Journal of Neuroscience*, 25: 11757–11767.

Roese, N.J. (1997) 'Counterfactual thinking', *Psychological Bulletin*, 121: 133–148.

Roese, N.J. (1999) 'Counterfactual thinking and decision making', *Psychonomic Bulletin and Review*, 6. 570–578.

Roese, N.J. and Olson, J.M. (1997) 'Counterfactual thinking: the intersection of affect and function', *Advances in Experimental Social Psychology*, 29: 1–59.

Schultz, W. (2007) 'Behavioral dopamine signals', *Trends in Neuroscience*, 30: 203–210.

Singer, T., Seymour, B., O'Doherty, J., Kaube, H., Dolan, R.J. and Frith, C.D. (2004) 'Empathy for pain involves the affective but not sensory components of pain', *Science*, 303: 1157–1162.

Smallman, R. and Roese, N.J. (2009) 'Counterfactual thinking facilitates behavioral intentions', *Journal of Experimental Social Psychology*, 45. 845–852.

Sommer, T., Peters, J., Glascher, J. and Buchel, C. (2009) 'Structure–function relationships in the processing of regret in the orbitofrontal cortex', *Brain Structure and Function*, 213: 535–551.

Sutton, R.S. and Barto, A.G. (1998) *Reinforcement Learning: An Introduction*, Cambridge, MA: MIT Press.

Tversky, A. and Kahneman, D. (1974) 'Judgment under uncertainty: heuristics and biases', *Science*, 185: 1124–1131.

van Harreveld, F., van der Pligt, J. and Nordgren, L. (2008) 'The relativity of bad decisions: social comparison as a means to alleviate regret', *The British Journal of Social Psychology*, 47: 105–117.

von Neumann, J. and Morgenstern, O. (1944) *Theory of Games and Economic Behaviour* (1st edn 1944; 2nd expanded edn 1947), Princeton, NJ: Princeton University Press.

Wicker, B., Keysers, C., Plailly, J., Royet, J.P., Gallese, V. and Rizzolatti, G. (2003) 'Both of us disgusted in My insula: the common neural basis of seeing and feeling disgust', *Neuron*, 40: 655–664.

Zeelenberg, M. and Breugelmans, S.M. (2008) 'The role of interpersonal harm in distinguishing regret from guilt', *Emotion*, 8: 589–596.

Zeelenberg, M. and Pieters, R. (2007) 'A theory of regret regulation', *Journal of Consumer Psychology*, 17: 3–18.

Zeelenberg, M., van Dijk, W.W., van der Pligt, J., Manstead, A.S.R., van Empelen, P. and Reinderman, D. (1998) 'Emotional reactions to the outcomes of decisions: the role of counterfactual thought in the experience of regret and disappointment', *Organizational Behavior and Human Decision Processes*, 75: 117–141.

2 The influence of social value orientation on information processing in repeated voluntary contribution mechanism games

An eye-tracking analysis

Susann Fiedler, Andreas Glöckner, and Andreas Nicklisch

Introduction

Many everyday situations are characterized by a social dilemma structure. Imagine, for instance, a situation in which the inhabitants of two villages intend to build a bridge over a river that divides both villages. The bridge would be beneficial for both villages by improving trades and reducing traveling costs, and so on. Building the bridge would necessitate a certain amount of money, which people would have to contribute to the project in order to realize it. Everybody would potentially benefit from the bridge, so the social goals would be maximized if the bridge was built. Let us assume that all contributions are voluntary and it is not possible to force anybody to pay because there is no law that allows this. Let us further assume that no one can be effectively excluded from using the bridge. In such a situation, for each person it would be optimal to save their own share and to free-ride on other people's contributions. In abstract terms, a social dilemma is characterized by socially efficient behavior (here: all contribute money to the bridge) standing in conflict with individual interests (here: saving the money). It is surprising how many situations in the real world have such a structure. For example, actions of environmental protection (e.g., buying an electrically powered car or the more expensive natural deodorant), decisions about paying for public television or transportation, voting, or situations in your private entourage like investing in a group present for a friend's birthday. All of these examples have one thing in common: you can decide whether you want to cooperate or free-ride. Many of these situations occur repeatedly.

In highly controlled laboratory studies, behavior in social dilemma situations is often investigated in prisoner dilemma tasks (Rapoport and Chammah 1965) or, in their generalized form, public-good games.

There is much research on the factors influencing cooperation in public-good games. One of the crucial factors seems to be people's social orientations (Balliet *et al.* 2009; Fehr and Fischbacher 2002; Fischbacher and Gächter 2010; Offerman *et al.* 1996; Van Lange *et al.* 1997a). Social value orientation (SVO) is assumed to be some kind of enduring personality structure that can be measured by assessing the preferences for particular distributions of outcomes to oneself and others in so-called "decomposed games" (Kuhlman and Marshello 1975; Liebrand and McClintock 1988; Van Lange *et al.* 1997b).

However, one of the interesting findings is that SVO is mainly predictive for behavior in so-called one-shot games, but not for situations in which people play public-good games repeatedly (Park 1994; Renkewitz *et al.* 2011). Overall, relatively little is known about the underlying processes mediating the relation of SVO and contributions. In the current study, two goals are pursued: first, the study aimed at investigating people's willingness to contribute to public goods in repeated social dilemma situations, depending on their SVO. Second, and more importantly, the cognitive processes involved in decision-making in a social dilemma situation should be investigated using advanced eye-tracking technology.

Here, the relationship between people's SVO is of special interest, as well as the question of whether this orientation can relate to enduring characteristics of the information search processes. This is one of the first studies to investigate decision processes in strategic games on a fine-grained level using eye-tracking (but see Costa-Gomes and Crawford 2007; Crawford 2008; Knoepfle *et al.* 2009). This allows monitoring and analyzing subjects' information search processes as well as the arousal connected with certain types of behavior (e.g., free-riding vs. cooperating).

Social value orientation

In economics, rational choice theory is traditionally used to generate predictions for rational behavior. A multitude of findings indicates that it often failed to predict real behavior, in that people show systematic violations of rationality and a variety of biases (Simon 1955; Tversky and Kahneman 2000). For the area of social dilemma situations, Messick and McClintock (1968) already developed the idea that the contribution behavior is influenced by relatively time-invariant person-specific factors. They specifically assumed that people differ in their tendency to maximize only their own profit or to share money with other people. They postulate that people have specific preferences for the distribution of outcomes between themselves and others (see also Offerman *et al.* 1996).

Thus, they pointed out that people's SVOs are one important factor that determines the behavior in social dilemmas. SVO is thereby basically explained by differences in weighting positive and negative outcomes for oneself and the other people against each other. The literature separates eight different social orientations (Figure 2.1), four of which occur most frequently in empirical studies: cooperative, individualistic, altruistic, and competitive orientation. SVO is often measured by people choosing between two options that contain outcomes for the person herself and for another person.

Several different methods have been developed to measure SVO (see Van Lange *et al.* 1997a; Liebrand and McClintock 1988; Kuhlmann and Marshello 1975). The measurement procedure is a decomposed game, which means that

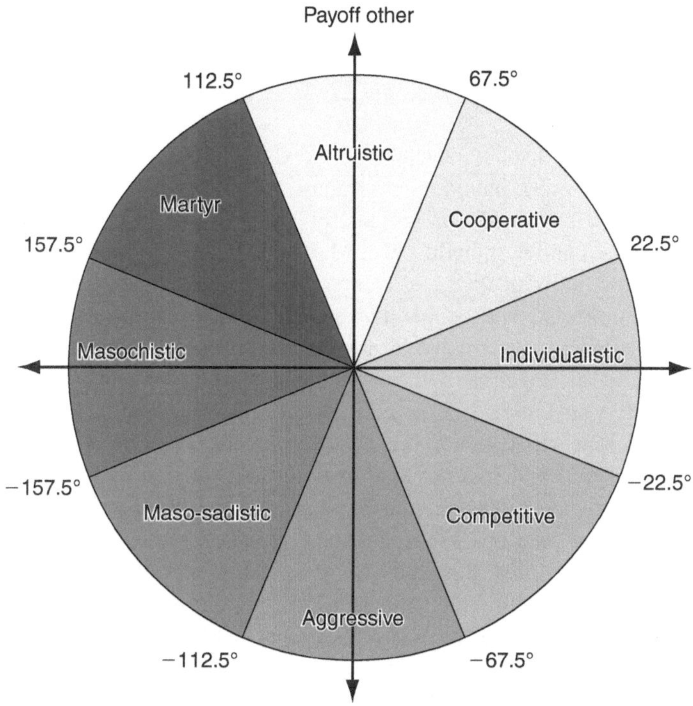

Figure 2.1 Social value orientations chart showing classes of dominant social values.

the participants make choices that determine their own payoff and the outcomes of the other players. Every participant has to choose one alternative from each of the pairs, such as those given in Table 2.1.

For the three pairs given from the first to the last: an altruist would always choose option A because they want to maximize others' payoffs regardless of their own; individualists only care about their own outcomes and would have chosen B, A, B; for competitors the most important goal is to maximize the difference between their own and others' payoffs so they would choose: B, A, A.

Table 2.1 Examples for outcome distributions in the ring measure of social values

	Option A	*Option B*
Self	€2.60	€2.90
Other	€1.50	€0.80
Self	€2.10	€1.50
Other	–€2.10	–€2.60
Self	–€3.00	–€2.90
Other	€0.00	€0.80

Cooperators, however, would pick A, A, B to maximize their own and others' outcome.

Predictive validity of SVOs

Researchers in economics and social psychology showed that SVO is predictive for behavior in social dilemmas, including environmental scenarios (Cameron *et al.* 1998), negotiation (De Dreu and Van Lange 1995) and also in abstract social dilemma games (Kuhlman and Marshello 1975; McClintock and Liebrand 1988). In general it is found that individualists and competitive people contribute less to public goods, whereas altruists and cooperative people tend to contribute more (see Balliet *et al.* 2009). SVO is predictive for the contributions in various public-good games, especially in one-shot games (De Cremer and van Dijk 2002; Smeesters *et al.* 2003; Van Lange 1999). Interestingly, Parks (1994) tested the same relationship in a repeated voluntary contribution mechanism (VCM) paradigm (see Isaac *et al.* 1985) and was not able to find the former results, in that there was no relation between SVO and contributions (see also Renkewitz *et al.* 2011). This divergence between one-shot games and repeated games is particularly relevant for this chapter. First, this study wants to add empirical evidence to this issue by investigating the predictive value of SVO for a one-shot as well as a repeated VCM game. However, the study will also go beyond this mere replication and try to capture differential aspects in the information search process that might remain in repeated VCM games, even if there are no differences in choices between them.

Information processing in strategic games

The mere level of contributions is only a very rough measure for the specific strategy a person uses in playing a strategic game. In many cases, the same behavioral pattern might be produced by rather different strategies (see, for example, Glöckner 2009, 2010; Martignon and Hoffrage 1999). The missing connection between choices and decision strategies in some cases suggests that contributions are insufficient to classify the behavior of players in strategic games. In order to investigate the underlying processes, it becomes necessary to take into account further measures such as response latencies as well as process-tracing measures. With regard to the body of evidence concerning the partially missing differences between contributions of people with different SVOs, it would be worth striving for a more specified model for these games. To make a start in this direction, the following study will investigate if there are traceable differences in information search and integration to create a foundation for developing such process models for strategic game situations.

The idea of looking at differences in information processing in economic decision-making is not generally new. Liebrand and McClintock (1988) showed that individualistic and altruistic players need less decision time to decide between the two outcome alternatives in the decomposed game of the social ring measure because they ignore (assign zero weight to) the others' (individualism) or their own (altruism) outcomes. Their results, hence, support their differential hypotheses concerning different information processing that is dependent on a person's SVO. In the current study, this important empirical finding is used as a starting point for a more differentiated investigation of the information search and processing in VCM games.

Assessing information processing

To explain decision behavior by sufficiently precise process models, it is helpful not only to analyze the final decision concerning, for example, objects or contributions, but also to investigate how a decision was formed. It might be helpful to know which information was used and in which order. Both measures are indicative for the information integration (Payne 1976). In research on judgment and decision-making, various methods were developed to assess information processing and to gain insights about the decision-making process (for reviews see Glöckner and Witteman 2010). Methods that have been repeatedly used for process tracing were instruments like information boards (Payne 1976; Payne and Braunstein 1978) or mouselab (a computer-based version of an information board – see Johnson *et al.* 1986; Payne *et al.* 1993), but also verbal protocols (Payne 1976, 1994). These methods were an attempt to focus more directly on the process between the informational input and a decision outcome to endorse mathematical models of decision-making (Svenson 1979). These basic assumptions about the information search are important in order for one to draw inferences about the mental representation. Svenson (1979) summarized them as follows: (1) the information a person looks at is assumed to be processed at a cognitive level; (2) the attention given to a certain piece of information reflects that this information is necessary for the decision; and (3) a longer period of attention given to a specific piece of information is linked to a more complex cognitive process than a shorter fixation.

Even though methods such as mouselab or verbal protocols are very helpful tools, they have one important disadvantage, namely that they might interrupt the decision-making and information acquisition process while trying to track it (Billings and Marcus 1983; Glöckner and Betsch 2008). Russo and Rosen (1975) already stated in their paper that eye fixations are preferable because they give more detailed information about the search process and are unobtrusive and difficult to misrepresent. The usage of eye-tracking has become increasingly popular in judgment and decision-making research. In this chapter we apply it to strategic VCM games.

Eye-tracking as a measure of information processing

According to the eye–mind hypothesis (Just and Carpenter 1976), fixations are linked to cognitive processes. Just and Carpenter (1976) postulate that the length of a fixation is closely related to the actual length of the underlying cognitive processes. But they add for consideration that the fixation duration may overestimate the processing time because components of other processes, such as the planning of the next fixation, might also take place during a fixation on the previous information. More recently, Velichkovsky (2001: 54) argued that "one can expect that higher levels of encoding, i.e., those emphasizing processes that are predicated to be metacognitive, communicative, or involved in a conscious decision, may be correlated with a higher proportion of longer fixations." In line with this argument, for the domain of decision-making Horstmann *et al.* (2010) show that deliberate calculations of weighted sums are connected with longer fixation times, whereas intuitive decisions are related to relatively short fixations. Based on that literature (see Pomplun *et al.* 1996; Rayner 1998), it seems reasonable to distinguish cognitive processes like conscious information integration vs. automatic processing by fixation duration. This study will investigate whether in repeated VCM games individuals mainly scan information or whether they process information on a higher level of attention.

Some studies already used eye movements and pupil responses as a measure of cognitive processes (see, for example, Beatty 1982; Bierman 2004; Glöckner and Herbold 2011; Hochman and Yechiam 2010; Horstmann *et al.* 2010; Renkewitz and Jahn 2010; Wang *et al.* 2010). Based on Velichkovsky's work and the empirical evidence in various studies in the field of usability research, the following assumptions are made: (1) longer fixations (overall) correspond to an increased level of processing and longer cognitive processes (Just and Carpenter 1976; Velichkovsky 2001); (2) longer fixations or a high amount of fixations on a particular piece of information correspond to the relative importance of the information (Jacob and Karn 2003; Poole *et al.* 2005); and (3) the number of fixations is related to the number of components that a person is required to process (Goldberg and Kotval 1999). With these assumptions in mind, it is possible to infer differences in cognitive processes by measuring eye movements.

Arousal measure via pupil diameter

Besides fixations, pupil dilations as a direct measure of arousal might be informative for processing in VCMs because they help to understand the affective component of contribution decisions.

In a classic work, Hess and Polt (1960) claimed that pupils dilate in response to positive affect and constrict to negative. Different studies, however, indicated that this assumption was wrong and that the relation between pupil diameter and affect might be better described by a U-shaped function (e.g., Janisse 1977). Steinhauer *et al.* (1983) showed that largest dilations were evoked by stimuli reported as most aversive or most pleasant and only small dilations occurred when the stimulus was neutral. Hence, the intensity of affective stimulation seems to be related to pupil dilation, regardless of the valence of the information. In recent studies, the diameter of the pupillary aperture of the eye has been repeatedly used as a measure of affective arousal (Bradley *et al.* 2008; Partala and Surakka 2003; Wang *et al.* 2010). In a first attempt to use the same measure in interactive games, Wang and colleagues (2010) tracked the pupil dilations while their participants sent deceptive messages in a sender–receiver game. Their results show that pupils dilate when the participants fool their opponents and that the magnitude of the dilation is increasing with the amount involved in the deception. For the current study, it is therefore assumed that pupil dilation increases with increasing affective arousal.

Eye-tracking in public-good games

Similar to the classic paradigms in judgment and decision-making research, in the last decades economists started to use data about the information search to improve their understanding of the processes underlying behavior on strategic games as well. In a first step, they used the mouselab paradigm in different strategic games to test their theories – for example, in repeated Cournot Oligopoly (Bigoni 2008), sequential bargaining (Camerer *et al.* 1993; Johnson *et al.* 2002), normal-form games[1] (Costa-Gomes *et al.* 2001) and VCM games (Kurzban and Descioli 2008). More recent studies (Chen *et al.* 2009; Knoepfle *et al.* 2009; Wang *et al.* 2010) use eye-tracking technology to investigate the information acquisition and cognitive processes while taking part in strategic games.

Coming from a rational-choice point of view, economists developed models of cognition and search (Costa-Gomes and Crawford 2007; Costa-Gomes *et al.* 2001) based on the first findings with process-tracing methods. In their perspective, information search is just another kind of rational decision that is determined by the trade-off between the benefits of making better decisions and the costs of search and storing numbers in working memory (see Beach and Mitchell 1978; Payne *et al.* 1988). In an open VCM game that will be used in the following study, the costs of look-ups are very small, because all information is directly available at all times (Glöckner and Betsch 2008). From a classic cognitive costs perspective (Lohse and Johnson 1996; Newell and Simon 1972; Payne *et al.* 1988), cognitive costs might mainly arise from keeping numbers in working memory and from integrating them. It seems plausible that in such a paradigm people prefer to look up information repeatedly, rather than storing all information in memory. Hence, in line with the eye–mind assumption one can assume that eye-fixations are indicative for the information that is currently considered.

In line with the general ideas of classic models for adaptive decision-making (Payne *et al.* 1988), two of the main ideas of the model by Costa-Gomes and colleagues are occurrence and efficiency, which means, on the one hand, that a rational player looks up all the available information that is costless and relevant for his decision (occurrence) and, on the other hand, that the player minimizes costs (for storage and information inspection) by processing the basic operations needed to evaluate the decision task without using unnecessary information (efficiency) (Costa-Gomes *et al.* 2001).

Seen from this perspective, eye-tracking is a valuable method to understand the strategies used in public-good games. In order to explain and to predict behavior in a VCM game and its relation to SVO, the method will be used in the following study to measure information search and arousal.

Research questions and predictions

Given that in many studies concerning the influences of SVO the social preferences are additionally pooled into two categories (*pro-social* and *pro-self*), some of the following research questions refer to this classification. Individualists and competitors are pooled as pro-self individuals, whereas cooperators and altruists are summarized under the category of pro-social individuals.

In the current study, we assess the information search process and arousal in a repeated VCM game. Based on assumptions about the information acquisition process (Svenson 1979) and the main ideas of the cognitive models by Costa-Gomes and colleagues (2001, 2007), it is tested whether differences in SVOs correspond to differences in the decision-making process. According to the findings reported above and concerning systematic decision time differences (Liebrand and McClintock 1988) one might assume that people with different SVOs also show systematic differences in the information search patterns, including fixation durations, the number of fixations, and the content on which they focus. Furthermore, one might assume that cooperative and competitive people inspect more information compared to individualistic and altruistic persons because of their attempt to make completely informed contributions and because they try to take into account the consequences for the other person. Individualist people should only care about their own outcomes, whereas altruists are only interested in the outcomes for the others. Both groups should show less information search and a strong focus on their own (others') outcome. According to the concept of SVO, cooperative and competitive players should pay attention to all the outcomes, whereas individualistic players are only interested in their own outcome and altruistic players in the outcomes of others. Finally, there might be differences in arousal while people decide about their contribution, which could depend on specific aspects of the situation and SVO.

To test these predictions, the following measures were analyzed: fixation duration, the number of fixations, the proportion of small and long fixations, the amount of inspected information, the proportion of inspections of payoff and contribution information, and pupil dilation. As a basic measure, we were interested in data about the contribution patterns as well.

Based on the empirical results concerning one-shot and repeated games, presented above, the following hypotheses were constructed.

Contributions

Hypothesis 1a: Pro-self-oriented participants contribute less in a one-shot VCM game than pro-social players do.

Hypothesis 1b: There are no systematic differences in mean contributions of pro-social- and pro-self-motivated participants in a repeated VCM game.

Additional to the contribution patterns the study investigates the information search process. For the eye-tracking measures described above, the following hypotheses were generated.

Information search and arousal

Cooperative and competitive participants consider information more intensely than individualistic and altruistic persons. Consequently, they should show longer considerations of information and a higher level of cognitive processing than individualistic and altruistic participants. This would result in:

> Hypothesis 2a: Cooperative and competitive individuals show longer decision times, mean fixation durations, and a higher proportion of medium and long fixations, as compared to altruistic and individualistic persons.

Information search of individualistic and altruistic participants is less comprehensive than in cooperative and competitive participants, resulting in:

> Hypothesis 2b: Cooperative and competitive individuals show a higher number of fixations per decision and a higher amount of inspected information, as compared to individualistic and altruistic persons.

Information search of participants with individualistic and competitive motives (pro-self individuals) is more focused on the payoff information than on feedback about the contributions, because their only aim is to maximize their own outcome, hence:

> Hypothesis 2c: Pro-self individuals show a higher proportion of the fixations on payoff information in relation to contribution information, as compared to pro-social (altruistic and cooperative) individuals.

Information search of individualistic participants should mainly focuses on information about themselves, hence:

> Hypothesis 2d: Individualistic individuals should show a stronger focus on their own payoff and contribution information, as compared to persons with other SVO.

Aside from information search, the study will focus on differences in arousal due to situational factors and SVO. We are particularly interested in arousal measures in participants deciding about their own contribution, which should reflect tension due to risk taking. Arousal is expected to be particularly high in two kinds of situations. First, if individuals have previously cooperated and now decide to exploit the other persons, they should be particularly aroused. Second, higher arousal might be experienced if people decide to contribute more than the average of previous rounds, so as to motivate other persons to start cooperation again. Both kinds of situation are characterized by people contributing considerably less/more than the average contribution in the previous period, resulting in Hypothesis 3.

Hypothesis 3: Arousal increases with increasing difference from the previous level of contributions.

Method

Participants and design

Thirty-six residents of Bonn, most of them students aged 19–65 (average age was 25.75 years and 45.5 percent of participants male), took part in the

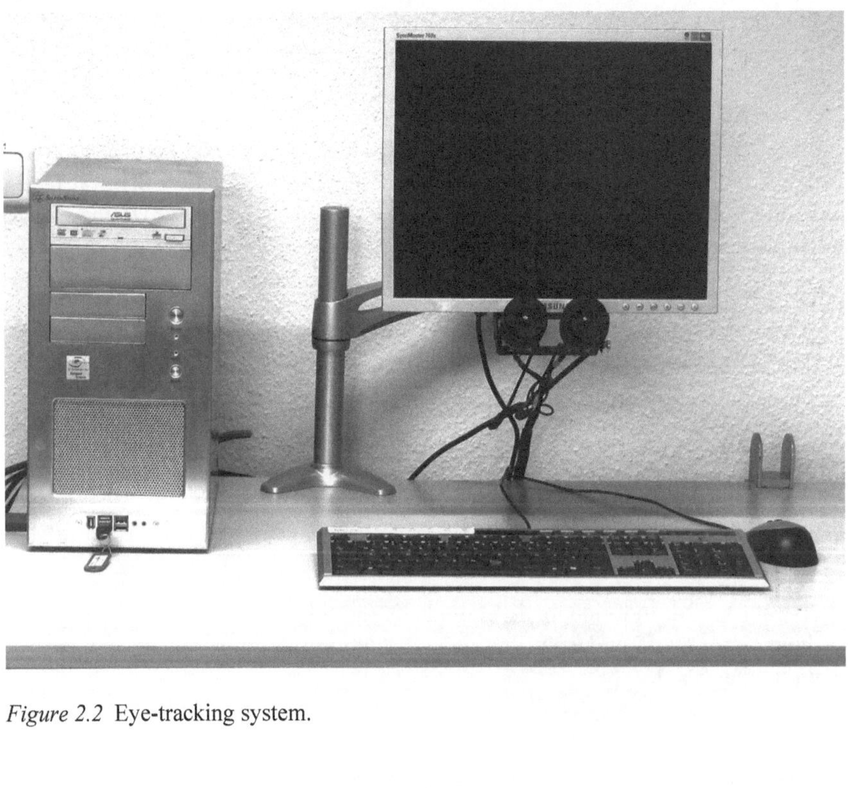

Figure 2.2 Eye-tracking system.

experiment. Volunteer subjects were recruited via Orsee (Greiner 2004) and most parts of the experiment were programmed in zTree (Fischbacher 2007). The experiment lasted 90–120 minutes. Participants received performance-dependent payments (average payment: €18) for their participation in the experiment. They were randomly assigned to their seats in the laboratory so that a later assembly in groups was independent of a person's show-up time (position in the line). Twelve participants worked on the tasks of the experiment simultaneously and three of them worked on a computer equipped with an eye-tracking tool.

Apparatus

The eye movements were recorded using a remote system based on a camera installed underneath the presentation monitor. The Eyegaze Analysis System used is a binocular system with a 0.45° accuracy and 120 Hz sampling rate. The computer monitor was used to present the VCM game. The head movement was prevented through a chin rest. Eye fixations and pupil diameter were recorded using the screen recording tool Nyan 2.0, provided by Interactive Minds.

Materials

VCM game

In the experiment, a common linear public-good game was used, which had already been used in Reuben and Riedl (forthcoming – see the normal group condition without punishment). A group of three participants play a VCM game in which the players have to decide how much they want to contribute to a common pool and how much they want to keep for themselves (*contribution stage;* see Figure 2.3a). The initial endowment per period is 20 Tokens.[2] All of the participants decide simultaneously about the amount of Tokens they want to contribute to the public good. All participants know the interest rate for the Token contributed to the common pool and that the pool will be split evenly by all the players in one group. Tokens in the private account have no interest rate. The payoff for every participant is calculated by:

> Payoff = 20 − own contribution to the common pool + 0.6 × sum of all contributions in the common pool.

The game structure is the same for the applied one-shot and repeated VCM game. In the one-shot game, the participants decide just once about their contribution and do not receive feedback about their payoffs. In the repeated VCM game, on the other hand, participants have to decide about their contribution repeatedly for ten periods, with immediate feedback about the behavior of the other players and the payoffs. After each period, the players get feedback about the contribution and payoffs for themselves, the other players, and the group (sum and average) (*feedback stage*; see Figure 2.3b). During the game, communication between the

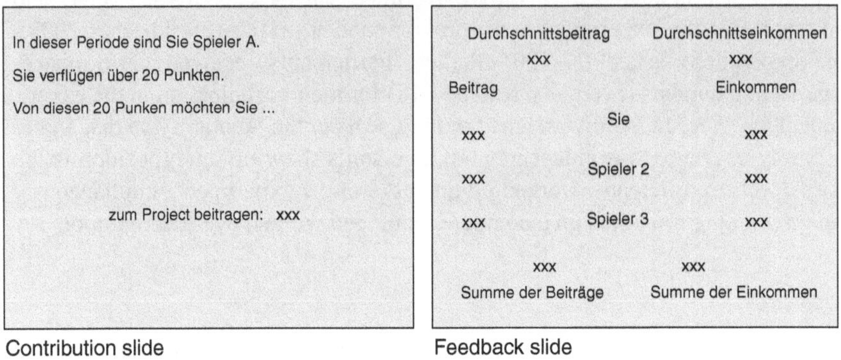

Figure 2.3 Presentation slides of the VCM game (all instructions and information were presented in German).

players is not allowed. The payoffs derived by any participant from this game depend on his or her contribution decisions and the decisions of the other two players.

Areas of interest

Ten areas of equal size (156 × 142 points) were defined on the screen. They captured the areas in which information about the contributions and payoffs of the last period were provided (i.e., own contribution/payoff, individual contribution/payoff of the other players, sum of contributions/payoffs, average contribution/payoff). These areas are relevant for testing Hypotheses 2c and 2d. For investigating the differences in attention for contribution and payoff information, areas of interest (AOIs) that included information about the payoffs (light gray) and the ones that contained information about the contributions (dark gray) were pooled (see Figure 2.4).

Assessment of SVO: the ring measure of social values

In order to investigate the social preferences of the players, the SVO of the participants was accessed by using the ring measure of social values (Liebrand and McClintock 1988).

Participants are classified as belonging to one of the groups (see Figure 2.1). Not only their SVO (vector angle), but also the consistency of their choices are important measures while using the social value questionnaire (length of the vector). A pattern is classified as inconsistent if the length of the vector is smaller than 1.8 (60 percent of the choices have to be in line with one SVO; see Liebrand *et al.* 1986). Participants who showed inconsistent choice patterns were sorted out, because it is assumed that the answers do not reflect a specific SVO. It could be the case in which a pattern is simply the result of a participant who

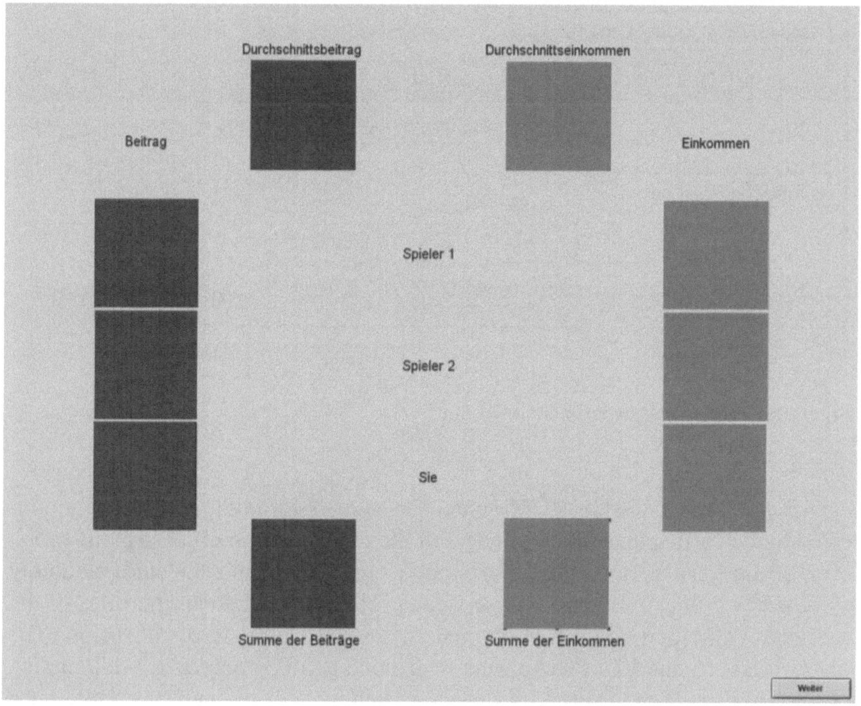

Figure 2.4 Definition of the areas of interest (dark gray AOIs contained contribution information, light gray AOIs contained payoff information).

did not understand the structure of the decomposed game, had no consistent contribution preference or chose randomly.

As mentioned before, in many studies concerning the influences of SVO the social preferences are additionally dichotomized into two categories (*pro-social* and *pro-self*). Participants were classified as pro-social when the vector angle was between 22.5° and 112.5°. This includes the orientations: cooperation, equality, and altruism. Participants with an individualistic or competitive orientation were classified as pro-self, which means they had a vector angle between 22.5° and –67.5° (see Figure 2.1).

Procedure

The experiment consisted of five different parts (the overall procedure is summarized in Figure 2.5). All participants took their seats (one in front of the eye tracker) after signing the official consent form and were instructed to take part in different experiments and economic games. They first completed the social value questionnaire (Liebrand and McClintock 1988, Appendix B); afterwards they were randomly assigned to groups of three people that had to give a

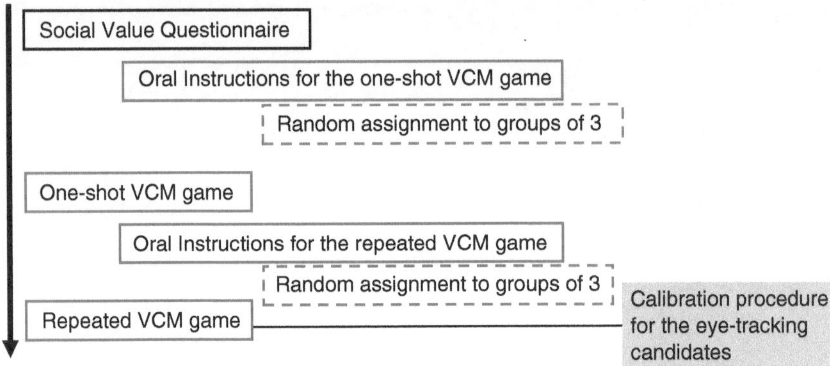

Figure 2.5 The overal experiment procedure.

contribution to a one-shot VCM game. The payoff for both was not communicated to the participants before the end of the experiment in order to avoid mood effects. In a next step, they were once again anonymously and randomly assigned to groups with three players each. They learned about the rules of the repeated VCM game and then started to play ten periods of the game. The instructions[3] for the VCM game were read aloud to all participants. Additionally, comprehension of the instructions was checked by control questions. Only once all participants had answered the questions correctly were the games started. All parts of the experiment were incentivized, so that every decision was payoff-relevant.

Results

As mentioned above, 36 participants took part in the study overall. For 12 of them (i.e., one person in each group) eye-tracking data were recorded in the repeated VCM. Hence, our first set of hypotheses concerning contributions was tested with 36 participants, whereas the hypotheses concerning information search and the exploratory analysis concerning arousal rested on 12 participants only. They will be reported in this order. All analyses were performed with Stata 10.1 using standard corrections for dependencies due to repeated measurement in regressions if indicated (see below).

Cooperation behavior and SVO

Classification by the ring measure of social values

Of the 36 participants, 15 were classified as pro-social and 17 as pro-self (see Figure 2.6). Three people could not be classified because the length of their vector was shorter than 1.8 (60 percent consistency) and one person was dropped

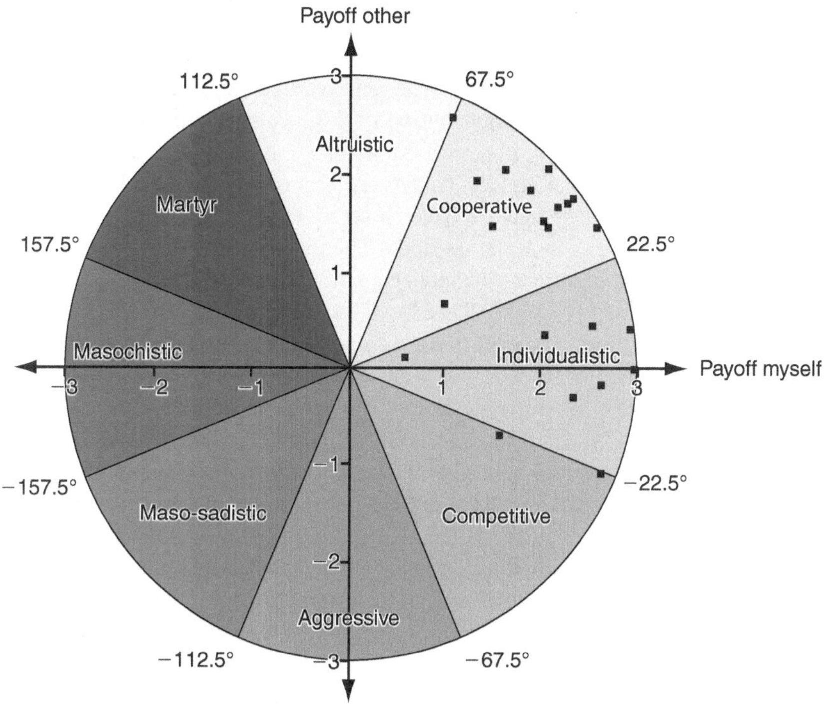

Figure 2.6 Results in the value orientation circle.

because he did not complete the form. This proceeding is in line with Liebrand *et al.* (1986), who included only participants that answered 60 percent of the choices in a manner consistent with one value orientation.

For the subsample of eye-tracking candidates, eight pro-self participants (all of them are individualists) and four pro-social participants (all of them are cooperators) were classified. Because none of the participants in the eye-tracking sample was classified as a competitor or altruist, the eye-tracking analysis refers to individualists and cooperators directly.

Predictions of the SVO for the repeated VCM game and the one-shot VCM game

The first hypothesis stated that SVO should be predictive for contributions in one-shot VCM games. Specifically, pro-social persons should contribute more to the public good as compared to pro-self persons in one-shot games. This was the case. The pro-social players contributed 14.34 (SD=5.78) Tokens on average, whereas the pro-self players contributed 9.47 (SD=8.2) Tokens on average. This difference turned out to be significant according to a one-sided t-test ($t(30)=1.96$, $p=0.03$, $d=0.7$), supporting Hypothesis 1a.

However, this was not the case in repeated VCM games (Figure 2.7). The overall results show that the temporal patterns and mean contributions in the ten-period VCM game are similar to previous findings (Keser and van Winden 2000; Weimann 1994). Contributions start with an average of 12.28 Tokens and decline smoothly to an average contribution of 7.81 Tokens (Figure 2.7). There was considerable heterogeneity in contribution behavior. Individual average contributions varied between 0.4 and 20 Tokens. A total of 47.2 percent ($n = 32$) of the subjects contributed less than 10 Tokens on average. Two participants contributed exactly 20 Tokens in all ten periods. The mean contribution over all ten periods did not differ significantly between both pro-social ($M_{Pro\text{-}social}=11.53$, SD=6.97) and pro-self ($M_{Pro\text{-}self}=9.97$, SD=6.38) people ($t(30)=0.66$, $p=0.25$, $d=0.24$ (one-tailed)). Interestingly, there was not even a difference in the first period. Pro-social people started out with a contribution of 12.0 (SD=7.2) Tokens, whereas pro-self players started out with a contribution of 12.5 (SD=7.3)); $t(30)=-0.21$, $p=0.58$, $d=-0.07$ (one-tailed). The results confirm Hypothesis 1a and Hypothesis 1b in that the social value questionnaire is predictive for behavior in one-shot VCM games, but not for contributions in a repeated VCM game.

Considering the 12 eye-tracking persons only, the pattern remained mainly the same, although they even showed an overall trend toward lower mean contributions of cooperative (pro-social) as compared to individualistic (pro-self) persons ($t(12)=1.34$, $p=0.89$, $d=-0.9$ (one-tailed)).

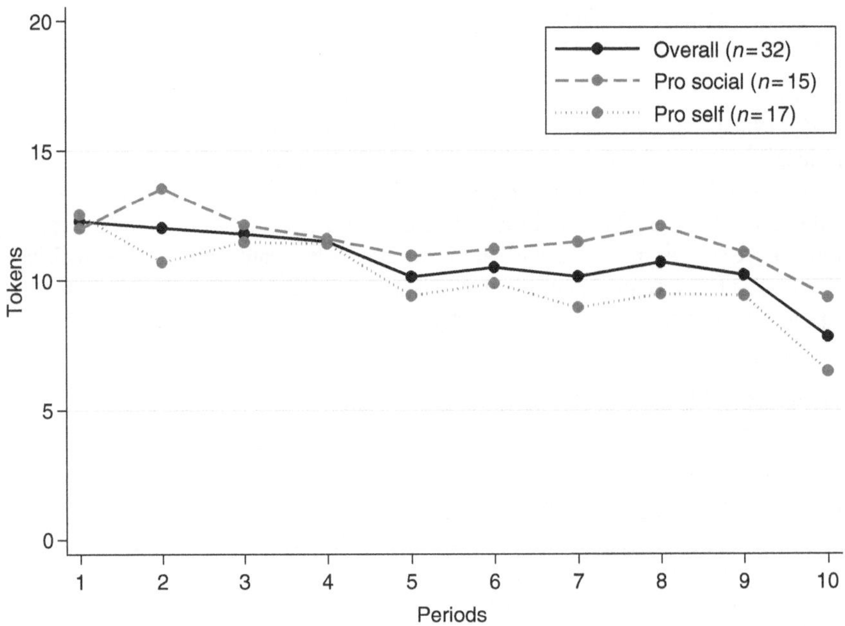

Figure 2.7 Average contributions over time for all subjects classified by SVO.

Information search and arousal

Decision and fixation times

Our first information search, Hypothesis 2a, stated that cooperative persons show longer decision times, mean fixation durations, and a higher proportion of medium and long fixations as compared to individualistic persons.[4] First decision time differences for the contribution decision were tested, and it was found that cooperative persons ($M_{cooperative}=5.66$ s, SD=1.55) indeed showed longer decision times as compared to individualistic persons ($M_{individualistic}=4.74$ s, SD=1.38) but the difference turned out not to be significant ($t(10)=1.05$, $p=0.15$, $d=0.70$ (one-tailed)). However, if merely the time spent looking at the screen is used as the data basis for the analysis, the result shows a statistically meaningful difference even with only 12 observations. Cooperators ($M_{cooperative}=4.66$ s, SD=1.67) indeed showed longer decision times than individualistic ($M_{individualistic}=3.34$ s, SD=9.18) persons ($t(10)=1.8$, $p=0.05$, $d=1.2$ (one-tailed)). Hence, the data supports the first part of Hypothesis 2a and is in line with Liebrand *et al.* (1988). As mentioned above, the duration of single fixations is an indicator for the level of processing – in other words, the intensity or depth in which information is considered – and it is assumed that cooperators process information more intensely. Clear support for this prediction was found. Overall, fixation durations are highly variable, ranging from 50 ms to 1,125 ms, with a median of 192 ms (considering fixations inside the defined AOIs in the feedback screen only).[5] They show a typically positively skewed distribution.[6] More importantly, cooperators show on average longer single fixations as compared to individualistic persons (Figure 2.8a) and seem to be stable over time (Figure 2.8b). A 2 (player type: cooperative vs. individualistic) × 10 (period) repeated measurement ANOVA with the log-transformed mean fixation duration as the dependent variable was conducted. The factor period is a within-participants factor that presents the different periods of the VCM game. The main effect of player type was significant, $F(1, 10)=7.36$, $p=0.022$, $\eta^2=0.424$. Additionally, there was a significant interaction effect between period and player type, $F(9, 89)=2.41$, $p=0.02$, $\eta^2=0.14$, the main effect of period was not significant, $F(9, 89)=0.50$, $p=0.873$, $\eta^2=0.33$. Hence, in support of Hypothesis 2a, mean fixation durations are higher in cooperative players than in individualistic players. Additionally, the difference between cooperative and individualistic players increases over time (see Figure 2.8b).

To investigate the influence of the player type on the single fixation duration in more detail and to test the third aspect of Hypothesis 2a, we tested for differences in the overall proportion of short, medium, and long fixations. Single fixations were categorized in short (<150 ms), medium (≥ 150 ms and <500 ms) and long (≥ 500 ms) fixation durations (Velichkovsky 1999). The results show that there are differences in the distribution of short, medium, and long fixations for the different player types (Figure 2.9).

The results of two one-sided *t*-tests for independent samples indicate that there is a statistically significant relationship between the player type and the

(a)

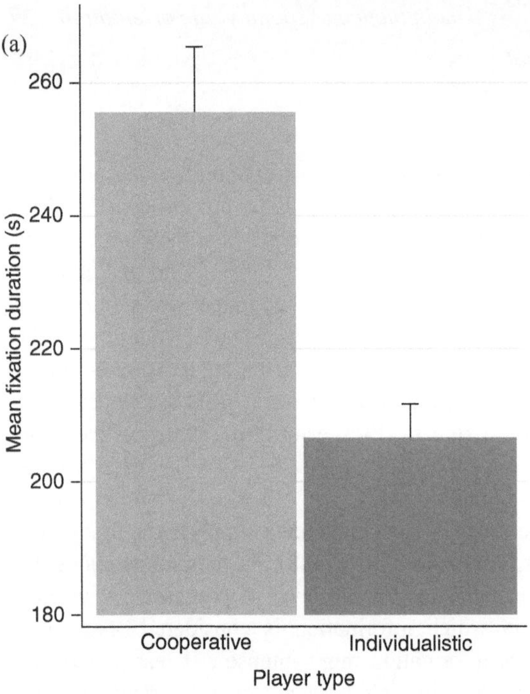

By player type

(b)

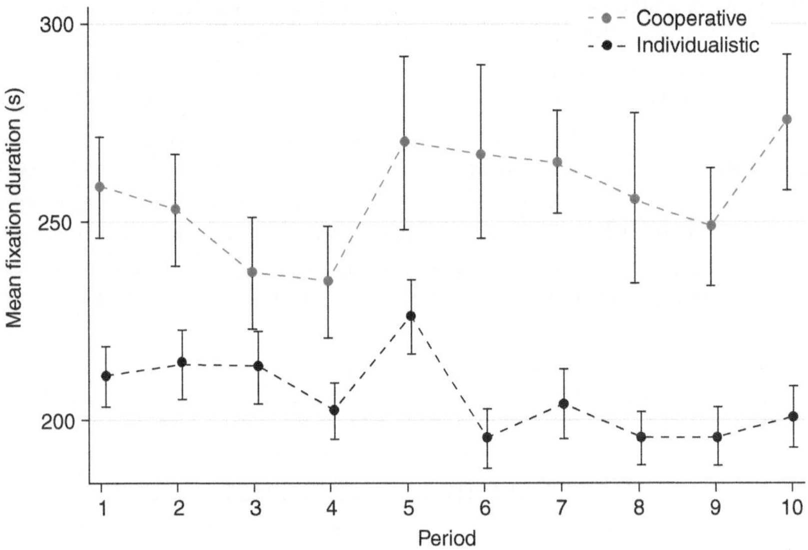

Over periods by player type

Figure 2.8 Mean fixation duration (with 95 percent confidence intervals).

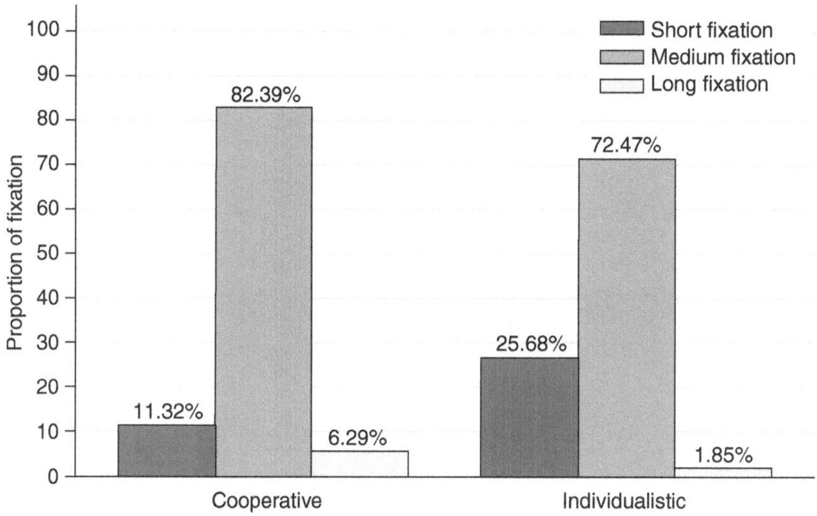

Figure 2.9 Distribution of short, medium, and long fixation for all classified player types in percent (bar labels indicate the proportion of fixation for each category).

proportion of small, medium, and long fixations. Subjects classified as cooperative players by the ring measure of social values showed a bigger proportion of long ($M_{cooperative}$=5.31 percent (SD=3.42) vs. $M_{individualistic}$=1.78 percent (SD=1.44); $t(10)=2.58$; $p=0.014$, $d=1.73$) and medium ($M_{cooperative}$=82.76 (SD=3.26) vs. $M_{individualistic}$=71.48 (SD=9.67); $t(10)=2.22$, $p=0.025$, $d=1.49$) fixations than subjects who were classified as individualistic.

Based on these results, all aspects of Hypothesis 2a are supported by the data in that cooperative individuals show longer decision times, longer fixation durations, and a higher proportion of long and medium fixations, compared to individualistic people.

It might additionally be interesting to see whether the relation between SVO and fixation duration can be approximated as a linear relation or has discontinuities caused by qualitative changes in processing. To shed some light on this question, a regression analysis with the interval-scaled SVO was conducted. The SVO score functioned as a predictor for the log-transformed mean fixation durations correcting for clusters in observations due to repeated measurement using the STATA option CLUSTER.[7] In line with previously reported analyses, SVO significantly predicted fixation duration, $\beta=0.004$, $t(10)=3.18$, $p=0.009$ and explains a considerable proportion of variance in fixation duration, $R^2=0.47$, indicating that the relation can be well approximated by a linear function (see Figure 2.10).

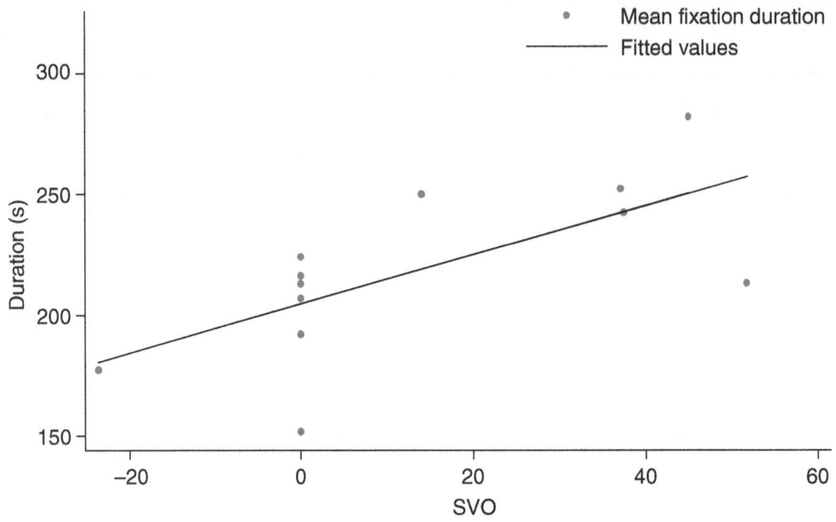

Figure 2.10 Average fixation duration and social value orientation with predicted regression line.

Note: For reasons of readability, we report the graphics based on the original values instead of the log-transformed values.

Number of fixations

The second information search of Hypothesis 2b states that cooperative persons show a higher number of fixations per decision and a higher amount of inspected information than individualistic persons. Again considering fixations to AOIs only, the number of fixations to the ten different pieces of information on the feedback screen varied considerably (between 2 and 47 fixations; M=17.64, SD=17.64, MD=17). Data did not support this hypothesis in that there were no significant difference between the average number of fixations for cooperative ($M_{cooperative}$=15.97, SD=8.62) and individualistic ($M_{individualistic}$=18.59, SD=6.74) individuals. ($t(10)=-0.58$, $p=0.71$, $d=0.39$).

The number of fixations is, of course, only partially informative concerning the question of how much of the total information was indeed taken into account, because people can look at information several times. Therefore, the proportion of information (every AOI that was investigated at least once) the participants looked at in each period was analyzed. In the current study participants inspected 6.85 (SD=2.37) (from ten) pieces of information on average which, however, also did not differ between types ($M_{cooperative}$=6.55 (SD=2.15) vs. $M_{individualistic}$=7.02 (SD=1.62); $t(10)=-0.42$; $p=0.68$, $d=-0.28$).

These somehow surprising results do not support Hypothesis 2b since the data do not show any statistically significant difference in the number of fixations and the amount of inspected information depending on the SVO.

Proportion of fixations on payoff and contribution information

To test Hypothesis 2c, which states that pro-self participants are more interested in payoff information than in contribution information, fixations to AOIs containing payoff and contribution information were compared to each other. Therefore, a percentage score indicating the proportion of fixations to payoff information was calculated. The result of a one-tailed t-test indicates that individualistic persons indeed focus more strongly on payoffs ($M_{individualistic}=62.07$ percent, SD=8.87) than cooperative ($M_{cooperative}=47.30$ percent, SD=18.28) persons, and the difference turns out to be significant ($t(10)=1.93$, $p=0.04$, $d=1.30$). Individualistic persons looked at payoffs more often, as compared to contributions (one-sampled test against $p=0.50$: $M_{individualistic}=58.81$ percent, SD=6.54, $t(7)=3.86$, $p=0.003$, $d=1.4$ (one-tailed)), whereas cooperative persons looked at both kinds of information equally often (one-sampled test against $p=0.50$: $M_{cooperative}=50.3$ percent, SD=16.05, $t(3)=0.04$, $p=0.486$, $d=0.02$ (one-tailed)), which supports Hypothesis 2c (see Figure 2.11).

Proportion of fixations on self and other referring information

Further, it was predicted that individualistic participants would focus more on information concerning themselves as compared to cooperative persons (Hypothesis 2d). To analyze this hypothesis, we calculated a score which indicated the

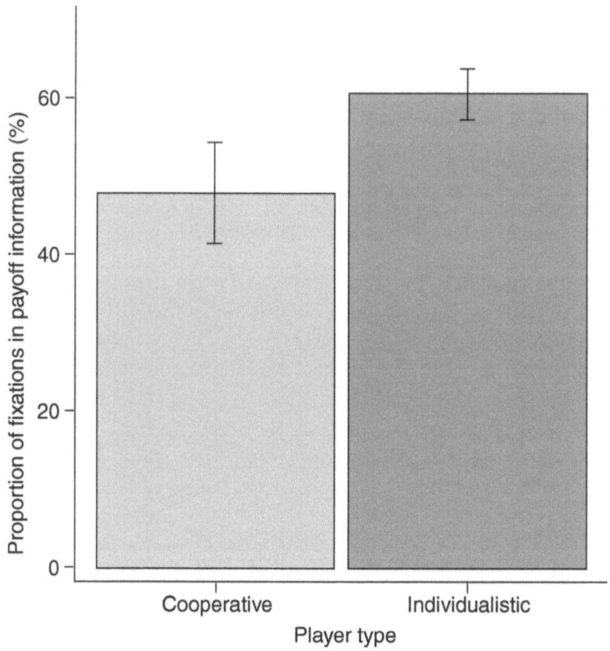

Figure 2.11 Proportion of fixations on payoffs (in percent).

proportion of information about oneself (again only considering fixations to AOIs so that proportions of fixations to self- and other-relevant information add up to 1). There was no difference between the proportion of fixations to self-relevant information between cooperative ($M_{cooperative}$=22.78 percent (SD=5.73)) and individualistic persons ($M_{individualistic}$=25.91 (SD=5.14)); $t(10)=-0.96$; $p=-0.36$, $d=-0.64$). Hence, overall the data does not support Hypothesis 2d.

To improve the understanding of the processes, we additionally investigated the development of proportion of fixations on own data over time. Figure 2.12 indicates that there is a tendency for all participants to start with a low interest in self-referring information and an increase of this attention until the fifth period, from where it starts to decrease slightly until the end of the VCM game. Hence, although Hypothesis 2d cannot be confirmed overall, Figure 2.13 reveals that mean differences show, and that pro-self participants look proportionally more often at self-referring AOIs than pro-social participants (particularly in the middle periods). Splitting data further into contribution and payoff information reveals that differences mainly prevail for payoff information (Figure 2.13).

Pupil size

In addition to the measures of fixations, we were interested in the variations in pupil dilations as a measure of arousal in different decision situations. Hypothesis 3, which states that arousal increases with an increasing difference in the current contribution as compared to the previous level of contributions, was investigated by analyzing pupil radius during the contribution phase in the VCM game (see Figure 2.3a). In other words, arousal was measured when persons reflected on their current contribution. In the analysis, extreme outliers[8] were excluded. The pupil radius was comparable to previous studies MD=2.62 mm).

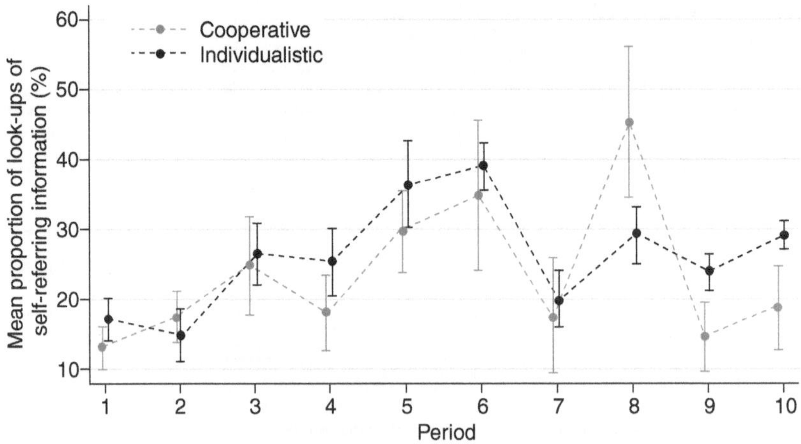

Figure 2.12 Proportion of look-ups in self-referring AOIs (payoff and contribution information) with 95 percent confidence intervals.

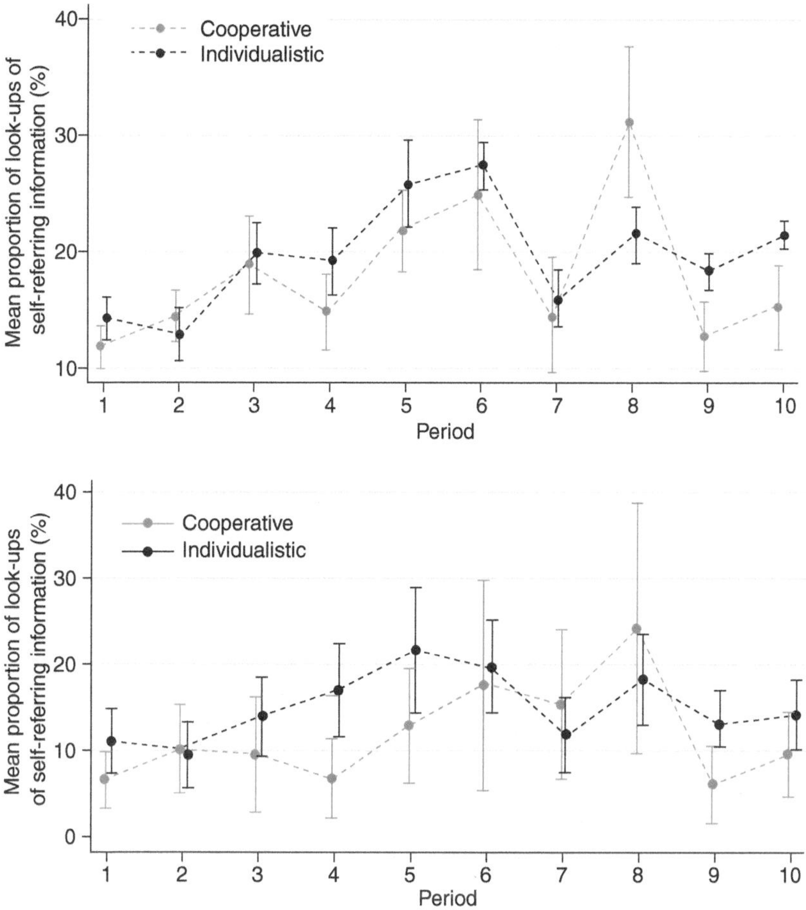

Figure 2.13 Proportion of look-ups in self-referring AOIs (payoff and contribution information) with 95 percent confidence intervals for contribution and payoff information.

A robust regression analysis predicting pupil radius by the absolute difference in contribution from the average contribution of the other two players in the previous period and SVO value, as well as their interaction as independent variables, was conducted to test Hypothesis 3. The main effect of absolute difference turned out marginally significant in support of Hypothesis 3 (Table 2.2, model 1). Separate analyses for situations in which individuals undercut the other person (Table 2.2, model 2) or try to motivate them to cooperate (Table 2.2, model 3) indicate that the main effect was mainly driven by the latter situations (see Figure 2.14b). Interestingly, there was an interaction with SVO in the other situation (see Figure 2.14a).

Table 2.2 Regression table for the pupil size predicted by the SVO value and absolute difference

	Model 1 overall	*Model 2 diff ≥ 0*	*Model 3 diff < 0*
Absolute difference[a]	1.688+	2.790**	–0.422
	(2.04)	(4.18)	(–0.46)
SVO value[a]	–1.000**	–0.828**	–1.167**
	(–3.84)	(–4.05)	(–4.40)
Absolute difference[a]	0.00712	–0.00569	0.0717+
× SVO-Value[a]	(0.35)	(–0.53)	(2.00)
Constant	267.0**	262.5**	275.2**
	(38.41)	(49.34)	(37.75)
Observations	108	60	48
Adjusted R^2	0.516	0.596	0.519

Note

Values refer to unstandardized regression weights. The *t*-statistics are given in parentheses. Pupil size regressions were corrected for 12 clusters in observations (Rogers 1994) and robust standard errors were used (Hayes and Cai 2007). Significance levels are indicated by +. $p<0.10$,* $p<0.05$, ** $p<0.01$, [a] values are centered

More pro-self participants showed pupil dilations while deciding about their contribution for the next period. However, since these differences could be due to individual differences in pupil size only the within comparisons can be meaningfully interpreted. That includes comparisons between situations where the absolute difference between the contribution of the others and the own contribution is high and situations where this difference is low as well as the interactions with the SVO. Nevertheless, it is interesting that SVO has such a strong linear effect on arousal and that the model overall accounts for such a high proportion of the variance. But further studies are necessary to replicate and investigate the relation.

Discussion

The current study investigated the relationship between SVO and contributions, characteristics of the information search process, and arousal. We were able to replicate the finding that SVO can predict contribution patterns in one-shot VCM games but not in repeated VCM games (Parks 1994). In line with Cohen (1988), SVO had a medium effect on the amount of contributions when there was no repetition, but had no significant effect on the average contribution and not even on the contributions in the first period of these repeated games.

Based on these results, the question arises as to whether or not these similarities in contribution indicate that people with different SVOs differ in their information processing in repeated VCM games. The study was able to answer this question based on the data on information search and arousal.

Most of the information search parameters differ between individuals with different SVOs, although there are no differences in contributions. In line with the hypotheses, cooperative persons show longer decision times, longer mean

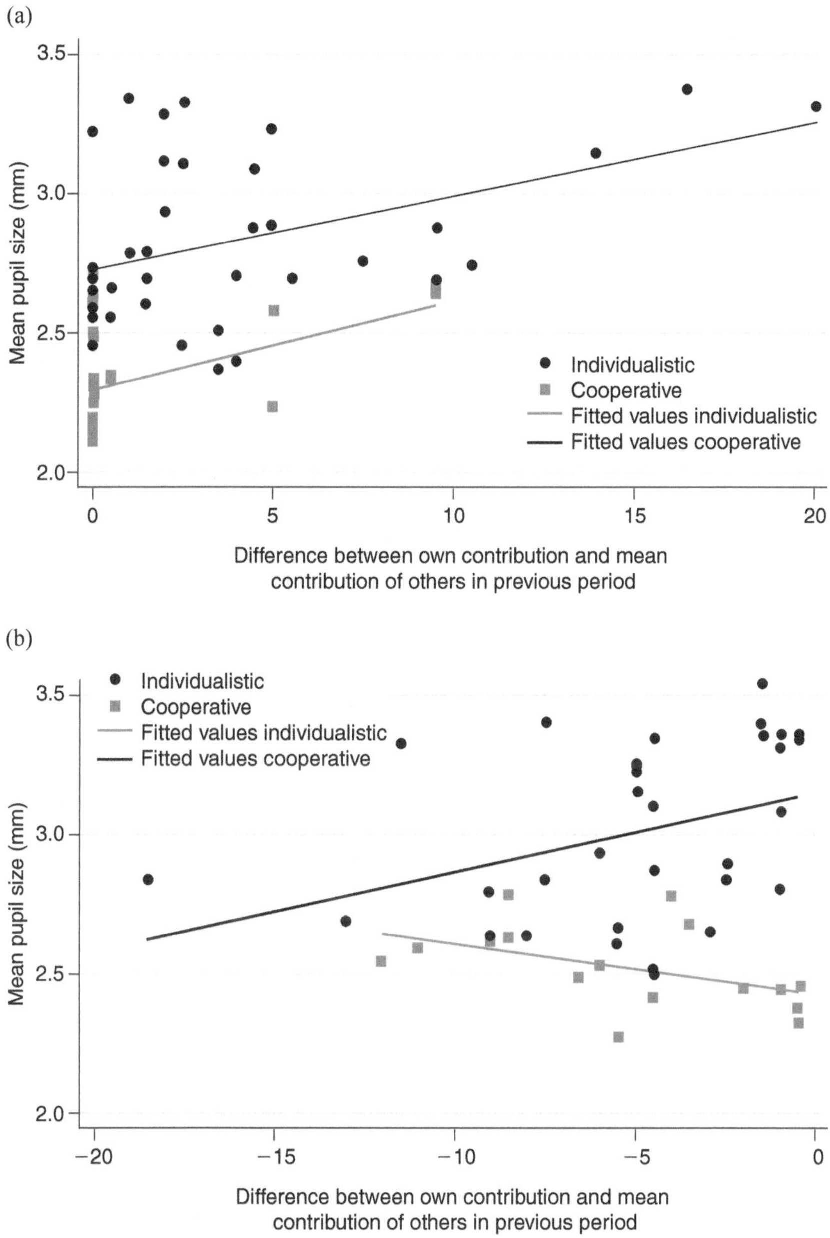

Figure 2.14 Mean pupil size as a function of player type (cooperative and individualistic) and the absolute difference between the own and the mean previous contribution of the other players.

fixation durations, and a higher proportion of long fixations than individualistic persons. The study, however, did surprisingly not find support for the hypothesis that individualistic persons look up less pieces of information (overall).

Results also showed that cooperative persons fixate more on contributions compared to individualistic persons, who mainly look at payoffs. However, we did not find differences in the proportion of look-ups of self-relevant information dependent on SVO. Furthermore, it was found that arousal increases with an increasing absolute difference between the current contribution and previous contribution levels. This effect is particularly driven by situations in which persons make lower contributions than had been previously provided on average – that is, they defect.

Overall, our findings indicate that individuals with different SVOs show considerable difference in information processing, even though we observe no differences in contributions in repeated VCM games. This indicates that pro-social persons still think pro-socially and cooperatively in repeated VCMs, but their choices are finally very similar to those made by pro-self persons. This might be due, for instance, to behavioral constraints and strong situational determination of behavior. Hence, depending on their SVO, people focus on different parts of the information and process the presented information differently. People's contributions and their overall strategy, however, seem to be dependent on their general assessment of the situation which, in turn, depends on the behavior of the other players. That means that even though people enter a VCM game or a real-life interaction with specific social preferences, they do not just follow their initial social tendency, but react to the environment surrounding them. Notwithstanding that a person cares only about his own payoffs, it is often a beneficial and even a rational strategy to cooperate in a repeated public-good game, because this, in turn, increases the other players' willingness to contribute – an aspect one might exploit later on (e.g., in the last rounds). A different effect might hold for cooperators: if they experience that one or all of the other players are free-riding on their behalf, then they might react radically and not cooperate any more. Further research is necessary to disentangle these effects of interdependency.

Relation to previous findings and possible directions for further research

The study at hand extends prior research findings (Bekkers 2004; Liebrand and McClintock 1988) on the validity of the social value construct. The results show that differences in social orientation can explain, at least partially, inter-individual differences in information acquisition and integration. There has been some discussion as to whether the root of cooperative behavior is really the interest in a public good (payoffs of others) or whether the cooperative behavior is just a sign for strategic acting with the goal to maximize one's own long-term payoffs. The recent research provides substantial evidence in support of the idea that SVO determines the mental representation of a decision situation (see, for example, De Dreu and Van Lange 1995). The data reveal that even when the players showed no differences in contributions they still displayed differences in information search and processing. Based on general assumptions concerning information processing (Svenson 1979; Velichkovsky 2001), the results can be interpreted as evidence that cooperative people take longer to make their decisions than individualistic persons. Considerations of fairness and reciprocity, as well as the interest in the well-being of others, seem to come along with more complex calculations and weightings.

Additionally, the current study revealed that individualistic people focus more on payoff than on contribution information, which is consistent with parts of the theoretical assumptions and previous findings that show individualistic players to be interested primarily in their own payoffs and not in the outcomes of other players (Liebrand and McClintock 1988; Messick and McClintock 1968; Van Lange 1999). The recent findings indicate that sometimes even individualistic persons are interested in the payoff information of the other players.

Together with the findings that SVO influences fixation duration, decision times, and the proportion of long and medium fixations, these results are additional evidence of the fact that SVO deeply and sustainably influences people's cognitive process of information search.

Based on these findings, the differences in information search and processing for persons with different SVO can be summarized as follows: Cooperators seem to use the same amount of information as individualists, but they invest more time to process this information. But why is it that cooperators need more time and more intense cognitive processes while deciding about their next contribution? One possible explanation could be that they evaluate the given feedback about the other players more thoroughly and thereby take into account more than one period. They might try to memorize the contributions of the other players to remember them in the next period. Additionally, it is possible that individualists only scan all pieces of information without really using them, as cooperators might do. For cooperators it is important to know and to take into account how all players behave in the game.

Pro-social individuals focus more on information about the contributions than pro-self persons. How can this be the case? A possible explanation could be their higher concern about fairness causing an increased interest in cheating detection for which contributions are the relevant source. Pro-self individuals focus more on the payoff of every player and themselves. Overall, considering these findings it might be promising to develop process models of decision-making in strategic games that take into account differences in how thoroughly different pieces of information are considered and what information a decision is mainly based on.

Additionally, this study sheds light on the relation between contributions and arousal and how it is influenced by SVO. The overall results are in line with Wang *et al.* (2010), who show that the magnitude of arousal depends on the absolute difference of the own contribution and the average previous contribution. Our findings indicate that the defection (i.e., giving less than others and benefiting from their contribution) increases arousal independently of SVO. Giving more than others, on the other hand, is different for pro-social and pro-self people. It remains to be seen whether this differential interaction effect is replicated in further studies.

Limitations of the study

Overall, this is one of the first studies that uses eye-tracking for investigating cognitive processes in strategic games. It has to be kept in mind that fixations and pupil diameter are only vague proxies for underlying processes. A replication of the study is needed to test the stability of the results. Further research will improve our understanding of the validity of these cues in decision tasks in general and specifically in strategic games (see, for example, Horstmann *et al.* 2010).

For pupil dilation, the problem is even more severe than for other fixation parameters. It has been shown that – besides being linked to arousal – pupil dilation is connected with stress, pain, and cognitive load (Hess and Polt 1964; Kahneman *et al.* 1969; Klingner *et al.* 2008). Future research should focus on methodological issues of the measurement of pupil dilations in strategic games.

This study shows that SVO sustainably influences information search processes in repeated VCM games. This could be a good starting point for further, more differentiated investigations of cooperation behavior and the development of more detailed process models. Eye-tracking has been proven to be an interesting method for achieving this goal.

Acknowledgments

The authors thank Frank Renkewitz for his helpful comments on a previous draft of this chapter.

Notes

1 Payoff information in these games is presented in a matrix, so that all strategies and their corresponding payoffs are included.
2 One Token corresponds to a specific amount of money. The exchange rate is stable and known by the participants.
3 Please contact the author for supplementary materials (fiedler@coll.mpg.de).
4 There will be no reports on altruistic and competitive persons because only individualistic and cooperative behavior was observed in the ring measure of social values.
5 This is an already adjusted dataset (adjustment: median ±3 standard deviations).
6 The common observation that fixation duration distributions are not normally distributed can be produced by the combination of different mechanisms of information processing; the duration of each may by itself be normally distributed (Unema *et al.* 2001).
7 The observations within one person are not independent of each other (repeated measure). Within a person this could lead to dependent residuals, which is why a robust regression with a cluster option is used to indicate that the observations have to be clustered within persons and that these observations may be correlated among each other. A random-effects model was used to correct for these dependencies. This model allows for different correlations between error terms for each individual. To account for the violations of the homoscedasticity assumption, Huber–White robust standard errors were used. Both corrections are recommended standard functions within STATA and are implemented in supplementing regression commands by the options *cluster(subject)* and *robust* (Hayes and Cai 2007; Rogers 1994).

8 Outliers are defined as extreme values if they are outside the range of median ±3 standard deviations.

References

Balliet, D., Parks, C. and Joireman, J. (2009) "Social value orientation and cooperation in social dilemmas: a meta-analysis," *Group Processes and Intergroup Relations*, 12 (4): 533.

Beach, L.R. and Mitchell, T.R. (1978) "A contingency model for the selection of decision strategies," *Academy of Management Review*, 3 (3): 439–449.

Beatty, J. (1982) "Task-evoked pupillary responses, processing load and the structure of processing resources," *Psychological Bulletin*, 91 (2): 276–292.

Bekkers, R. (2004) *Stability, Reliability and Validity of Social Value Orientation*, unpublished manuscript, Utrecht University.

Bierman, D.J. (2004) *Non Conscious Processes Preceding Intuitive Decisions*, Paper presented at the Proceedings of Bial Foundation 5th Symposium: Behind and Beyond the Brain, Porto, Portugal.

Bigoni, M. (2008) *Information and Learning in Oligopoly: An Experiment*, unpublished manuscript.

Billings, R.S. and Marcus, S.A. (1983) "Measures of compensatory and noncompensatory models of decision behavior: process tracing versus policy capturing," *Organizational Behavior and Human Performance*, 31 (3): 331–352.

Bradley, M.M., Miccoli, L., Escrig, M.A., and Lang, P.J. (2008) "The pupil as a measure of emotional arousal and autonomic activation" *Psychophysiology*, 45: 602–607.

Camerer, C., Johnson, E., Rymon, T., and Sen, S. (1993) "Cognition and framing in sequential bargaining for gains and losses," in K. Binmore, A. Kirman, and P. Tani (eds.), *Frontiers of Game Theory*, Cambridge, MA: MIT Press.

Cameron, C.F., Brown, P.M., and Chapman, J.G. (1998) "Social value orientations and decisions to take proenvironmental action," *Journal of Applied Social Psychology*, 28: 675–697.

Chen, C.T., Huang, C.Y., and Wang, J.T. (2009) *A Window of Cognition: Eyetracking the Reasoning Process in Spatial Beauty Contest Games*, unpublished manuscript, Taiwan University.

Cohen, J. (1988) *Statistical Power Analysis for the Behavioral Sciences*, Hillsdale, NJ: Lawrence Erlbaum Associates.

Costa-Gomes, M. and Crawford, V. (2007) *Studying Cognition via Information Search in Two-Person Guessing Game Experiments*, unpublished manuscript.

Costa-Gomes, M., Crawford, V.P., and Broseta, B. (2001) "Cognition and behavior in normal-form games: an experimental study," *Econometrica*, 69 (5): 1193–1235.

Crawford, V. (2008) "Look-ups as the windows of the strategic soul: studying cognition via information search in game experiments," in A. Caplin and A. Schotter (eds.), *Perspectives on the Future of Economics: Positive and Normative Foundations*, New York: Oxford University Press.

De Cremer, D. and van Dijk, E. (2002) "Perceived criticality and contributions in public good dilemmas: a matter of feeling responsible to all?," *Group Processes and Intergroup Relations*, 5 (4): 319–332.

De Dreu, C. and Van Lange, P. (1995) "The impact of social value orientation on negotiator behavior and cognition," *Personality and Social Psychology Bulletin*, 21: 1178–1188.

Fehr, E. and Fischbacher, U. (2002) "Why social preferences matter: the impact of non-selfish motives on competition, cooperation and incentives," *Economic Journal*, 112: 1–33.

Fischbacher, U. (2007) "Z-Tree: Zurich toolbox for ready-made economic experiments," *Experimental Economics*, 10 (2): 171–178.

Fischbacher, U. and Gächter, S. (2010) "Social preferences, beliefs and the dynamicy of free riding in public good experiments," *American Economic Review*, 100: 541–556.

Glöckner, A. (2009) "Investigating intuitive and deliberate processes statistically: the multiple-measure maximum likelihood strategy classification method," *Judgment and Decision Making*, 4 (3): 186–199.

Glöckner, A. (2010) "Multiple measure strategy classification: outcomes, decision times and confidence ratings," in A. Glöckner and C. Witteman (eds.), *Tracing Intuition: Recent Methods in Measuring Intuitive and Deliberate Processes in Decision Making*, London: Psychology Press and Routledge.

Glöckner, A. and Betsch, T. (2008) "Multiple-reason decision making based on automatic processing," *Journal of Experimental Psychology: Learning, Memory and Cognition*, 34 (5): 1055–1075.

Glöckner, A. and Herbold, A.K. (2011) "An eye-tracking study on information processing in risky decisions: evidence for compensatory strategies based on automatic processes," *Journal of Behavioral Decision Making*, in press.

Glöckner, A. and Witteman, C. (2010) "Beyond dual-process models: a categorisation of processes underlying intuitive judgement and decision making," *Thinking and Reasoning*, 16 (1): 1–25.

Goldberg, J.H. and Kotval, X.P. (1999) "Computer interface evaluation using eye movements: methods and constructs," *International Journal of Industrial Ergonomics*, 24 (6): 631–645.

Greiner, B. (2004) "The online recruitment system ORSEE 2.0: a guide for the organization of experiments in economics," *University of Cologne, Working Paper Series in Economics*, 10.

Hayes, A.F. and Cai, L. (2007) "Using heteroskedasticity-consistent standard error estimators in OLS regression: an introduction and software implementation," *Behavior Research Methods*, 39 (4): 709–722.

Hess, E.H. and Polt, J.M. (1960) "Pupil size as related to interest value of visual stimuli," *Science*, 132 (3423): 349–350.

Hess, E.H. and Polt, J.M. (1964) "Pupil size in relation to mental activity during simple problem-solving," *Science*, 143 (3611): 1190–1192.

Hochman, G. and Yechiam, E. (2010) *Loss Aversion in the Eye and in the Heart: The Autonomic Nervous System's Responses to Losses*, unpublished manuscript.

Horstmann, N., Ahlgrimm, A., and Glöckner, A. (2010) "How distinct are intuition and deliberation? An eye-tracking analysis of instruction-induced decision modes," *Judgment and Decision Making*, 4: 335–354.

Isaac, R.M., McCue, K.F., and Plott, C. (1985) "Public goods provision in an experimental environment," *Journal of Public Economics*, 26 (1): 51–74.

Jacob, R.J.K. and Karn, K.S. (2003) "Eye tracking in human–computer interaction and usability research: ready to deliver the promises," *Mind*, 2 (3): 573–605.

Janisse, M.P. (1977) *Pupillometry: The Psychology of the Pupillary Response*, New York: Halsted Press.

Johnson, E.J., Payne, J.W., Schkade, D.A., and Bettman, J.R. (1986) *Monitoring Information Processing and Decisions: The Mouselab System*, Unpublished manuscript, Center for Decision Studies, Fuqua School of Business, Duke University.

Johnson, E.J., Camerer, C., Sen, S., and Rymon, T. (2002) "Detecting failures of backward induction: monitoring information search in sequential bargaining," *Journal of Economic Theory*, 104 (1): 16–47.

Just, M.A. and Carpenter, P.A. (1976) "Eye fixations and cognitive processes," *Cognitive Psychology*, 8: 441–480.

Kahneman, D., Tursky, B., Shapiro, D., and Crider, A. (1969) "Pupillary, heart rate and skin resistance changes during a mental task," *Journal of Experimental Psychology*, 79 (1): 164–167.

Keser, C. and van Winden, F. (2000) "Conditional cooperation and voluntary contributions to public goods," *Scandinavian Journal of Economics*, 102 (1): 23–39.

Klingner, J., Kumar, R., and Hanrahan, P. (2008) *Measuring the Task-evoked Pupillary Response with a Remote Eye Tracker*, Paper presented at the Proceedings of the 2008 Symposium on Eye Tracking Research and Applications, Savannah.

Knoepfle, D.T., Tao-yi Wang, J., and Camerer, C.F. (2009) "Studying learning in games using eye-tracking," *Journal of the European Economic Association*, 7 (2–3): 388–398.

Kuhlman, D.M. and Marshello, A.F. (1975) "Individual differences in game motivation as moderators of preprogrammed strategy effects in prisoner's dilemma," *Journal of Personality and Social Psychology*, 32 (5): 922–931.

Kurzban, R. and Descioli, P. (2008) "Reciprocity in groups: information-seeking in a public goods game," *European Journal of Social Psychology*, 38 (1): 139–158.

Liebrand, W.B.G. and McClintock, C.G. (1988) "The ring measure of social values: a computerized procedure for assessing individual differences in information processing and social value orientation," *European Journal of Personality*, 2 (3): 217–230.

Liebrand, W.B.G., Jansen, R., Rijken, V.M., and Suhre, C.J.M. (1986) "Might over morality: social values and the perception of other players in experimental games," *Journal of Experimental Social Psychology*, 22 (3): 203–215.

Lohse, G.L. and Johnson, E.J. (1996) "A comparison of two process tracing methods for choice tasks," *Organizational Behavior and Human Decision Processes*, 68 (1): 28–43.

McClintock, C.G. and Liebrand, W.B.G. (1988) "Role of interdependence structure, individual value orientation and another's strategy in social decision making: a transformational analysis," *Journal of Personality and Social Psychology*, 55 (3): 396–409.

Martignon, L. and Hoffrage, U. (1999) "Why does one-reason decision making work," in G. Gigerenzer and P.M. Todd (eds.), *Simple Heuristics that Make Us Smart*, New York: Oxford University Press.

Messick, D. and McClintock, C.G. (1968) "Motivational bases of choice in experimental games," *Journal of Experimental Social Psychology*, 4 (1): 1–25.

Newell, A. and Simon, H.A. (1972) *Human Problem Solving*, Englewood Cliffs, NJ: Prentice-Hall.

Offerman, T., Sonnemans, J., and Schram, A. (1996) "value orientations, expectations and voluntary contributions in public goods," *Economic Journal*, 106 (437): 817–845.

Parks, C. (1994) "The predictive ability of social values in resource dilemmas and public goods game," *Personality and Social Psychology Bulletin*, 20 (4): 431–438.

Partala, T. and Surakka, V. (2003) "Pupil size variation as an indication of affective processing," *International Journal of Human-Computer Studies*, 59 (1–2): 185–198.

Payne, J.W. (1976) "Task complexity and contingent processing in decision making: an information search and protocol analysis," *Organizational Behavior and Human Performance*, 16 (2): 366–387.

Payne, J.W. (1994) "Thinking aloud: insights into information processing," *Psychological Science*, 5 (5): 241–248.

Payne, J.W. and Braunstein, M.L. (1978) "Risky choice: an examination of information acquisition behavior," *Memory and Cognition*, 6 (5): 554–561.

Payne, J.W., Bettman, J.R., and Johnson, E.J. (1988) "Adaptive strategy selection in decision making," *Journal of Experimental Psychology: Learning, Memory and Cognition*, 14 (3): 534–552.

Payne, J.W., Bettman, J.R., and Johnson, E.J. (1993) *The Adaptive Decision Maker*: Cambridge, MA: Cambridge University Press.

Pomplun, M., Ritter, H., and Velichkovsky, B. (1996) "Disambiguating complex visual information: towards communication of personal views of a scene," *Perception*, 25: 931–948.

Poole, A., Ball, L.J., and Phillips, P. (2005) "In search of salience: a response-time and eye-movement analysis of bookmark recognition," *People and Computers*, 18: 363–378.

Rapoport, A. and Chammah, A.M. (1965) *Prisoner's Dilemma: A Study in Conflict and Cooperation*, Ann Arbor, MI: University of Michigan Press.

Rayner, K. (1998) "Eye movements in reading and information processing: 20 years of research," *Psychological Bulletin*, 124 (3): 372–422.

Renkewitz, F. and Jahn, G. (2010) "Tracking memory search for cue information," in A. Glöckner and C. Witteman (eds.), *Foundations for Tracing Intuition: Challenges and Methods*, Hove: Psychology Press.

Renkewitz, F., Fuchs, H. and Fieldler, S. (2011) "Is there evidence for publication biases in JDM research?" *Judgment and Decision Making*, 6: 870–881.

Reuben, E. and Riedl, A. (forthcoming) "Public goods provision and sanctioning in privileged groups," *Journal of Conflict Resolution*, in press.

Rogers, W. (1994) "Regression standard errors in clustered samples," *Stata Technical Bulletin*, 13: 19–23.

Russo, J.E. and Rosen, L.D. (1975) "An eye fixation analysis of multialternative choice," *Memory and Cognition*, 3 (3): 267–276.

Simon, H.A. (1955) "A behavioral model of rational choice," *Quarterly Journal of Economics*, 69 (1): 99–118.

Smeesters, D., Warlop, L., Van Avermaet, E., Corneille, O., and Yzerbyt, V. (2003) "Do not prime hawks with doves: the interplay of construct activation and consistency of social value orientation on cooperative behavior," *Journal of Personality and Social Psychology*, 84 (5): 972–987.

Steinhauer, S.R., Boller, F., Zubin, J., and Pearlman, S. (1983) "Pupillary dilation to emotional visual stimuli revisited," *Psychophysiology*, 20: 472.

Svenson, O. (1979) "Process descriptions of decision making," *Organizational Behavior and Human Performance*, 23 (1): 86–112.

Tversky, A. and Kahneman, D. (2000) "Judgment under uncertainty: heuristics and biases," in T. Connolly, H.R. Arkes and K.R. Hammond (eds.), *Judgment and Decision Making: An Interdisciplinary Reader*, New York: Cambridge University Press.

Unema, P.J.A., Dornhoefer, S.M., Steudel, S., and Velichkovsky, B.M. (2001) "An attentive look at driver's fixation durations," *Vision in Vehicles-VIII*. Amsterdam: Elsevier Science Ltd.

Van Lange, P. (1999) "The pursuit of joint outcomes and equality in outcomes: an integrative model of social value orientation," *Journal of Personality and Social Psychology*, 77 (2): 337–349.

Van Lange, P., Otten, W., De Bruin, E.M.N., and Joireman, J.A. (1997a) "Development of prosocial, individualistic and competitive orientations: theory and preliminary evidence," *Journal of Personality and Social Psychology*, 73: 733–746.

Van Lange, P., Agnew, C.R., Harinck, F., and Steemers, G.E.M. (1997b) "From game theory to real life: how social value orientation affects willingness to sacrifice in ongoing close relationships," *Journal of Personality and Social Psychology*, 73: 1330–1344.

Velichkovsky, B.M. (1999) "From levels of processing to stratification of cognition," in B.H. Challis and B.M. Velichkovskii (eds.), *Stratification in Cognition and Consciousness*, Amsterdam: John Benjamins.

Velichkovsky, B.M. (2001) "Levels of processing: validating the concept," in F.I.M. Craik, M. Naveh-Benjamin, and M. Moscovitch (eds.), *Perspectives on Human Memory and Cognitive Aging: Essays in Honour of Fergus Craik*, New York: Psychology Press.

Wang, J.T., Spezio, M., and Camerer, C.F. (2010) "Pinocchio's pupil: using eyetracking and pupil dilation to understand truth-telling and deception in games," *American Economic Review*, 100 (3): 984–1007.

Weimann, J. (1994) "Individual behaviour in a free riding experiment," *Journal of Public Economics*, 54: 185–200.

3 Gaze bias reveals different cognitive processes in decision-making under uncertainty

Pietro Piu, Francesco Fargnoli and Alessandra Rufa

Introduction

The dual process theory differentiates two cognitive systems: System 1, which is heuristic; and System 2, which is analytic. This theoretical framework may be adapted for resolving behavioural differences in decision-making (DM) processes (Kahneman 1999).

It is generally assumed that every living being, including humans, tends to maximize the expected positive outcome of an action such as utility, gain or pleasure. In this respect, standard economic theory emphasizes the role of analytic processes and rational behaviour in guiding human decisions by maximizing the sum of utilities for various outcomes weighted by their probabilities (expected utility theory) (Lee 2006). However, the rationality in DM is limited by the uncertainty (i.e. incompleteness of information), the cognitive capabilities of the subjects to retain and elaborate the information and the finite time allowed to take the decision (De Martino *et al.* 2006). Thus, according to the concept of 'bounded rationality' (Simon 1957, 1991), the DM, instead of producing the maximization of some function of utility, may return a sub-optimal solution that is an 'approximate' but satisfactory result. In this respect, when decisions are taken in contexts where available information is too complex or incomplete, people tend to approximate the optimal choice using simplified heuristic routines, often driven by the emotional system.

Uncertainty in the DM arises from noisy inputs or the noisy perception of the inputs (the brain is inherently noisy) and from the lack of complete knowledge of the outcomes (Hsu *et al.* 2005). Thus, DM under uncertainty also needs probabilistic rules and it may be handled by means of informational cascade (IC). IC occurs when the subjects consider the final decisions of the participants ahead, independently of their own private signal. Individuals in an IC typically mimic the behaviour of other components of the cascade, but it is not mindless imitation – rather, it is the result of drawing rational inferences from a restricted amount of information (Banerjee 1992; Bikhchandani *et al.* 1992).

The analysis of gaze may reveal some mechanisms underlying the DM process (Trommershäuser *et al.* 2009). Laboratory evidence shows the accumulation of continuous engagement of gaze-related brain areas in both perceptual- and value-based DM (Wang 2008; Serences 2008). Indeed, choices are made in frontal parietal networks, including perceptual- and eye movement-related areas (Kiani and Shadlen 2009), and it is also demonstrated that attention orienting and saccade planning occur in early stages of the DM process. Thus, it is plausible that the gaze orienting supports the brain in making decisions by increasingly looking at the eventually chosen target and decreasing inspection time over less relevant details. Moreover, it has been reported that the exogenous manipulation of the visual attention may modulate the final choice. Finally, Shimojo *et al.* (2003) showed a *gaze cascade* effect which is an increasing gaze bias towards a chosen target in a two-alternative forced-choice preference task.

We used an eye-tracking setting to study whether gaze orienting reveals differences in DM behaviour between subjects embedded within an IC. We expected to find gaze biases among subjects taking into account the IC and those deviating from the IC.

Methods

Participants

Participants were 72 healthy volunteers (35 males and 37 females, mean age 22.4 years), with normal or corrected-to-normal vision. Subjects were recruited from graduate and undergraduate students of the University of Siena through notices posted on university web pages. All were naïve to the purpose of the study. None of the subjects was on drugs influencing DM in any way. Participants were required to avoid alcohol, caffeine and smoking for four hours before the experiment. All volunteers were guaranteed a baseline fee of €5 for participation in the study, in addition to the money gained during the task. Informed written consent was obtained from all participants. The study was performed according to the criteria of the Declaration of Helsinki and was approved by the local Ethics Committee.

Gambling task

In the game paradigm, subjects were instructed to make a prediction in a probabilistic game with a monetary reward of €5 in the case of a correct answer. The experimental design comprised eight experimental sessions, each involving nine participants. Subjects were randomly assigned to one of the eight groups. Sessions were performed on three different days. Before starting each session, the experimenter showed the nine participants the content of two envelopes marked with a red square and a red circle, respectively. The envelope with the square contained two square forms and one round form, while the envelope with the circle contained two round forms and one square form. The experimenter draws randomly, in a separate box obscured to the players, one out of the two envelopes, which will be the object of the bet. The nine subjects were randomly arranged in sequence and asked to predict which envelope had been drawn on the basis of two different kinds of information. First, a private signal, which is a form, for each subject independently and randomly drawn out of the chosen envelope, with a two-thirds chance of indicating the correct event. Second, the former choices (but not the private signals) made by all the players, who previously betted in the sequence. To monitor the gaze, the prediction was made separately by each subject looking at an LCD screen displaying the information in an eye-tracking setting. At the beginning of each trial, the subject stared at a central fixation cross. After a time interval of 500 ms the fixation cross was switched off and the private signal of the subject (a red square or a red circle) was shown on the left-hand side of the screen, separated through a vertical central bar by the empty right-hand side. After a time interval of 1,000 ms, the private signal disappeared and the choices of the previous subjects were displayed on the right-hand side of the screen. Each prediction was shown for a time of 1,000 ms as a red square (corresponding to the square-marked envelope) or a red circle (circle-marked envelope) marked with the position of the related player in the session, following the sequence. Subjects were instructed to make their decision during the last screen, lasting 5,000 ms, where the private signal was placed on the left-hand side and the opposite form on the right side, in such a way that the possible final screen displayed the couple square–circle or circle–square for each player. Timing of the game was calculated to force the choice during the last screen, avoiding a scenario in which participants made decisions while information was given.

Participants were instructed to state their prediction, whichever envelope had been drawn, as quickly as possible after the last screen. Immediately after the response, each subject was required to fill out a brief structured questionnaire, explaining the main reason of the choice selecting among four possibilities: (1) private signal; (2) choices of the previous subjects in the sessions; (3) probability calculation; (4) random/casual answer.

During each session it was strictly forbidden for participants to talk to each other about any information regarding the experiment, particularly signals and choices made.

The items shown on the screen were reversed in sessions 4–6, in which the private signal was shown on the right-hand side and the previous choices on the left, to check whether the left–right orientation of reading could have some systematic effect on gaze direction.

Subjects were provided with a written description of the condition of the game, which was read and explained by an experimenter to all the participants, who had the option to ask questions. To ensure that participants fully understood the rules of the task, a brief simulation of the experimental condition was shown on a screen prior to the session. A fundamental explanation about the eye-tracking techniques and the calibration procedure was also provided to subjects.

Experimental setting and eye-movement recording

All experiments were carried out in complete darkness. Subjects were head restrained by means of a frontal support at a fixed view distance of 68 cm. All images were presented to subjects on a 31 × 51 cm LCD screen with a resolution of 1024 × 768 pixels and a monitor refresh rate of 60 Hz. Each stimulus had an overall size of 8 × 8 (horizontal × vertical) degrees of visual angle. Eye movements were recorded using a high-speed remote infrared eye-tracker, ASL 504 model (Applied Science Laboratories, Bedford, MA) with an ASL 5000 series controller provided by the Department of Neurology of the University of Siena. Eye positions were sampled at 240 Hz, and data were processed by means of the dedicated eye-tracker software, developed by the Eye-tracking Visual Application Lab (EVALAB) of the University of Siena (Rufa *et al.* 2005). Eye movements were recorded from either the right or the left eye, but viewing was always binocular. Gaze signal was calibrated at the beginning of each experiment using interactive dedicated software, by a nine-point calibration and a three-point control. The guidelines of the University of Siena Standing Committee on Laboratory Experiments were followed throughout the experiments.

Data pre-treatment

Data analysis was conducted offline using an automatic algorithm. All computation was done with Matlab software (The MathWorks Inc., Natick, MA). We focused our analysis on the later 5 s of data recoded array when the subject made the decision. Data were sampled every 36 ms, so 136 sub-samples per subject were extracted.

We determined the fixation point using a dispersion-based algorithm (Gelman 2002) and saccades using a velocity-based algorithm. We previously verified that sampling points were within a fixation region so we could exclude that they were saccades crossing the midline.

We first analysed 72 choices. We assigned a true value (1) to every sampling point if the observer's gaze was directed towards the chosen stimulus, and a false value (0) if the gaze was towards the other stimulus (Shimojo *et al.* 2003). We calculated the likelihood that gaze was directed to the stimulus eventually chosen (Simion and Shimojo 2006).

The subjects were split into two groups (A and B) based on their overt choice and verbal report. Group A based decisions on the private signal, while group B considered both the private signal and the previous choices following the IC. We analysed separately the gaze of the two groups and then compared them.

Statistical analysis

The DM under uncertainty needs a probabilistic approach; we can then try to read the eye movements under Bayesian theory.

In its more general formulation, Bayes' theorem (Equation 3.1) provides a measure of the reliance upon a certain hypothesis or model, based on the acquired data:

$$p(\text{hypothesis} \mid \text{data}) = \frac{p(\text{data} \mid \text{hypothesis}) \cdot p(\text{hypothesis})}{p(\text{data})} \tag{3.1}$$

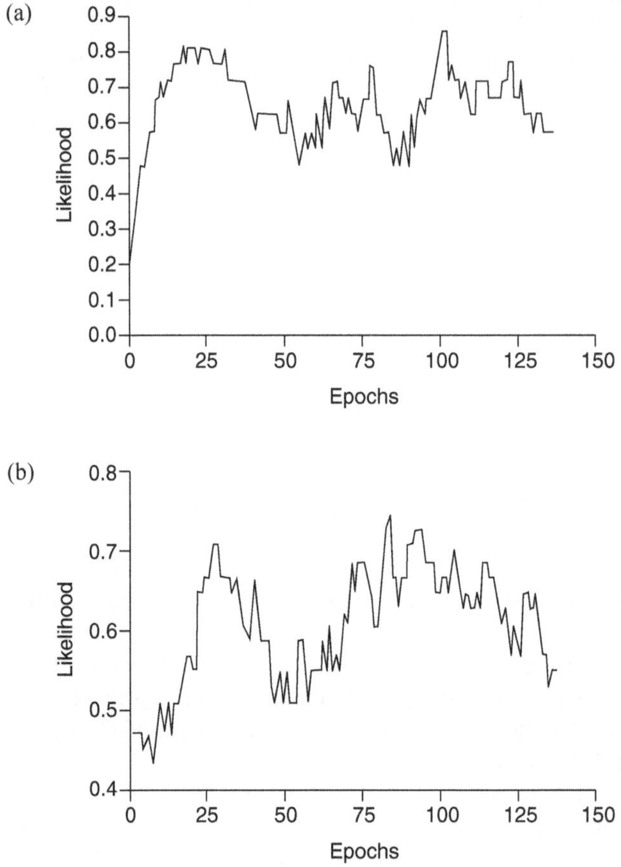

Figure 3.1 The likelihood of the observed gaze conditional to the given final chosen signal (group A in the top panel, group B in the bottom panel).

The left term of Equation 3.1 is called the *posterior probability*, which is the probability that, having observed a certain dataset, data could have been generated according to the hypothesis taken. The Bayesian inference refers to the *principle of inverse probability* in the form: 'the posterior probability is proportional to the product of the *prior probability* and the *likelihood*' (Jeffreys 1961), where the likelihood represents the compatibility of the observed data with the hypothesis and the prior is the inherent likelihood that is the probability associated to that hypothesis. The decisional process was studied as the time course of the *likelihood* of gazing at the ultimate selected item (square vs circle).

The distribution of the likelihood for groups A and B appeared significantly bimodal according to Hartigan's dip test (Hartigan and Hartigan 1985; Mechler and Ringach 2002), which returned the statistics dip=0.0882 and 0.0662 for A and B, respectively, with p-value=0 for both groups.

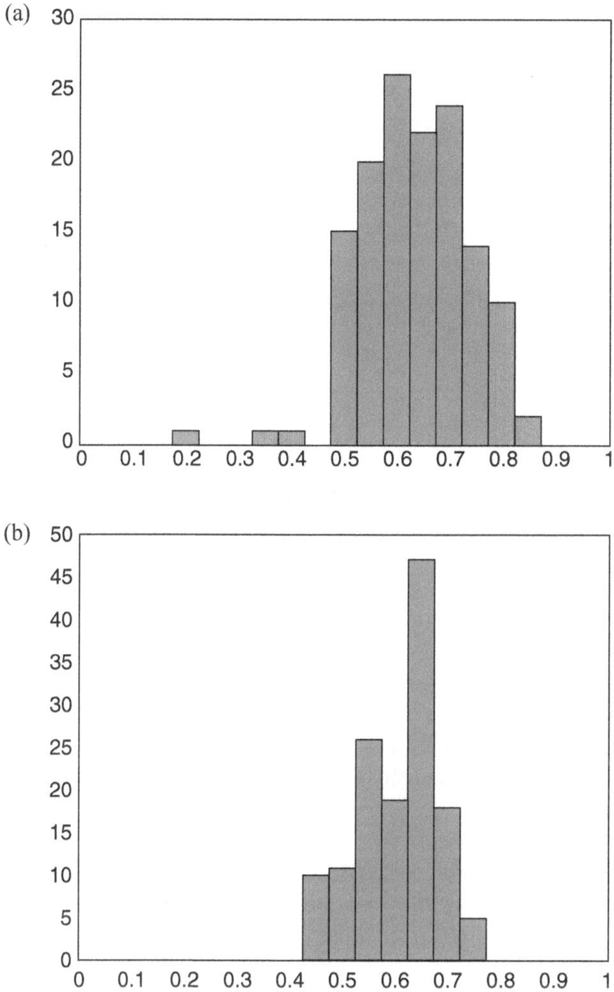

Figure 3.2 The results of the Hartigan's tests applied to group A (top panel) and group B (bottom panel).

The likelihood expresses a conditional probability, whose functional form, because of its possible non-unimodality, may even not adhere the more usual probability distribution. Therefore, the adoption of *basis functions* comes in handy for estimating the distribution of the likelihood series (y). The basis functions give rise to a superposition of a number M of non-linear kernel functions $\varphi_j = \varphi(|z - \mu_j|)$ where μ_j is a template vector of size n (with $n \in \mathbb{N}^+$) for the observed variable $z \in \mathbb{R}^n$ in the j-th basis function φ_j (see Equation 3.2). The functions φ_j depend on the distance (let's take for example the L^2-norm) between z and μ_j, thus the vector μ_j acts as the centre of the kernel φ_j. It is possible to verify that $y = f(z)$ may be written as:

$$y = f(z) = \sum_{j:1}^{M} \alpha_j \cdot \phi\left(\left\| z - \mu_j \right\|\right) \tag{3.2}$$

The superposition in Equation 3.2 is also known as the mixture model and, provided the number of kernels M is sufficiently high, it can approximate any continuous density function to arbitrary accuracy (Bishop 1995). If we take a Gaussian function, i.e. a radial function for the φ, then we obtain a radial basis function model that holds the property of best approximation (Girosi and Poggio 1990), that is the Gaussian mixture model (GMM):

$$y = f(z) = \sum_{j:1}^{M} \alpha_j \cdot \frac{e^{\left(-\frac{(z-\mu_j)' \cdot \Sigma_j^{-1} \cdot (z-\mu_j)}{2}\right)}}{(2\pi)^{\frac{n}{2}} \cdot \sqrt{\det(\Sigma_j)}} \tag{3.3}$$

where $\det(\Sigma_j)$ is the determinant of the variance–covariance matrix of the j-th kernel and $\sum_{j:1}^{M} \alpha_j = 1$ with $\alpha_j \geq 0 \ \forall j$. Thus, the conditions of non-negativity and of summation to the unit over the weights $(\alpha_1, \ldots, \alpha_M)$ make them the prior probabilities of the data point having been generated from the components of the mixture. The parameters of a GMM are then the mean and variance–covariance matrix of the kernels, the number of kernels M and the vector of weights $\alpha = (\alpha_1, \ldots, \alpha_M)$.

GMM may be applied not only for density estimation but also for classification problems (McLachlan and Peel 2000), and this application may be called *GMM classification* or *GMM clustering*. In fact, Bayes' decision rule implies the assignment of an (n-dimensional) input vector z to a certain class C, which gives rise to the highest posterior probability $P(C|z)$ of observing that value of z. The posterior probability is proportional to the product of the a priori probability of that class and the class-conditional probability density function (pdf). In the GMM approach to classification, the class-conditional pdf for each class C is $f_C(z) = \sum_{j:1}^{m_C} \alpha_{Cj} \phi_j$, which is a superposition of a number m_c of n-variate Gaussians φ. Thus, since each class is described by the composition of different mixture densities, which provides flexible models for $P(C|z)$ (Hastie *et al.* 2001), the GMM classification can deal with non-normality, non-linear class edges and clustered classes (Calò 2007).

The number of kernels may be determined with the Bayesian information criterion (BIC) or other goodness-of-fit indices, e.g. the root mean square error (RMSE).

The BIC penalizes the models with higher free parameters while the preferable model would show the lower value of BIC. The RMSE is the quadratic mean of the residuals of the model; thus the lower its value the better the fitting of the corresponding model. By observing the data reported in Table 3.1, we realize

Table 3.1 Selection of the basis functions for the Gaussian mixture models

Group	*No. kernels*	*RMSE*	*BIC*
A	2	0.0657	–5.2371
	3	0.4613	–4.7796
B	2	0.0454	–6.2032
	3	0.0312	–6.3492

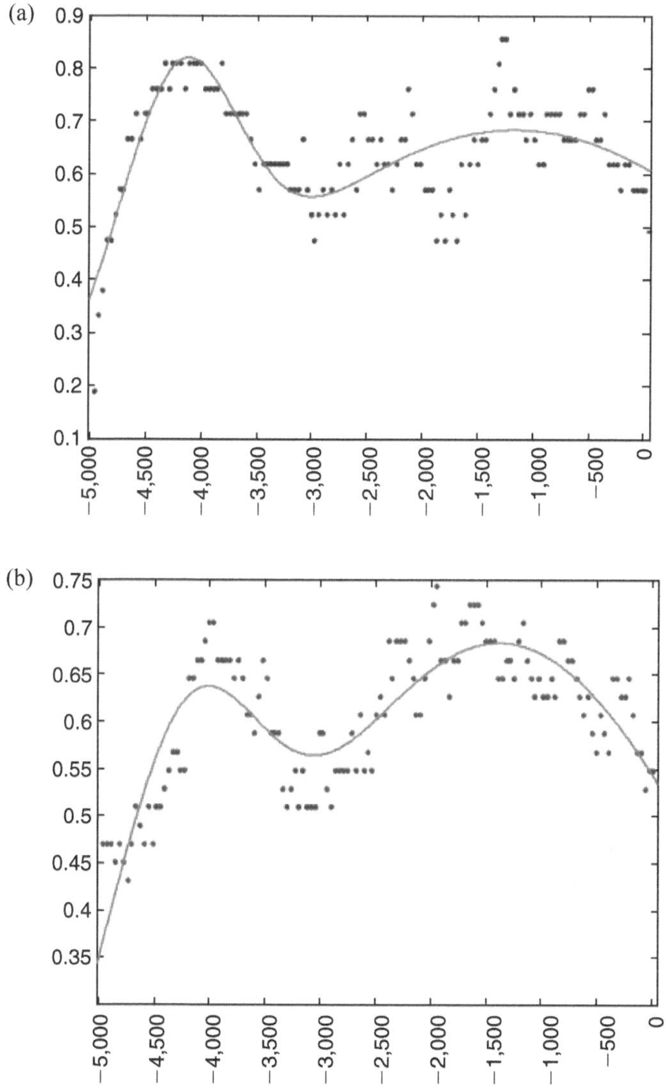

Figure 3.3 Likelihood time series (group A in the top panel, group B in the bottom panel) fitted by two Gaussians.

that two components for the GMM is optimal for group A and quasi-optimal for group B. For the latter, in fact, the absolute values of BIC and RMSE associated to the case of two kernels are higher than the ones associated to the three kernels model. But since the differences are just minor then by recalling the principle of minimal complexity (Occam's razor), according to which simpler models should be preferred to complex models, we may consider suitable the two components GMM also for group B.

Given the bimodality of the distributions of the likelihood, we considered Gaussian mixtures made of two components. Within group A and B the two bivariate Gaussian components, coming from the GMM, were only mildly overlapped, while their peaks were still distinct. Therefore, both datasets could be split consistently into two clusters. Points had been associated to clusters on the basis of estimated posterior probability that a point came from a component, namely each point had been assigned to the cluster corresponding to the highest posterior probability.

The GMM was iterated several times (n=1,000), whereas a limited number of cluster configurations came out. Table 3.2 reports the means and standard deviations of the centroids of the clusters (i.e. means of the mixture components).

Moreover, along all the iterations we observed fixed couples of the centroids. The most replicated matching of the centroids were for group A (16–0.68 and 83–0.64), and 44–0.58 and 111–0.64 for group B. Figure 3.4 shows the GMM clustering of the likelihoods for the two groups. Each cluster corresponds to one of the bivariate normal components in the mixture distribution. The points (i.e. likelihood observed over time) are associated to clusters on the basis of estimated posterior probability that a point came from a component. Each point is assigned to the cluster corresponding to the highest posterior probability.

The clusters are expressed by the ellipsoids that are centred on the vectors of means of the GMM components, and whose extensions are proportional to the eigenvectors of the variance–covariance matrices.

Table 3.2 Configurations of the centroids obtained after several iterations (1,000) of the GMM

A: mean and std dev. of centroids		*B: mean and std dev. of centroids*	
Time	*Likelihood*	*Time*	*Likelihood*
16 (0.0172)	0.68 (0.00001)	35 (0.0472)	0.53 (0.0002)
23 (0.0024)	0.75 (0.000012)	44 (0.0116)	0.58 (0.000025)
51 (0.0057)	0.64 (0.000005)	86 (0.0346)	0.65 (0.000054)
59 (0.0896)	0.70 (0.0002)	111 (0.015)	0.64 (0.000024)
73 (0.0283)	0.65 (0.0221)		
76 (0.0508)	0.61 (0.0001)		
80 (0.0027)	0.62 (0.000005)		
83 (0.0247)	0.64 (0.0001)		
118 (0.0021)	0.68 (0.000003)		

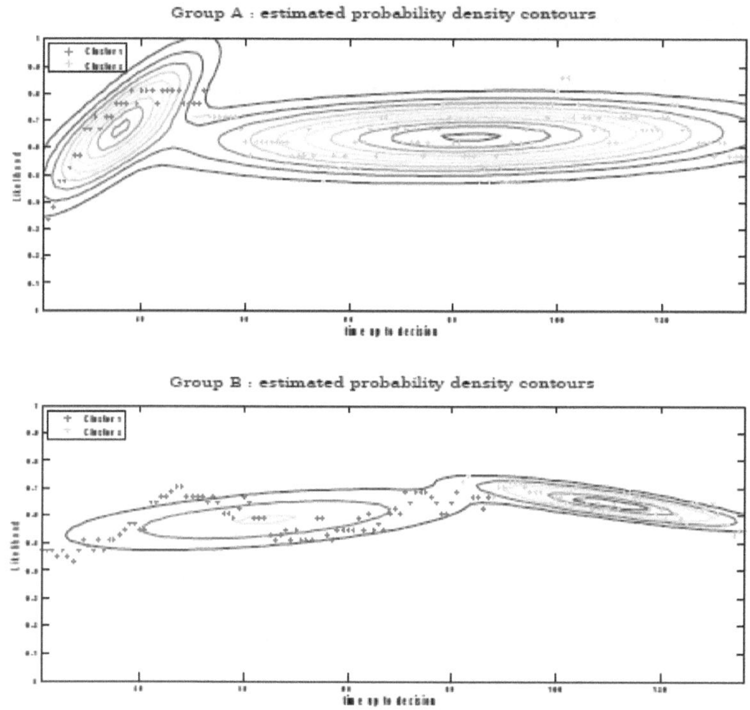

Figure 3.4 GMM clustering.

In Table 3.3 the parameters of the two-components GMM obtained for groups A and B are reported. The values of the weights indicate that the probability of membership to component 1 for group A likelihood data is only one-third of the corresponding membership probability for group B. This fact made the first

Table 3.3 Parameters of the GMMs

Component	*Weight*	*Mean vector*			
		Time	*Likelihood*	*Variance–covariance matrix*	
Group A					
1	21.93%	16.1462	0.6783	83.1550	1.2252
				1.2252	0.0261
2	78.07%	83.2079	0.6410	964.5427	0.3404
				0.3404	0.0063
Group B					
1	63.60%	44.1486	0.5857	661.6446	1.0007
				1.0007	0.0053
2	36.40%	111.0486	0.6446	231.6585	–0.6227
				–0.6227	0.0025

cluster for group A narrower than the homologous cluster of group B. Of course, the complementary considerations may be done for the weights recorded for the second components.

For both groups the (null) hypotheses of equal mean vectors and covariance matrices between the two components of the mixtures were rejected (see Table 3.4).

Hence, as a general outcome, we assess that the two components of the mixtures both in group A and in group B showed significant differences in the moments (at least up to the second order), therefore the two clusters (i.e. the class-conditional pdf for each class) were well separated. In other words, from the application of the GMM it emerged that the decisional processes in the two groups A and B were characterized by two distinct time-dependent structures (clusters) and the next step was to determine if there were differences between clusters induced by the group label. For this purpose we first compared the GMM estimated likelihood distributions of A and B (see Figure 3.5). The Kolmogorov–Smirnov (KS) test rejected the null hypothesis of equal distributions of the likelihoods between the two groups even for the nearest GMM clusterings, i.e. the ones referred to the A pdf with centroids at times (16, 83) and B pdf with centroids at times (35, 86) (KS_stat=0.2794; *p*-value=3.4635e-05).

Table 3.4 Results of the test for the null hypotheses of equal vectors of the means and equal matrices of variance–covariance for the two groups

A Tests for difference in covariance and mean between clusters			
H0: $\Sigma_1 = \Sigma_2 = \Sigma$	Stat = 99.75	(χ^2_3)	*p*-value = 0
H0: m1 = m2	Staat = 262.04	$(F_{2.121})$	*p*- value = 0
B Tests for difference in covariance and mean between clusters			
H0: $\Sigma_1 = \Sigma_2 = \Sigma$	Stat = 97.93	(χ^2_3)	*p*- value = 0
H0: m1 = m2	Staat = 218.37	$(F_{2.115})$	*p*- value = 0

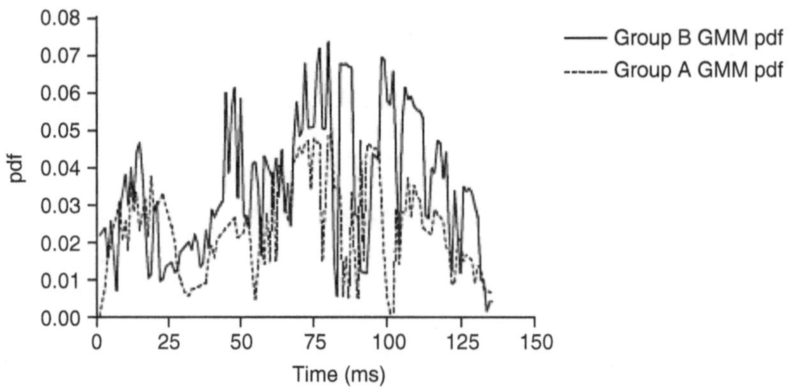

Figure 3.5 The probability density functions estimated by the two-component GMM for the two groups A and B at their specified closest centroid.

The result of the KS test implies that the distributions of the likelihoods were significantly different between the two compared groups over the whole duration (5,000 ms) of the experiment for the nearest configurations of the centroids.

Furthermore, we measured the Bhattacharyya distances (d_B) within and between the estimated GMM class-conditional pdf of the likelihood of the two groups which supported the cluster detachment. We can think of the d_B as a measure of the similarity of two probability distributions. The distance d_B may be written as:

$$d_B = -\log\left(BC\left(p,q\right)\right) \tag{3.4}$$

where $BC(p,q)$ is the Bhattacharyya coefficient between the distributions p and q, which for continuous distributions is given by:

$$BC\left(p,q\right) = \int \sqrt{p\left(x\right)\cdot q\left(x\right)}dx \tag{3.5}$$

For multivariate Gaussian distributions $x_i \sim N(m_i,S_i)$, where m_i are the vectors of the means and S_i the matrices of variance–covariance of the distributions, the distance d_B is given by:

$$d_B\left(p,q\right) = \frac{1}{8}\cdot\left(m_1 - m_2\right)'\cdot S^{-1}\cdot\left(m_1 - m_2\right) + \frac{1}{2}\cdot\log\left(\frac{\det\left(S\right)}{\sqrt{\det\left(S_1\right)\cdot\det\left(S_2\right)}}\right) \tag{3.6}$$

So, the BCs are an approximate measurement of the amount of overlap (or relative closeness) between two statistical samples. Hence, BC ranges in the interval [0, 1], where the value 0 corresponds to the event of no overlap and the value 1 stands for perfect overlap.

Figure 3.6 shows the BCs between the mixture components of the GMM applied both to the components of the GMM within each group and then between the homologue components of the groups that were calculated on the basis of Equation 3.6.

From Figure 3.6 we note that within each group the BC values were proximal to zero, thus revealing absence of significant overlap between the two clusters of the GMM models, while the comparison between the correspondent components of the GMM of groups A and B yielded relatively higher values of BC, wherein specifically the matching between components at time 83 (for group A) and 86 (for group B) provided all the values of BC greater than 0.3 (Figure 3.7).

The particular matching of centroids that would produce, over the iterations of the GMM, the BC measures greater than 0.3 occurred only 57 times, i.e. around 5 per cent of the iterations gave rise to relatively high overlapping (BC=0.5987). On the contrary, the BC between the first mixture components and between the second mixture components values were on average 0.0417 (SD=0.1347) and 0.0450 (SD=0.1393), respectively. Finally, recalling that both the test for the equality among mean vectors and the test for the equality among covariance matrices resulted in the rejection of the null hypothesis even for the

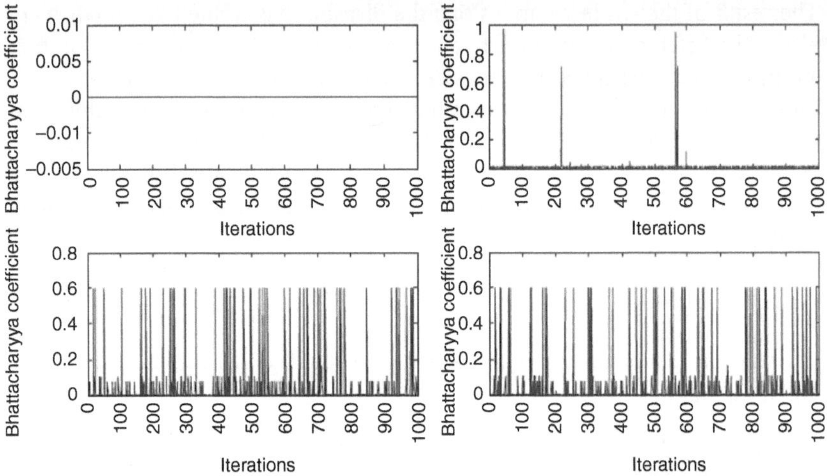

Figure 3.6 The BCs computed between the two components of the GMM (group A in the top-right panel, group B in the top-left panel). The BCs were also measured to compare the homologues components of groups A and B (the BCs for the first components in the lower-left panel, and for the second components in the lower-right panel).

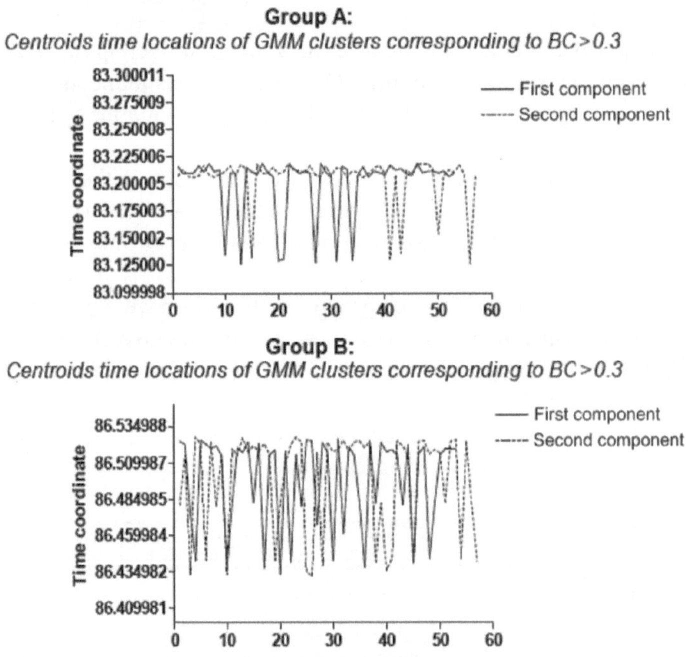

Figure 3.7 Centroids corresponding to the highest values of BC between homologue components of GMM.

closest GMM clustering configurations, it seems reasonable to consider the decisional paradigms described by GMM for group A and group B as distinct ones. In fact, the differences between groups A and B appear not only in terms of the distributions of the likelihood series, but also by considering the characterizations of the GMM (weights, centroids and dispersions).

Discussion

The main result of our study is that the gaze behaviour differs between subjects who deviated from the IC and subjects who followed the IC. Nevertheless, similarly to the gaze bias in preference tasks observed by Shimojo *et al.* (2003), in both groups a *gaze cascade effect* was evident. This suggests that the gaze cascade effect may occur also in DM under uncertainty. Unlike Shimojo, who elaborated the model by considering the last two seconds before the final decision, we developed our model by taking into account the last five seconds before the overt decision. In this period of time, the likelihood of gaze showed in both groups a bimodal distribution. However, even if the bimodality characterized both groups, the distributions of the likelihood were significantly different between groups. This would imply the occurrence of two different *phases* of cognitive process supporting a decision. Thus the components of the GMM model that we elaborated may reveal the characteristics of these phases through the centroids and the variance–covariance matrices. Our results showed significant differences in likelihood and time of centroids within and between groups. Group B showed an increase of the likelihood from the first to the second component of the GMM, while group A showed a decreased likelihood at the second component (Table 3.3). A possible explanation of this difference between groups may be related to the effect of *socially mediated positive reinforcement* (Heal and Kunreuther 2008). This process occurs when the probability of a certain behaviour (in our experiment, the gaze likelihood) increases conditionally based on the decisions of other subjects (Sanfey 2007). In our experiment this kind of reinforcement was represented by the IC. Therefore, only in group B, which showed an increment of the second component likelihood, could the socially mediated positive reinforcement be effective. Thus, in group B the reinforcement could improve the ability to overcome the uncertainty through the probabilistic computation of the IC. On the contrary, in group A, which showed a decrement of the likelihood in the second component, the positive reinforcement mediated by social interaction seemed to be ineffective. This could reveal the inability of this group of subjects to extract the probabilistic structure of the IC, their tendency to interpret the IC as an ambiguous signal and their tendency to avoid this consequent ambiguity (uncertainty with unknown probabilities). The aversion to ambiguity may lead to preference reversals (Trautmann *et al.* 2011) and it is possible that group A shifts towards the private signal, whose uncertainty could be resolved with an easier probabilistic computation.

When considering the differences in the time variable of the centroids, we observed that centroids were anticipated in group A. We interpreted this finding in terms of the dual theory through the interaction between System 1 and System 2. Since System 1 includes automatic and heuristic processes activated immediately by external stimuli, the first centroid may represent the prevalence of System 1 over System 2 (see Table 3.3). On the contrary, in group B, where both centroids were postponed, they may express the prevalence of the slower analytic process of System 2 over System 1. Actually, this aspect confirms the phenomenon of the socially mediated positive reinforcement conveyed by IC.

In conclusion, the analysis of eye movements may provide insights into the mental processes underlying DM since differences in gaze bias may be observed in preference and rational behaviour, including DM under uncertainty.

References

Banerjee, A.V. (1992) 'A simple model of herd behavior', *Quarterly Journal of Economics*, 107: 797–817.

Bikhchandani, S., Hirshleifer, D. and Welch, I. (1992) 'A theory of fads, fashion, custom, and cultural change as informational cascades', *Journal of Political Economy*, 100: 992–1026.

Bishop, C.M. (1995) *Neural Networks for Pattern Recognition*, Oxford: Oxford University Press.

Calò, D.G. (2007) 'Gaussian mixture model classification: a projection pursuit approach', *Computational Statistics and Data Analysis*, 52 (1): 471–482.

De Martino, B., Kumaran, D., Seymour, B. and Dolan, R.J. (2006) 'Frames, biases and rational decision making in the human brain', *Science*, 313: 684–687.

Gelman, D.R. (2002) 'ILAB: a program for post experimental eye movement analysis', *Behavior Research Methods, Instruments, and Computers*, 34 (4): 605–612.

Girosi, F. and Poggio, T. (1990) 'Networks and the best approximation property', *Biological Cybernetics*, 63: 169–176.

Hartigan, J.A. and Hartigan, P.M. (1985) 'The dip test of unimodality', *Annals of Statistics*, 13: 70–84.

Hastie, T., Tibshirani, R. and Friedman, J. (2001) *The Elements of Statistical Learning*, New York: Springer.

Heal, G. and Kunreuther, H. (2008) 'Social reinforcement: cascades, entrapment and tipping', *American Economic Journal: Microeconomics, American Economic Association*, 2 (1): 86–99.

Hsu, M., Bhatt, M., Adolphs, R., Tranel, D. and Camerer, C.F. (2005) 'Neural systems responding to degrees of uncertainty in human decision making', *Science*, 310: 1680–1683.

Jeffreys, H. (1961) *Theory of Probability*, 3rd edn. Oxford: Oxford University Press.

Kahneman, D. (1999) 'New challenges to the rationality assumption', *Journal of Institutional and Theoretical Economics*, 150: 18–36.

Kiani, R. and Shadlen, M.N. (2009) 'Representation of confidence associated with a decision by neurons in the parietal cortex', *Science*, 324: 759–764.

Lee, D. (2006) 'Neural basis of quasi-rational decision making', *Current Opinion in Neurobiology*, 16 (2): 191–198.

McLachlan, G.J. and Peel, D. (2000) *Finite Mixture Model*, New York: John Wiley & Sons.

Mechler, F. and Ringach, D.L. (2002) 'On the classification of simple and complex cells', *Vision* Research, 42: 1017–1033.

Rufa, A., Mariottini, G.L., Prattichizzo, D., Alessandrini, D., Vicino, A. and Federico, A. (2005) 'Video-based eye-tracking: our experience with advanced stimuli design for eye-tracking software', *Annals of the New York Academy of Sciences*, 1039: 575–579.

Sanfey, A.G. (2007) 'Social decision making: insights from game theory and neurosciences', *Science*, 318: 598–602.

Serences, J.T. (2008) 'Value-based modulations in human visual cortex', *Neuron*, 60: 1169–1181.

Shimojo, S., Simion, C., Shimojo, E. and Scheier, C. (2003) 'Gaze bias both reflects and influences preference', *Nature Neuroscience*, 6: 1317–1322.

Simion, C. and Shimojo, S. (2006) 'Early interactions between orienting, visual sampling and decision making in facial preference', *Vision Research*, 46: 3331–3335.

Simon, H. (1957) *Models of Man*, New York: John Wiley & Sons.

Simon, H. (1991) 'Bounded rationality and organizational learning', *Organization Science*, 2 (1): 125–134.

Trautmann, S.T., Vieider, F.M. and Wakker, P.P. (2011) 'Preference reversals to explain ambiguity aversion', *Management Science*, 57: 1320–1333.

Trommershäuser, J., Glimcher, P.W. and Gegenfurtner, K.R. (2009) 'Visual processing, learning and feedback in the primate eye movement system', *Trends in Neurosciences*, 32 (11): 583–590.

Wang, X.J. (2008) 'Decision making in recurrent neuronal circuits', *Neuron*, 60: 215–234.

Part II

Emotions and morality in decision-making

4 Moral sentiments

A behavioral economics approach

Marcel Zeelenberg, Seger M. Breugelmans, and Ilona E. de Hooge

The moral sentiments

Ever since Adam Smith (1759) proposed his *Theory of Moral Sentiments* it has been known that people are not strictly self-regarding, but also other-regarding. This other-regarding aspect of humans is important in creating a sustainable, livable, and sociable society. According to Smith, moral sentiments play a pivotal role in this. He also made it explicit that in his view moral sentiments are a universal aspect of humans; in us is rooted the ability to feel emotions about the fortune and misfortune of others, and our behavioral choices reflect this. Put differently, our other-regarding preferences stem from moral sentiments. The opening paragraph of Smith's book (1759: 9) reads:

> How selfish soever man may be supposed, there are evidently some principles in his nature, which interest him in the fortunes of others, and render their happiness necessary to him, though he derives nothing from it, except the pleasure of seeing it. Of this kind is pity or compassion, the emotion we feel for the misery of others, when we either see it, or are made to conceive it in a very lively manner. That we often derive sorrow from the sorrows of others, is a matter of fact too obvious to require any instances to prove it; for this sentiment, like all the other original passions of human nature, is by no means confined to the virtuous or the humane, though they perhaps may feel it with the most exquisite sensibility. The greatest ruffian, the most hardened violator of the laws of society, is not altogether without it.

Moral sentiments and pro-social behavior

Interestingly, the interest in the fortune of others violates the assumption in traditional economics and rational choice theory that people are strictly selfish (i.e., they only care about material outcomes for themselves). Nowadays, in both economics and psychology, many empirical demonstrations can be found of people actually choosing courses of action that benefit others, even at the expense of oneself (see for reviews, Batson 2011; Gintis *et al.* 2005; Henrich *et al.* 2004). Consistent with the ideas of Adam Smith, these other-regarding preferences are often explained by referring to the emotions, in particular moral emotions, that decision-makers can experience when confronted with such choice situations in which they have to balance their own outcomes and those of others. Moral emotions are those that are linked to the interests or welfare of society as a whole or of other people (Haidt 2003). They are thought to originate in social relationships and are built on reciprocal evaluations and judgments of the self and others (Tangney and Fischer 1995). The typical moral emotions are guilt, shame, and embarrassment, but one may also include anger (Berkowitz 1990), remorse, and regret (Zeelenberg and Breugelmans 2008).

Moral emotions can thus lead people to focus on the other and on how one's own behavior affects the other's well-being. For example, in situations where there is a conflict between the self-interest of a person and interest of a group (a so-called "social dilemma"), moral emotions have been claimed to motivate people to act in favor of other people's interests (Smith 1759; see also Frank 1988; Ketelaar 2004). In this way, moral sentiments should motivate cooperative behaviors.

The economist Robert Frank (1988, 2004) elaborated on the cooperative effect of moral emotions in his commitment theory. His reasoning is as follows: Often we are confronted with situations in which we need to choose between, on the one hand, immediate individual rewards that are costly for the group and, on the other hand, cooperation that is costly for the individual in the short run, but beneficial for the group and the individual's self-interest in the long run. People's self-regarding preferences may seduce them to choose the attractive immediate reward at the expense of long-term benefits. Emotions, according to Frank, may come in handy here. They can act as commitment devices that help us to solve these social dilemmas. Choosing defectively (i.e., immediate individual rewards) may give rise to negative moral emotions such as guilt, regret, shame, and embarrassment. These negative emotions create disutility and as a result they make defection less attractive. People are aware of the fact that they will feel bad about behaving egoistically (maybe by learning from experience, by mentally simulating such events, or by experiencing these emotions vicariously [Welten *et al.* 2012]), and that by choosing to avoid this behavior they also avoid feeling bad. In such a way moral emotions may commit people to choose for cooperation, for long-term outcomes or for the group's interest.

Recent research has documented the role of emotions in eliciting these prosocial behaviors. For example, Ketelaar and Au (2003) hypothesized that guilt would increase cooperation especially for people who already have a tendency to act uncooperatively. These people (hereafter referred to as pro-selfs) would perceive their feelings of guilt as a consequence of their negative behavior and use this as information about future costs of pursuing an uncooperative strategy. This would lead them to act more cooperatively compared to pro-selfs who do not experience guilt. People with the general tendency to act cooperatively (hereafter referred to as pro-socials) would already act cooperatively and thus not use the negative feeling state as an inference about their strategy. These findings of Ketelaar and Au were recently replicated by Nelissen *et al.* (2007), who studied the influences of fear and guilt on cooperation in a one-shot give-some dilemma game. They hypothesized and found guilt mainly to motivate cooperation for pro-selfs, as pro-socials would already have cooperation as a chronically accessible goal activated in cooperation situations. Contrary to guilt, the induction of fear (arguably a non-moral emotion) decreased cooperation for pro-socials and not for pro-selfs. Also, Miettinen and Suetens (2008) measured the experience of guilt in a prisoner's dilemma experiment that allowed for pre-play communication. They found that guilt arose in the case of unilateral defection and it was strongest when players had initially agreed to cooperate (thus, when people behaved immorally by both lying and choosing egoistically).

We ran experiments similar to those of Ketelaar and Au (2003) and Nelissen *et al.* (2007) and found similar pro-social effects for guilt. But, and this is interesting, we did not find any support for shame, one of the other prototypical moral emotions, to promote pro-social behavior (De Hooge *et al.* 2007). In follow-up studies that we review later in this chapter we also found situations in which guilt did not produce socially beneficial outcomes, and sometimes even outcomes that were arguably asocial. Together, this line of research begged the question as to whether moral emotions are of a special kind, requiring special theory to understand them (as implied by Adam Smith and by most moral emotion researchers), or whether they behave like any other emotion that can be understood with general emotion theory. We now believe that there is nothing intrinsically moral about moral emotions, and that the workings of the so-called moral emotions can be apprehended by applying theory that was developed to describe and predict the impact of emotion on behavioral decision-making. The fact that moral emotions are regarded as special and in need of unique theorizing is, in our view, the result of these emotions being typically felt when others' outcomes are at stake (hence these moral emotions are also sometimes called social emotions). However, as we will show by applying our emotion-behavior theory, we were able to predict, find, and understand instances in which moral emotions promote amoral and even immoral behaviors. Let us first describe what emotions are and our approach for understanding them, and then turn to the empirical studies.

Understanding how and why emotions impact decision-making: feeling-is-for-doing

Emotions are studied by psychologists, philosophers, and many other scholars, and there has always been dispute concerning the exact definition (Kleinginna and Kleinginna 1981). Nevertheless, there is enough consensus on important aspects of emotion such that the study of its behavioral consequences is warranted. Emotions are momentary experiences: we feel them in the here and now. They are about something or someone: you are shamed about something you did, feel guilty toward someone, regret a choice, etc. Emotions arise when we evaluate events or outcomes as relevant for our concerns or preferences (i.e., they stem from appraisals) and therefore we do not become emotional over trivial things. Emotions are also to some extent under cognitive control, but not completely. We cannot simply choose to become or not become emotional, given that certain things that happen are relevant for our goals or concerns. But we can regulate our emotion experiences and try to attenuate them or use them strategically. We believe that much of the impact of emotion on behavior actually stems from such regulative attempts (Baumeister *et al.* 2007; Zeelenberg and Pieters 2007).

Emotions are best conceptualized as multi-component experiences, manifesting themselves in different psychological subsystems, such as cognitive appraisals, hedonic experiences, bodily sensations, motivational goals, and action tendencies (Breugelmans and Poortinga 2006; Frijda *et al.* 1989; Roseman *et al.* 1994). In our approach, that we refer to as the feeling-is-for-doing approach, we built on this and elaborate on what this means for understanding decision-making.

We first presented our approach in Zeelenberg and Pieters (2006), and refer the reader to that chapter for an elaborated exposition (see also Zeelenberg *et al.* 2007, 2008). Our approach has its roots in the philosophy of pragmatism of William James (1907, 1909). The core element of our approach is that emotion has evolved for reasons of behavioral guidance. Emotions may help us to overcome the cognitive limitations within ourselves and constraints placed upon us within the decision environment. We think emotions serve this function because emotions prioritize certain goals and thereby mobilize energy and give direction to behavior (Bagozzi *et al.* 2000; Frijda 1986, 2006). Behavior, therefore, should be central in understanding emotion. A summary of our approach in five broad propositions is presented in Table 4.1 and explained below.

We conceptualize emotions as motivational constructs (*proposition 1*). This is not new, but in behavioral decision research it has often been neglected. Emotions prioritize action, that is, commit decision-makers to certain courses of action by providing control precedence (Frijda 1986). Emotions bring forward an associated goal that may overrule other goals. For example, when one is fearful, running away from the fear-evoking stimulus has priority. Different emotions are associated with different goals (e.g., Nelissen *et al.* 2007) and thus

Table 4.1 Propositions summarizing the "feeling-is-for-doing" perspective

1	The emotional system is the primary motivational system for goal-directed behavior.
2	Each specific emotion serves distinct motivational functions in goal striving.
3	These motivational functions cannot be reduced to the overall valence of the specific emotions.
4	The distinct motivational functions are rooted in the experiential qualities of the specific emotions.
5	Emotions can be either endogenous (an integral part) or exogenous (environmentally invoked) to the goal-striving process, their effect on behavior being contingent on their perceived relevance to the current goal.

Source: adapted from Zeelenberg and Pieters 2006.

it follows that different emotions have their idiosyncratic impact on decision-making (*proposition 2*). For example, anger motivates us to move against the source of our anger, whereas fear motivates us to move away. The feeling-is-for-doing approach thus puts emphasis on the forward-looking, motivational function of emotions (see also Zeelenberg *et al.* 2007). It explains how emotions may be instrumental in achieving the goal one is striving for. That is, emotions provide information about how one is currently doing. This affective feedback informs us about the extent of goal progress (e.g., *I am still not safe!*). But the impact of emotion goes further in that it provides the decision-maker with clear guidelines for how to attain these goals (e.g., *I better climb up that tree*).

Proposition 3 states that the motivational function of emotion cannot be reduced to the overall valence of the specific emotions. This is important, because often emotion is equated with affect and only the affect dimension is taken into account. Such a hedonic approach was already favored by Freud (1920: 365, emphasis in the original), who argued that "our entire psychical activity is bent upon *procuring pleasure* and *avoiding pain.*" However, research has now convincingly shown that different specific emotions are associated with different behaviors that cannot be reduced to the valance of the emotion (e.g., Lerner and Keltner 2001; Zeelenberg and Pieters 1999).

The experiential content of emotion, how it is felt and what thoughts, feelings and motivations come with it (Roseman *et al.* 1994), is the source of the differential motivational functions (*proposition 4*). The specific relation between emotion, motivation, and behavior is slightly more complex as the same specific emotion in different situations may activate different behaviors, depending on the overarching goal that people strive toward and the opportunities that are present in the environment. Put differently, emotions do not automatically call for a specific action, but rather they reflect a concern of the decision-maker that is potentially threatened (in the case of negative emotions) or served (in the case of positive emotions). The emotion then facilitates behavior that is in line with our concerns and that is aimed at closing the gap between the current situation and the goal strived for (Frijda and Zeelenberg 2001). Depending on the situation one is in, different behaviors can fulfill this role ("many roads lead to Rome"), but which action will be performed is based on their accessibility, acceptability, and instrumentality to the current overarching goal. Thus, because of the specific meaning they convey to the decision-maker, specific emotions may help us to better understand the goals and motivations of the decision-makers and hence better predict the specific behaviors the decision-makers engage in or refrain from.

Proposition 5 differentiates between endogenous and exogenous influences of emotion. Emotions are endogenous when the experience is relevant to the decision at hand, and they are thus an integral part of the goal-setting and goal-striving process. For example, the disgust experienced when thinking about dirty streets may impact littering behavior. Likewise, the anger about goal frustration is endogenous when it influences future behavior with respect to that goal. But disgust felt while watching a horror movie may perhaps spill over to behaviors later on, and may, for example, eventually cause one to get rid of garbage more quickly even when this means littering. Such an impact of emotion, which is not directly related to inducing situations and the motivations that were relevant then, is referred to as exogenous. Exogenous emotions, or emotional influences, are those that are not related to the current decision, and are external to the actual goal-setting and goal-striving process, although they may – exogenously – influence this. The distinction is relevant as research has often studied the effects of emotions, feelings, or moods that should be irrelevant for the current decision. As a consequence, we know much about the inadequacies of the system, but too little about how and when the emotional system works in the service of decision-making. In sum, an endogenous emotion is part of the current goal pursuit, while an exogenous emotion comes from outside the situation, and its effects may spill over and influence current decisions. Many effects of exogenous emotions that seem erratic at first sight can be understood if one is aware of the effects of endogenous emotions.

How moral emotions are for doing

We have applied the reasoning outlined above to many emotional experiences and also studied extensively how moral emotions have influenced decision-making. Below we review some of our work and demonstrate how these emotions can induce amoral or immoral behavior. We start with shame.

Shame

Shame is perhaps the most complicated moral emotion. It is "one of the most powerful, painful, and potentially destructive experiences known to humans" (Gilbert 1997: 113). Shame arises after a moral transgression or incompetence (Keltner and Buswell, 1996). The emotion leads to a threatened self-view and a heightened degree of self-awareness and awareness of others around us (Welten *et al.* 2011). Ashamed people often feel small, alone, powerless, helpless, and inferior to others (Tangney 1995, 1999). This can be expressed in bodily posture: After a shame experience the body is often collapsed with the shoulders falling in, and the eyes are lowered with the gaze downwards (Keltner and Buswell 1996; Lewis 2003).

Shame has had a bad reputation in emotion research, as researchers have argued that it has primarily a negative influence on behavior. It makes speech, movement, and action more difficult and less likely (Gilbert 1997), and would be related to submission, social avoidance, withdrawal, rejection, and disengagement from others (e.g., Lewis 2003; Probyn 2004). According to Tangney (1999), shame motivates behaviors that "are likely to sever or interfere with interpersonal relationships." The thought behind these submissive and withdrawing behaviors is that they function as a form of appeasement, signaling to others that people are aware of their norm-violating behavior and will not fight back but will conform to the group standards.

Shame has been studied extensively, but there is hardly any empirical research on the behaviors elicited in attempts to regulate current experiences of shame. Even more, the few existing empirical studies on shame-induced behaviors produced contradicting results. Often, participants were asked to recall a situation in which they had experienced shame, and subsequently they rated what they felt, what they thought, and what they wanted to do after the described situation. On the one hand, findings of these studies suggest that shame promotes withdrawal and avoidance behaviors. For example, shame was found to be characterized by withdrawal tendencies compared to other emotions such as joy, anger, disgust, sadness, and fear (Scherer and Wallbott 1994). On the other hand, some studies suggest that shame can promote approach behaviors. For example, Tangney *et al.* (1996) showed that shame activated a higher willingness to make amends than to hide. In addition, some scholars such as Wicker *et al.* (1983) showed that shame experiences were rated neutral on items ranging from wanting to hide to making restitutions, while others such as Frijda *et al.* (1989) even found that shame activated *both* a desire to disappear from view and a desire to undo the situation compared to guilt and regret.

We studied shame by applying our feeling-is-for-doing approach and focusing on the emotion elements and the situation. In this way we can explain how shame can motivate seemingly contradictory behaviors. When we think back to the definition of shame, the central theme appears to be a negative or hurt self-image. One of the most important fundamental human motives is the desire to have a positive self-view. People compare themselves to others, make self-serving attributions, and they react defensively or act assertively to achieve and maintain such a positive view (Gibbons 1990). Exactly this positive view of the self is threatened during a shame experience (Lewis 1971), and this gives rise to feelings of inferiority and worthlessness, and to negative thoughts about the self and about what others would think about the self. When applying the feeling-is-for doing approach, it appears that the emotional goal of shame is to deal with the threatened self.

First, based on the emotion elements of shame, we suggest that shame motivates approach behaviors to restore the self, and when this is not possible or too risky, it motivates avoidance behaviors to protect the self. In other words, the behaviors following from shame are first and foremost approach behaviors. Because having a positive self-view is a fundamental motive, people experiencing shame will be motivated to restore that positive self-view. This restore motivation will elicit approach behaviors such as entering achievement situations, performing new challenges, and undertaking reparative actions. But when, for any reason, it is impossible or too risky to restore the self, we suggest that shame will motivate withdrawal behaviors instead of approach behaviors to protect the threatened self from more possible harm. Thus, shame "can prompt behaviors to protect the self from additional scrutiny or self-threatening exposure" (Ferguson 2005: 378). This was recently supported by findings showing that shame activates both a restore motive and a protect motive, which then motivate approach behavior (De Hooge *et al.* 2010, 2011b).

Second, we suggest that the approach behavior motivated by shame depends on the situation and on whether the emotion is endogenous or exogenous to the decision at hand. We have reason to believe that shame induces approach behavior and, as discussed in the introduction, pro-social behavior is the approach behavior that moral emotions theory would predict (Frank 1988, 2004). But, when taking a close look at the psychology of shame, we would only expect pro-social behavior when the shame is endogenous to the situation. When shame is exogenous to the situation, the self threat is already different from the decision situation at hand, and we would expect no effect (explaining the findings reported in De Hooge *et al.* 2007). More recently, in a follow-up study (De Hooge *et al.* 2008), we found that shame does indeed also motivate pro-social behavior in situations related to the shame event, but does not motivate pro-social behavior in situations unrelated to the shame event.

These findings are consistent with our general approach to how emotions influence decision-making. Our approach also predicts and explains how the moral emotion shame operates, and allows us to combine seemingly contradicting findings. Let us now look at what we have learned about guilt.

Guilt

Where shame is a complex moral emotion, guilt might be the most prototypical, with extensive evidence for its pro-social consequences, as we described in the introduction to this chapter. Guilt is therefore seen as a much more positive emotion. Guilt mainly arises after a moral transgression in which people have hurt, intentionally or unintentionally, another person (Tangney 1991; Zeelenberg and Breugelmans 2008). Common causes of guilt are neglecting partners in close relationships and failing to live up to commitments or obligations to others (Baumeister *et al.* 1995). Whereas shame reflects badly upon the whole self, guilt only involves perceiving a behavior as bad, hurtful, or immoral (Lewis 1971). As a consequence, people are focused on the harm and distress they have caused others (Baumeister *et al.* 1994; Lewis 1987). After the transgression, people often feel tense, remorseful, worried and less competent (Ferguson *et al.* 1991; Lewis 1971).

Guilt has been linked to better perspective taking and feelings of empathy (Leith and Baumeister 1998; Tangney and Dearing 2002). It involves a desire to compensate the victim, and actions to repair the damage, to make amends, or to apologize (Caplovitz Barrett 1995; Lindsay-Hartz 1984). The function of guilt is to preserve and strengthen the hurt relationship by making up the past transgression and stimulating more appropriate behavior in the future (Amodio *et al.* 2007; Baumeister *et al.* 1994). Roseman *et al.* (1994) found that after a guilt experience participants felt like undoing their actions, punishing themselves, apologizing, and wanting to make up for their transgression and to be forgiven. Importantly, cross-cultural studies have shown that these characteristics of guilt are quite similar across a wide array of cultures (Breugelmans and Poortinga 2006; Fontaine *et al.* 2006), which is testimony to the universal character of guilt and in line with Adam Smith's ideas. The studies described in the introduction suggest that guilt appears to be a good, moral emotion that produces beneficial consequences for people in one's social surroundings.

However, when we applied the reasoning following from our feeling-is-for-doing approach and based predictions for behavior on the experiential characteristics of guilt, it became clear that guilt may not only have positive effects. Guilt revolves around a threatened relationship that needs to be dealt with and people feeling guilt are focused on the person hurt by their actions. In the words of Baumeister *et al.* (1994: 260, italics added): "After doing something bad to another person, people are motivated *to help that person* or comply with that person's wishes, apparently to rectify any inequity and to repair any damage to the relationship." Interestingly, we reasoned that in situations in which the victim is present this will indeed result in reparation and pro-social behavior toward the victim. But, what would happen with others that are present as well? In daily life people interact with multiple others at the same time, while in the research thus far, the studies were limited to dyadic situations. We reasoned that the dyadic preoccupation that is central to experiences of guilt can lead to behavior that is negative for the outcomes of others around us. When focusing on repairing the hurt relationship, people temporarily pay less attention to others and generally compensate at the expense of the resources allocated to other people rather than those allocated to themselves. In other words, guilt may lead to an extra investment in the relationship with the victim but someone else will have to pay the bill. Indeed, recent studies showed that in three-person dictator games, guilt motivated pro-social behavior toward the hurt other at the expense of the third one around and not at the expense of oneself (De Hooge *et al.* 2011a).

In another line of research Nelissen and Zeelenberg (2009) show that guilt may induce self-punishment, which is not necessarily a moral thing to do. In a follow-up, Nelissen (2011) combines these discrepant views of guilt being an adaptive social emotion and guilt being a maladaptive emotion producing negative self-directed responses. Nelissen reveals that even these negative self-directed responses that can be associated with guilt may serve an adaptive social function by acting as signals of remorse. Such seemingly contradictive patterns of behavior cannot be understood by portraying guilt as uniquely moral. However, from our perspective this fits nicely with how guilt is experienced.

Summary and conclusions

In this chapter we have reviewed our motivational account of the effects of emotion on decision-making that we refer to as the feeling-is-for-doing approach, and applied it to the domain of moral emotions. We have done so in order to answer the question of whether moral emotions are of a special kind and we conclude that they are not. Our approach recognizes that emotions arise when events or outcomes are relevant for one's concerns or preferences and they prioritize behavior that acts in service of these concerns. As such, emotions can be understood as functional programmes for decision-making, imposing upon the decision-maker inclinations for action that, in a given situation, serve current goals. We believe that such a general approach to how emotions influence behavior should be preferred over more limited approaches that only look at moral emotions. A more general approach allows us to see communalities between the different emotional states and their behavioral consequences. It brings us closer to a more coherent theory of behavior. Put differently, when we realize that feeling is here for the sake of our doing, we also realize that progress in studying how people make decisions cannot be done without scrutinizing the functional role of emotion.

References

Amodio, D.M., Devine, P.G., and Harmon-Jones, E. (2007) "A dynamic model of guilt: implications for motivation and self-regulation in the context of prejudice," *Psychological Science*, 18: 524–530.

Bagozzi, R., Baumgartner, H., Pieters, R., and Zeelenberg, M. (2000) "The role of emotions in goal-directed behavior," in S. Ratneshwar, D.G. Micka, and C. Huffman (eds.), *The Why of Consumption*, London: Routledge.

Batson, C.D. (2011) *Altruism in Humans*, New York: Oxford University Press.

Baumeister, R.F., Stillwell, A.M., and Heatherton, T.F. (1994) "Guilt: An interpersonal approach," *Psychological Bulletin*, 115: 243–267.

Baumeister, R.F., Reis, H.T., and Delespaul, P.A.E.G. (1995) "Subjective and experiential correlates of guilt in daily life," *Personality and Social Psychology Bulletin*, 21: 1256–1268.

Baumeister, R.F., Vohs, K.D., DeWall, C.N., and Zhang, L.Q. (2007) "How emotion shapes behavior: feedback, anticipation, and reflection, rather than direct causation," *Personality and Social Psychology Review*, 11: 167–203.

Berkowitz, L. (1990) "On the formation of anger and agression: a cognitive neo-associationistic analysis," *American Psychologist*, 45: 494–503.

Breugelmans, S.M. and Poortinga, Y.H. (2006) "Emotion without a word: shame and guilt with Rarámuri Indians and rural Javanese," *Journal of Personality and Social Psychology*, 91: 1111–1122.

Caplovitz Barrett, K. (1995) "A functionalist approach to shame and guilt," in J.P. Tangney and K.W. Fischer (eds.), *Self-conscious Emotions: The Psychology of Shame, Guilt, Embarassment, and Pride*, New York: The Guilford Press.

De Hooge, I.E., Zeelenberg, M., and Breugelmans, S.M. (2007) "Moral sentiments and cooperation: differential influences of shame and guilt," *Cognition and Emotion*, 21: 1025–1042.

De Hooge, I.E., Breugelmans, S.M., and Zeelenberg, M. (2008) "Not so ugly after all: when shame acts as a commitment device," *Journal of Personality and Social Psychology*, 95: 933–943.

De Hooge, I.E., Zeelenberg, M., and Breugelmans, S.M. (2010) "Restore and protect motivations following shame," *Cognition and Emotion*, 24: 111–127.

De Hooge, I.E., Nelissen, R.M.A., Breugelmans, S.M., and Zeelenberg, M. (2011a) "What is moral about guilt? Acting 'prosocially' at the disadvantage of others," *Journal of Personality and Social Psychology*, 100: 462–473.

De Hooge, I.E., Zeelenberg, M., and Breugelmans, S.M. (2011b) "A functionalist account of shame-induced behavior," *Cognition and Emotion*, 25: 939–946.

Ferguson, T.J. (2005) "Mapping shame and its functions in relationships," *Child Maltreatment*, 10: 377–386.

Ferguson, T.J., Stegge, H., and Damhuis, I. (1991) "Children's understanding of guilt and shame," *Child Development*, 62: 827–839.

Fontaine, J.R.J., Luyten, P., De Boeck, P., Corveleyn, J., Fernandez, M., Herrera, D., *et al.* (2006) "Untying the gordian knot of guilt and shame: the structure of guilt and shame reactions based on situation and person variation in Belgium, Hungary, and Peru," *Journal of Cross-Cultural Psychology*, 37: 273–292.

Frank, R.H. (1988) *Passions Within Reason: The Strategic Role of the Emotions*, New York: W.W. Norton.

Frank, R.H. (2004) "Introducing moral emotions into models of rational choice," in A.S.R. Manstead, N. Frijda, and A. Fischer (eds.), *Feelings and Emotions: The Amsterdam Symposium*, Cambridge: Cambridge University Press.

Freud, S. (1920/1952) *A General Introduction to Psychoanalysis*, New York: Washington Square Press.

Frijda, N.H. (1986) *The Emotions*, New York: Cambridge University Press.

Frijda, N.H. (2006) *The Laws of Emotion*, Mahwah, NJ: Erlbaum.

Frijda, N.H. and Zeelenberg, M. (2001) "Appraisal: what is the dependent?," in K.R. Scherer, A. Schorr, and T. Johnstone (eds.), *Appraisal Processes in Emotion: Theory, Methods, Research*, New York: Oxford University Press.

Frijda, N.H., Kuipers, P., and Ter Schure, E. (1989) "Relations among emotion, appraisal and emotional action readiness," *Journal of Personality and Social Psychology*, 57: 212–228.

Gibbons, F.X. (1990) "The impact of focus of attention and affect on social behaviour," in W.R. Crozier (ed.), *Shyness and Embarrassment: Perspectives from Social Psychology*, Cambridge: Cambridge University Press.

Gilbert, P. (1997) "The evolution of social attractiveness and its role in shame, humiliation, guilt, and therapy," *British Journal of Medical Psychology*, 70: 113–147.

Gintis, H., Bowles, S., Boyd, R., and Fehr, E. (eds.) (2005) *Moral Sentiments and Material Interests*, Cambridge, MA: MIT Press.

Haidt, J. (2003) "The moral emotions," in R.J. Davidson, K.R. Scherer, and H.H. Goldsmith (eds.), *Handbook of Affective Sciences*, Oxford: Oxford University Press.

Henrich, J., Boyd, R., Bowles, S., Camerer, C., and Fehr, E. (2004) *Foundations of Human Sociality: Ethnography and Experiments in Fifteen Small-scale Societies*, Oxford: Oxford University Press.

James, W. (1907/1995) *Pragmatism*, New York: Dover.

James, W. (1909/2002) *The Meaning of Truth*, New York: Dover.

Keltner, D. and Buswell, B.N. (1996) "Evidence for the distinctness of embarrassment, shame and guilt: a study of recalled antecedents and facial expressions of emotion," *Cognition and Emotion*, 10: 155–171.

Ketelaar, T. (2004) "Ancestral emotions, current decisions: using evolutionary game theory to explore the role of emotions in decision-making," in C. Crawford and C. Salmon (eds.), *Darwinism, Public Policy and Private Decisions*, Mahwah, NJ: Lawrence Erlbaum Associates.

Ketelaar, T. and Au, W.T. (2003) "The effects of guilt on the behaviour of uncooperative individuals in repeated social bargaining games: an affect-as-information interpretation of the role of emotion in social interaction," *Cognition and Emotion*, 17: 429–453.

Kleinginna, P.R. and Kleinginna, A.M. (1981) "A categorized list of emotion definitions, with suggestions for a consensual definition," *Motivation and Emotion*, 5: 345–379.

Leith, K.P. and Baumeister, R.F. (1998) "Empathy, shame, guilt, and narratives of interpersonal conflicts: guilt-prone people are better at perspective taking," *Journal of Personality*, 66: 1–38.

Lerner, J.S. and Keltner, D. (2001) "Fear, anger, and risk," *Journal of Personality and Social Psychology*, 81: 146–159.

Lewis, H.B. (1971) *Shame and Guilt in Neurosis*, New York: International Universities Press.

Lewis, H.B. (1987) "Shame and the narcissistic personality," in D.L. Nathanson (ed.), *The Many Faces of Shame*, New York: The Guilford Press.

Lewis, M. (2003) "The role of the self in shame," *Social Research*, 70: 1181–1204.

Lindsay-Hartz, J. (1984) "Contrasting experiences of shame and guilt," *American Behavioral Scientist*, 27: 689–704.

Miettinen, T. and Suetens, S. (2008) "Communication and guilt in a prisoner's dilemma," *The Journal of Conflict Resolution*, 52: 945–960.

Nelissen, R.M.A. (2011) "Guilt-induced self-punishment as a sign of remorse," *Social Psychological and Personality Science*, in press.

Nelissen, R.M.A. and Zeelenberg, M. (2009) "When guilt evokes self-punishment: evidence for the existence of a Dobby effect," *Emotion*, 9: 118–122.

Nelissen, R.M.A., Dijker, A.J., and De Vries, N.K. (2007) "How to turn a hawk into a dove and vice versa: interactions between emotions and goals in a give-some dilemma game," *Journal of Experimental Social Psychology*, 43: 280–286.

Probyn, E. (2004) "Everyday shame," *Cultural Studies*, 18: 328–349.

Roseman, I.J., Wiest, C., and Swartz, T.S. (1994) "Phenomenology, behaviors, and goals differentiate discrete emotions," *Journal of Personality and Social Psychology*, 67: 206–211.

Scherer, K.R. and Wallbott, H.G. (1994) "Evidence for universality and cultural variation of differential emotion response patterning," *Journal of Personality and Social Psychology*, 66: 310–328.

Smith, A. (1759/1976) *The Theory of Moral Sentiments*, Oxford: Clarendon Press.

Tangney, J.P. (1991) "Moral affect: the good, the bad, and the ugly," *Journal of Personality and Social Psychology*, 61: 598–607.

Tangney, J.P. (1995) "Recent advances in the empirical study of shame and guilt," *American Behavioral Scientist*, 38: 1132–1145.

Tangney, J.P. (1999) "The self-conscious emotions: shame, guilt, embarrassment, and pride," in T. Dalgleish and M. Power (eds.), *Handbook of Cognition and Emotion*, Chichester: John Wiley & Sons.

Tangney, J.P. and Dearing, R.L. (2002) *Shame and Guilt*, New York: The Guilford Press.

Tangney, J.P. and Fischer, K.W. (1995) *Self-conscious Emotions: The Psychology of Shame, Guilt, Embarrassment, and Pride*, New York: The Guilford Press.

Tangney, J.P., Miller, R.S., Flicker, L., and Barlow, D.H. (1996) "Are shame, guilt, and embarrassment distinct emotions?", *Journal of Personality and Social Psychology*, 70: 1256–1269.

Welten, S.C.M., Zeelenberg, M., and Breugelmans, S.M. (2012) "Various shame," *Cognition and Emotion*, in press.

Wicker, F.W., Payne, G.C., and Morgan, R.D. (1983) "Participant descriptions of guilt and shame," *Motivation and Emotion*, 7: 25–39.

Zeelenberg, M. and Breugelmans, S.M. (2008) "The role of interpersonal harm in distinguishing regret from guilt," *Emotion*, 8: 589–596.

Zeelenberg, M. and Pieters, R. (1999) "Comparing service delivery to what might have been: behavioral responses to regret and disappointment," *Journal of Service Research*, 2: 86–97.

Zeelenberg, M. and Pieters, R. (2006) "Feeling is for doing: a pragmatic approach to the study of emotions in economic behavior," in D. DeCremer, M. Zeelenberg, and J.K. Murnighan (eds.), *Social Psychology and Economics*, Mahwah, NJ: Lawrence Erlbaum Associates.

Zeelenberg, M. and Pieters, R. (2007) "A theory of regret regulation 1.0," *Journal of Consumer Psychology*, 17: 3–18.

Zeelenberg, M., Nelissen, R.M.A., and Pieters, R. (2007) "Emotion, motivation and decision making: a feeling is for doing approach," in H. Plessner, C. Betsch, and T. Betsch (eds.), *Intuition in Judgment and Decision Making*, Mahway, NJ: Lawrence Erlbaum Associates.

Zeelenberg, M., Nelissen, R.M.A., Breugelmans, S.M., and Pieters, R. (2008) "On emotion specificity in decision making: why feeling is for doing," *Judgment and Decision Making*, 3: 18–27.

5 Neuropsychology of moral judgment and risk seeking: what in common?

A new look at emotional contribution to decision-making

Michela Balconi and Andrea Terenzi

Introduction: what role for emotions in moral decisional processes and gain-related behavior?

Contemporary decision research in economics, business, psychology, and neuroscience now accepts the idea that emotions play a significant role in decision-making. Specifically, it was supposed that emotional correlates intervene in decisional processes directed toward moral contexts and moral dilemmas. A second main domain where emotions are highly implicated regards the decisional mechanism related to tasks in which a gain or a loss is implicated. Both of these contexts require, in fact, a decision in which the subject is the direct agent of an emotional-relevant behavior.

Nevertheless, the implication of emotions into moral decisions and gain-related performance was discussed and criticized by some authors. Some models indicate that moral judgment is a rational, deliberative endeavor. In this perspective emotions generate reactive attitudes (Strawson 1960) on the basis of rational appraisals, but moral judgment is primarily a conscious process of deliberate reflection. Other models (Haidt 2001; Prinz 2006), by contrast, maintain that reason is the "slave of the passions," that moral psychology is essentially emotive and that deliberative mechanisms are recruited only to provide post-hoc rationalizations of moral judgments. Finally, other perspectives (Damasio 1994; Greene *et al.* 2001, 2004) have also been developed on the basis of recent neurophysiological data, indicating that both emotional and deliberative mechanisms are recruited in making moral judgments.

However, there are actually many theoretical positions consistent with a variety of conceptually and empirically distinct claims about the relationship between emotion and moral psychology, with at least three specifically implicated thus far:

1 Neuroscientific studies (Blair 1995; Greene *et al.* 2001, 2004; Greene and Haidt 2002) demonstrate that *emotional structures are recruited in making moral judgments*.

2 Morally relevant action is often *emotionally motivated*, appearing early in ontogeny and phylogeny (Gallese 2003; Hoffman 1982, 2000; Meltzoff and Moore 1977).
3 Perceived *moral violations* often evoke contempt, shame, anger, or disgust (Rozin 1997; Rozin *et al.* 1999).

In order to underline the significance emotions have for moral decisions, it should first be considered that emotional circuits are integral to evaluating morally salient stimuli. For example, judgments about morally salient claims (e.g., "Today people violate social values") show increased activity in the frontal polar cortex (FPC) and medial frontal gyrus, when compared to judgments about non-moral claims (e.g., "The football match was interrupted") (Moll *et al.* 2002). Moreover, morally salient stimuli evoke increased functional connectivity between the left FPC, orbital frontal (OFC), anterior temporal, and anterior cingulate cortices (ACC) and limbic structures such as the thalamus, midbrain, and basal forebrain (Moll *et al.* 2003).

A much stronger test of the hypothesis that emotion is the source of moral judgment is indicated by studies of patients with bilateral damage to the ventromedial prefrontal cortex (VMPC). These patients generally exhibit a flattening of their social emotions, indicated by behavioral and physiological measures, an inability to redeploy emotional representations previously associated with punishment and reward, an inability to anticipate future outcomes, punishments and rewards, and a lack of inhibitory control (Anderson *et al.* 2006; Damasio 1994; Damasio *et al.* 1990; Koenigs *et al.* 2007). Damasio (1994) argues that emotion is usually integral to cognition, and on this basis, hypothesizes that moral judgment is likely to rely on the emotional processes implemented in VMPC. Consistent with this hypothesis, frontotemporal dementia (FTD), resulting from the deterioration of the prefrontal and anterior temporal cortex, generates blunted emotion, disregard for others, and a willingness to engage in moral transgressions. Moreover, FTD patients show a pronounced tendency to adopt the utilitarian alternative in personal moral dilemmas such as the footbridge case (see below) (Mendez *et al.* 2005).

Taking into account the present conflictual hypotheses on the role emotions may have in determining (or influencing) the decisional orientation in moral contexts, we intend to explore what kind of relationship exists between decisional processes and emotions in moral decisions.

Second, our interest is devoted to testing the contribution of emotional correlates in contexts where no moral judgments are questioned, but instead subjects have to decide in favor or disfavor of a behavior that may have an effect on gain or loss of some money. That is, we compared moral dilemmas with a potentially more morally neutral context, in which subjects are not solicited to make a decision that implicates values or moral beliefs, but they are only required to take some risks in terms of gains or losses. Specifically, we try to relate more directly the moral choices with a decisional behavior in which the subject is required to maximize his gain by adopting a more or less risky strategy, as suggested in the Iowa Gambling Task paradigm (Bechara *et al.* 1994).

In this regard, Damasio and colleagues propose a neural model of decision-making processes in which emotions are the most important element in the interaction between environmental conditions and decision-making. In short, the emotions have the task of providing, knowingly or not, some additional information essential to making the best decision.

Our main interest was therefore to verify any analogy in decisional processes underlining these two tasks and to show any particular similarity in the emotional influence on decision-making. An analysis of decisional mechanisms in two different contexts, looking for similarities and differences, would make us better understand the role of emotions and of their relationship with other cognitive processes. A second related issue regards the possibility to test the role of unconscious emotional processes in decisions, taking into account the subjective psychophysiological responses, by monitoring some autonomic measures, in addition to the cortical brain responses, by analyzing ERP (event-related potential) modulation.

Greene model between cognition and emotion

The first part of our research concerning the moral dilemmas was inspired by the studies of Greene and his collaborators. Greene, through his research, introduced the double process theory (2001, 2007), according to which utilitarian judgments, such as that leading to approve the killing of one person to save many others, are driven by cognitively controlled processes. These cognitively controlled processes are intended to contain the emotional reaction, following the reading of the dilemma, and then to guide the subject toward a utilitarian response. On the contrary, deontological judgments, that leading to disapprove the killing of one person to save many others, are driven by automatic emotional responses.

As shown in Figure 5.1, Greene suggests (1) that contexts that direct attention to violations of moral rules generate deontology-consistent emotional reactions;

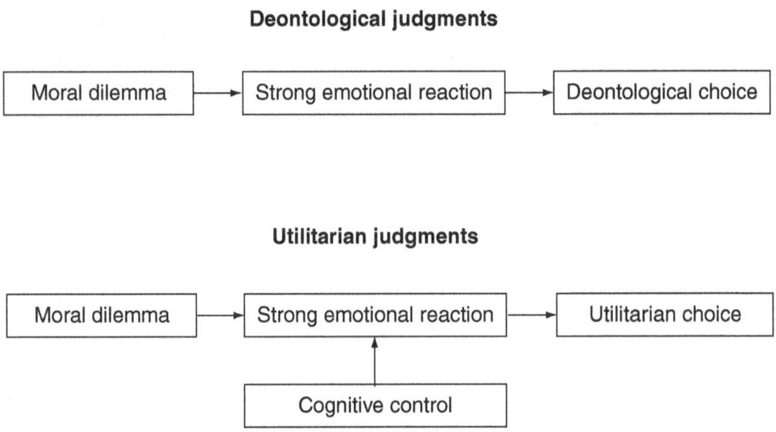

Figure 5.1 Representation of the double process theory.

(2) that deontological response is diminished in contexts that direct attention to utilitarian considerations; and (3) that contextual factors interact with situation-specific values and individual differences to shape moral judgment and choice.

Several lines of empirical research, including Greene's own fMRI studies of brain activity during moral decision-making, comprise strong evidence against the legitimacy of deontology as a moral theory (Greene *et al.* 2001, 2008; Haidt 2001; Moll *et al.* 2002, 2003). This is because the empirical studies establish that "characteristically deontological" moral thinking is driven by prepotent emotional reactions that are not a sound basis for morality, while "characteristically consequentialist" (or utilitarian) thinking is a more reliable moral guide because it is characterized by greater cognitive command and control.

Notwithstanding that, it was underlined that Greene did not always succeed in drawing a strong causal connection between prepotent emotional reactions and deontological theory, and, consequently, he did not undermine the legitimacy of deontological moral theories. In other words, the empirical evidences relied on from neuroscience and social psychology do not support the conclusion that consequentialism is superior to deontology (Dean 2010). We considered the main questions that may be deducted by Greene's considerations, pointing out their critical weakness.

Based on Greene's theory, the utilitarian choice would always be better than the deontological one because the first would be produced by strong, controlled reasoning and not by instinctive emotions. The critical nature of these conclusions has inspired the present research, since we agree with the idea that every moral choice is influenced by emotional reactions of varying intensity, even if we may also agree with the supposition that controlled cognitive processes should support final decisions. A first general consideration states that, as we know, in many cases focusing only on the practical implications of an action does not lead us to make the best choice. Also, as Dean (2010) reminds us, emotions lead us in many cases to violate our moral principles (as in the case of envy or anger).

The evidence for the theory of double process has been criticized by several authors. Greene takes as evidence the response times (RTs) recorded during the resolution of moral dilemmas, suggesting that people have longer RTs when deciding to violate the moral norm than when they decide not to violate it, and it is supposed there is a greater cognitive workload in responding to the personal dilemmas (Greene *et al.* 2001). Since the violation of moral norms is usually motivated by utilitarian considerations (such as saving more lives) Greene interprets these results as evidence that the utilitarian judgments are driven by controlled cognitive processes, whose involvement is demonstrated by longer RTs (Greene *et al.* 2001). Cognitive control processes intervene by dampening the rise of emotion resulting from the breach of a moral norm, allowing a choice of utilitarian type (see Figure 5.1). These control processes are not necessary for non-utilitarian choices in which moral norms are not violated and therefore would not lead to an increase in RTs.

Nevertheless, a recent study by McGuire and colleagues (2009) showed that the increase in RT for utilitarian responses is an artifact. In the subset of dilemmas in which there is a real conflict between utilitarian and deontological considerations (as in the footbridge dilemma in which subjects must decide whether to push a man down from a bridge to save four other men, or let them die but not knock the man) there is no significant difference between RTs. The apparent effect of longer RTs would be generated by the inclusion of some dilemmas in which a personal injury (such as, for example, pushing a man down from the bridge, which is the basis of personal dilemmas) has no convincing utilitarian justification. These dilemmas, prompting non-utilitarian quick responses, have introduced new variables that may have a direct effect on the observed data (that is the longer RTs). More generally, the RT data are also a weak index because they do not furnish direct evidence, but only the possibility of an increase in cognitive load by the subject.

Other data taken as proof of the theory of double process are based on neuroimaging techniques. Greene and his colleagues analyzed the brain processes using fMRI measures, while subjects responded to some personal moral dilemmas. The results showed an increased activity during these tasks in the ACC (Greene *et al.* 2004), a brain region associated with cognitive conflict such as the Stroop Effect and other tasks (Botvinick *et al.* 2001). In particular, this increased cortical activity was significantly higher for those individuals who produced the longest RTs when responding to these dilemmas (compared to those with shorter RTs).

Subjects with longer RTs also showed a comparatively increased activation of the dorsolateral prefrontal cortex (DLPFC), a brain area involved in the processes of abstract reasoning and cognitive control (Miller and Cohen 2001). The authors therefore come to a tentative conclusion that the lengthening of RTs in personal moral dilemmas is due to a conflict between a strong emotional reaction and abstract reasoning, with this conflict being resolved through specific processes of cognitive control.

In their view, this positive correlation between the activity of the DLPFC and the utilitarian solutions demonstrates that specific processes of control are working to counter the strong socio-emotional response due to personal dilemmas, in favor of a utilitarian response. So, in the case of a conflict between a strong emotional reaction and utilitarian reasoning, this conflict would be detected by the ACC, and consequently an appropriate cognitive control would intervene, performed thanks to the activity of the DLPFC. Thus, to provide utilitarian answers in difficult conditions (i.e. the personal moral dilemmas) it would be necessary for there to be an additional cognitive control that can overpower the strong emotional reaction.

Nevertheless, this conclusive remark does not take into account other recent research that did not result in the activation of DLPFC or ACC (Young *et al.* 2007). A second critical point is related to the functional significance of the activity of specific brain areas. As is well known, no brain area performs only a single function, so it is risky to take the activation of this brain area as evidence of the involvement of a cognitive or emotional process in absence of a clear dissociation between the different cognitive functions supported by this cortical site. For example, the right angular gyrus (RAG), a brain region that is strongly activated in the personal dilemmas task (Greene *et al.* 2001), is implicated in many cognitive and emotional processes in addition to those of moral decisions. The RAG is involved in perception of facial expression of emotions (Iidaka *et al.* 2002), in cognitive categorization tasks under conditions of uncertainty (Grinband *et al.* 2006), and during anticipation of risk (Fukui *et al.* 2005), as well as during processes that require inference regarding the subjective goals for implausible non-stereotypical actions (Liepelt *et al.* 2008). Part of these subcomponents are present in the moral dilemmas brought by Greene, whereas others are not present, making more dubious what kind of functional process is represented by RAG activation.

A third main problem to be considered regards the contribution of the individual differences in moral decisional processes. As suggested by Bartels (2008), the analysis of moral judgment processes should consider and identify universal principles of moral cognition (Hauser 2006; Mikhail 2007), which may be modulated by subjective value systems and personality components. The last point will be more largely discussed at the end of this chapter.

IOWA Gambling Task and unconscious contribution of emotions in decisions

As previously mentioned, we have chosen to compare the decisions made by individuals about moral dilemmas with those committed in the Iowa Gambling Task (IGT). In the IGT paradigm players are given four decks of cards, and they are told to play in order to minimize losses and maximize winnings (Bechara and Damasio 1997). At first, choosing a card from any deck will get an instant win (100 for decks A and B, 50 for decks C and D). Unexpectedly, however, in subsequent choices some cards may generate penalties (which are larger in decks A and B). When a subject mostly chooses cards from the disadvantageous decks (A and B) they experience a decrease in the initial capital, as opposed to using primarily the advantageous decks (C and D), which lead to increasing it. Players have no way to predict either the penalty that lies behind the choice of any deck in a given cluster nor to calculate with precision the total amount of losses and wins of any decks.

This task allowed Damasio to empirically support some basic principles implicated in decisional tasks when a gain/loss goal is included, such as the following:

1 Knowledge and reasoning are usually insufficient to make favorable decisions, so the role of emotions in decision-making has been underestimated.
2 Emotions have a positive effect when they are connected to the decision task (but may be harmful if not).
3 Unconscious processes are active in response to imminent choices, especially when a unfavorable option is being processed.

4 Some specific neural circuits subserve the decisional processes, which assure that mainly those unconscious emotional components will be active in normal subjects.

Damasio used IGT to compare the performance of healthy subjects with patients with a lesion to the ventromedial prefrontal cortex (VPFC) (Bechara *et al.* 1994). After suffering a few losses, normal participants began to generate an increased skin conductance response (SCR) before choosing a card from a disadvantageous deck and a preference to avoid such decks. Contrarily, VPFC patients did not show either of these two events. Based on these results the author proposed the existence of two processes largely parallel but interacting at times, responsible for decision-making. One of the two processes is the sensory representation of the situation or facts that generates a dispositional knowledge that is not declared, on the basis of previous emotional experiences in similar situations. Damasio suggested that it is precisely the VPFC structure which supports this dispositional knowledge. Following this phase, non-conscious signals (known as somatic markers) would act as a hidden bias in the circuits that support processes of cognitive evaluation and reasoning.

According to the author, his experiment indicates that in healthy participants activation of a non-conscious bias precedes the conscious reasoning on the facts available. This unconscious bias could assist the process of reasoning in a cooperative manner, which means that by itself it would not determine the decision, but it would make easier the processes of knowledge and logic needed to make informed decisions. The autonomic response observed in healthy subjects would therefore be evidence of an unconscious, complex signaling process reflecting access to memories of past personal experiences (specifically remembering about the wins and losses and the corresponding emotional states that were produced). Damage to the VPFC would prevent access to certain types of memories of past personal experiences considered highly relevant for that task.

The somatic marker hypothesis proposes a neuroanatomical and cognitive framework explaining the decision-making and influence made on it by emotion. The idea behind this hypothesis is that decision-making is influenced by marker signals generated by bioregulator processes, including those responsible for emotions and feelings, before the subject makes a final decision and performs a particular behavior. This influence can operate both consciously or unconsciously. Nevertheless, recent empirical evidence shows an increased autonomic activity (mainly represented by an increased SCR) also after that choice is performed (not only before, as supposed by Damasio). Thus emotion should be present throughout the entire decisional process, operating not only as an automatic marker able to direct future behavior, but also contributing to regulating the entire performed decisional behavior (Balconi and Pozzoli 2008; Balconi 2008).

The two decisional tasks: a comparison between morality and gain behavior

A main question to be answered relates to the influence of *emotions in decision-making processes*, taking into account contexts that are potentially more or less emotionally involving along a continuum (from more neutral to more involving). A second point of comparison between the two domains regards the *communality of the neural correlates* underlying decisions for both moral and gain tasks – as they are localized in the prefrontal cortex – as suggested by a vast amount of empirical research. Third, as supposed by the theoretical models for moral judgment and risk taking, both tasks foresee a significant intervention by *unconscious and automatic emotional mechanisms* able to induce a prompt and functional response to critical contexts. Specifically, like deontological choices, utilitarian choices could also be supported by unconscious emotion contribution, where subjects are required to potentially violate their own value systems; also, more general decisions require the contribution of *unconscious mechanisms* (as evidenced by the somatic marker hypothesis). Specifically, in addition to what was stated by previous models, we suppose that utilitarian contexts also require the contribution of unconscious emotional behavior that is represented as the emotional counterpart of a pragmatic behavior finalized to allow the subject to respond to moral requests in a prompt manner. In other words, both emotion and cognition intervene into the decisional processes, even if cognitive strategies may vary as a function of a more utilitarian or deontological goal (Figure 5.2).

We tried to demonstrate that emotional contribution is present in all our moral and risk-taking choices, it being also unconsciously processed by the subject, by using double neuropsychological measures: ERPs as a marker of a conscious emotional response and autonomic measures (SCR, body temperature, heart pulse, blood flow, and blood pressure) as a marker of the unconscious emotional reaction related to the arousal parameter.

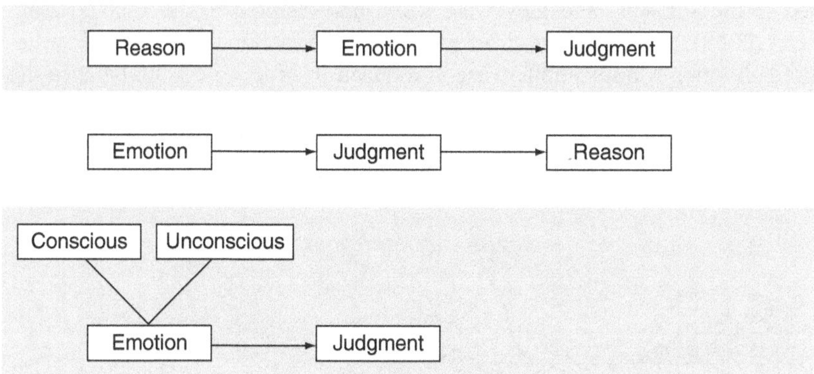

Figure 5.2 Three models of moral decision-making. The first and the second models evidence the contribution of emotion between reason and judgment, whereas the third introduces the conscious and unconscious distinction.

The empirical research

Method

Subjects

Twenty-five subjects (students) took part in the study (12 males and 13 females; age range 19–25, mean=22.37, SD=4.20). All subjects were right-handed and had normal or corrected-to-normal visual acuity. All subjects gave informed written consent for participating in the study. Exclusion criteria were history of psychopathology for the subjects or immediate family.

Procedure

The research was divided into the following phases:

- *Pre-experimental phase*: in this phase the stimuli used in the two experimental sections were created, selected, and validated.
- *Experimental phase*: execution of two experimental tasks (A – moral dilemmas; B – IGT) by subjects with a simultaneous recording of electrophysiological (only for moral dilemmas) and autonomic (for both tasks) indices.
- *Post-experimental phase*: a questionnaire, created to detect the subjective perception of the stimuli and the general task procedure, was submitted to the experimental subjects.

Moral dilemma

A PRE-EXPERIMENTAL PHASE

Moral dilemma stimuli Moral dilemmas formed the battery of stimuli presented to the subjects, and they were taken and adapted to our context from Bartels' (2008), and Greene *et al.*'s (2001) database (without altering their structural conditions). Modifications were introduced in order to counterbalance the influence of underlining variables (such as personal and impersonal dilemmas, which differ mainly for the direct or indirect harm produced by the subjects) (Greene *et al.* 2001). A figurative example of the typical dilemma is presented in Figure 5.3.

Figure 5.3 An example of moral dilemma: the trolley problem.

All moral dilemmas we have submitted to the subjects have the same structure, in which a person must choose one of two alternatives that oppose two principles: not to violate our moral values (deontological option) with negative consequence for other people; and to ensure that our acts have positive consequences by violating our own moral values (utilitarian option). One choice leads therefore to make an action morally right (in which we are not directly responsible for someone's death) but that leads to negative consequences (does not save lives); conversely, the other creates a morally wrong action (that makes us directly responsible for someone's death) with positive consequences (saves lives) (Kelly 1996). It is clear that the moral dilemma creates a situation that leads the subject to a mental conflict where they must choose which of the two principles outlined above is more important.

Stimulus validation Three independent judges were used to validate the moral dilemmas by asking them to state the degree of moral significance of each dilemma, their emotional value, and the complexity and comprehensibility of the content reported.

B EXPERIMENTAL PHASE

Experimental setting and procedure Subjects were seated comfortably in a moderately lit room with the monitor screen situated approximately 100 cm in front of them. Twenty-three dilemmas were presented in a randomized order in the center of the PC monitor using the STIM 4.2 software. During the experiment participants were asked to minimize blinking. Every moral dilemma was presented on the computer screen in the form of written text (always 10–15 lines). The instructions were presented in a written form prior to the registration session, and the subjects were told only that they have to express their opinion by using a mouse. This text remained on the screen until the subject performed a response. Following immediately after the scenario was a question related to the dilemma presented (e.g. "Do you choice to perform action *x*?" where *x* corresponds to killing one person to save others). This question also remains on the screen until the subject presses one of the two mouse buttons (right mouse button for a negative response, left button for a positive response).

The experimental session lasted approximately 90 minutes. Prior to beginning the experimental phase, subjects were familiarized with the overall procedure (training session). The duration of this phase was about three minutes, and every subject saw in a random order all the stimulus types presented in the successive experimental session. Two categories of subjects were successively created as a function of the prevalence of their choice (utilitarian vs. deontological). Subjects who responded in favor of the violation of moral norms with positive consequences were classified as utilitarian subjects; subjects who responded as not in favor of the violation of moral norms with negative consequences were classified as deontological subjects (for all the categories the subjects expressed and agreed with their choice type at least 80 percent of the time).

C POST-EXPERIMENTAL PHASE

Questionnaire and assessment of moral dilemmas In addition to the submission of the Ethics Position Questionnaire (EPQ) (Forsyth 1980) and the Moral Motives Scale (MMS) to detect specific psychometric characteristics of the subjects, a post-experiment questionnaire was given, which was created to assess the adequacy of the proposed stimuli during the task. This questionnaire was composed of eight questions, identical for each of the 23 moral dilemmas. The first seven were intended to verify that the definition of moral dilemma was suitable for each stimulus presented. This includes, for example, such questions that investigate the degree of relevance of the subjects' values generated by the stimuli. The last question investigates the difficulties experienced in understanding the situation. The subjects were asked to respond to each item using a seven-point Likert scale.

Section B IOWA Gambling Task

The submission of the IGT was made using the same procedure (PC and setting) as for the presentation of moral dilemmas. Each subject saw four decks on the screen and after each choice in the top of the screen subjects could see both points gained or lost and their total score. Once the subject had completed 100 choices, the program stopped automatically (for the entire procedure see Bechara *et al.* 1994). The two experimental sections (A and B) were randomized across the subjects.

Data reduction

EEG recording and ERP measures

The EEG was recorded with a 32-channel DC amplifier (SYNAMPS system) and acquisition software (NEUROSCAN 4.2). An ElectroCap with Ag/AgCl electrodes was used to record EEGs from active scalp sites referred to earlobe (10–20 system of electrode placement). Additionally, two EOG electrodes were put on the outer sides of the eyes. The data were recorded using a sampling rate of 501 Hz, with a frequency band of 0.1–60 Hz. The impedance of recording electrodes was monitored for each subject prior to data collection and it was always below 5 kΩ. An averaged waveform (offline) was obtained from about 17 artifact-free (trials exceeding 50 μV in amplitude were excluded from the averaging process) individual target stimuli for each subject. The EEG signals were visually scored on a high-resolution computer monitor and portions of the data containing eye movements, muscle movements, or other sources of artifacts were removed. Peak amplitude measurement was quantified relative to 100 ms pre-stimulus. Only some electrodes were used for the successive statistical analysis, respectively: F7, F3, FZ, F4, F8, FC3, FCZ, FC4 (for the frontal region); C3, CZ, C4, CP3, CPZ, CP4 (for the central region); P3, PZ, P4 (for the parietal region); T3, TP7, T5, T4, TP8, T6 (for the temporal region). In order to perform data analyses, eight regions of interest (ROIs) were identified (frontal L/R; central L/R; temporal L/R; parietal L/R) (Figure 5.4).

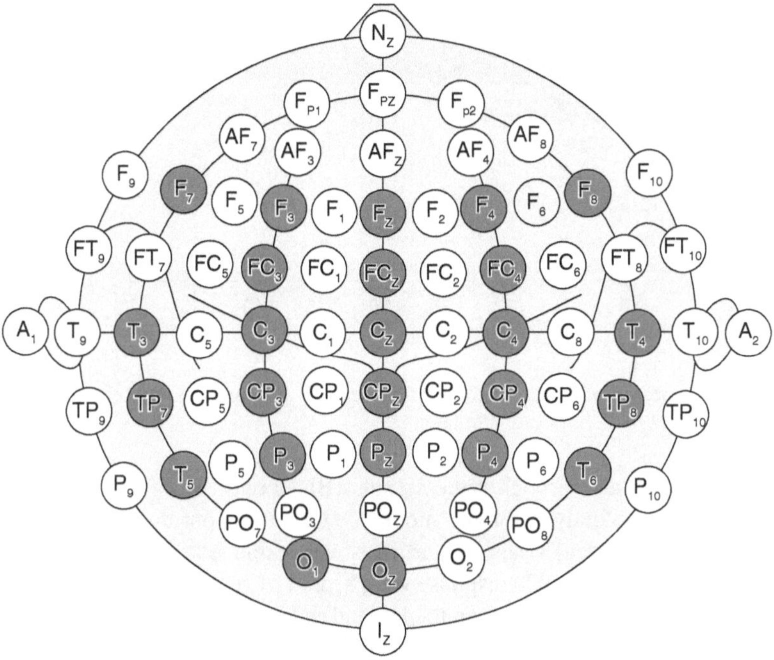

Figure 5.4 Black highlighting of the 25 electrodes used in the 10–20 system.

We then proceeded with the first step of morphological analysis consisting of a qualitative exploration of wave profiles in search of significant variations relative to response. We combined a visual exploration of the profiles with computerized peak detection (Edit Software NeuroScan 5.2) in order to find minimum and maximum values of peak intensity. Morphological ERP analyses showed a similar pattern of activation for utilitarian and deontological groups at different mean latencies of the wave. For statistical analyses, an N200 latency window (180–250ms) was considered, taking into account the functional significance of this deflection as an emotional marker. An example of N200 peak deflection is reported in Figure 5.5.

Biofeedback: registration of autonomic indices

During the performance of moral dilemmas and of the IGT task some psychophysiological indices were recorded: skin conductance response (SCR) and level (SCL), body temperature (TEMP), heart rate (pulse PULS), blood flow (PVA) and pressure (BVP) (for a detailed description of these measures see Balconi and Pozzoli 2007; Balconi *et al.* 2009). Autonomic indices were measured continuously with a constant voltage by Biofeedback (Biofeedback 2000, version X-pert). This is a modular feedback system so the radio technology allows transference of

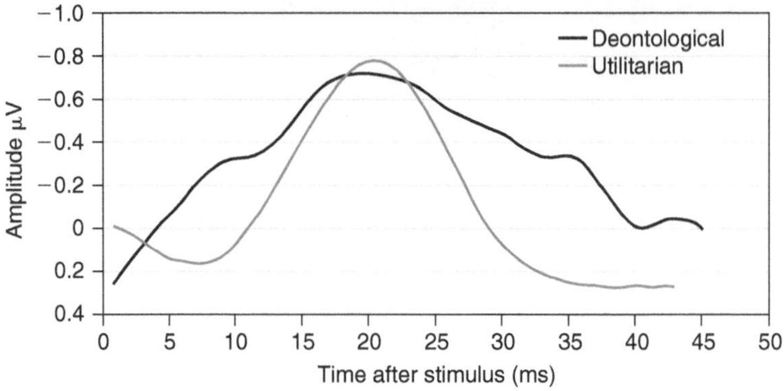

Figure 5.5 N200 peak amplitude recorded during the utilitarian and deontological responses to the moral dilemmas.

the data to the computer through radio signals (Bluetooth). The radio modules were positioned on the body: the radio module MULTI was put on the left wrist with a pulling action system. Trials with artifacts were excluded from the analysis, whereas trials with no detectable response were scored as zero. The electrocardiogram was recorded using electrodes on the left and right forearms. Inter-beat intervals of the EKG were converted to heart rate in beats per minute (PULS, scoring acceleration during the experimental phase). Autonomic measures were registered during the task execution (2 s before and 2 s after the subject's choice) in order to acquire their modulation along the entire performance.

Data analysis

Moral dilemmas

Different sets of ANOVA were performed, respectively for the moral dilemma and the IGT section.

For the first task ERP N200 modulation was assessed with three-factor (between-subject, group 2; within-group, site 4; and lateralization 2) mixed-measure ANOVA. With respect to the N200 profile, the group main effect was not significant ($F(1, 24)=1.50$; $p=0.31$; $\eta^2=0.12$) (Figure 5.6).

In addition, site main effect was significant $F(3, 24)=8.32$; $p=0.02$; $\eta^2=0.38$). Contrast analysis showed an increased frontal activation in comparison with the other sites (all comparisons $p\leq 0.01$). Moreover, a more right-side activation was observable by the cortical map displays (see Figure 5.7).

A successive ANOVA tested the significance of the differences between utilitarian and deontological choices with respect to RTs. As showed by the analysis, significant differences were found between groups ($F(1, 24)=8.32$; $p=0.02$; $\eta^2=0.38$), since the utilitarian group revealed reduced RTs in comparison with the deontological group (see Figure 5.8).

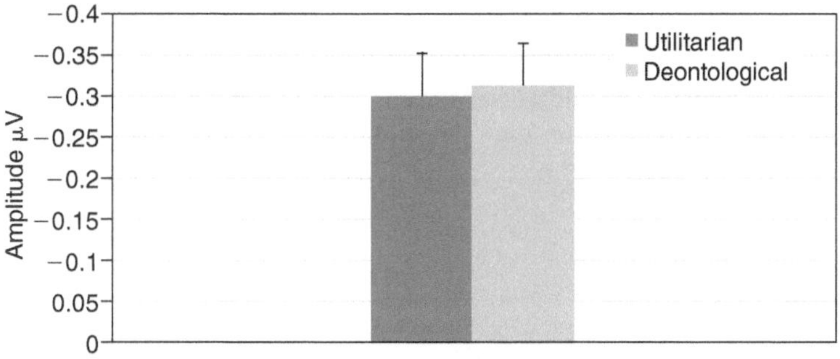

Figure 5.6 Mean amplitude of N200 effects observed during the moral dilemmas, divided by utilitarian and deontological responses.

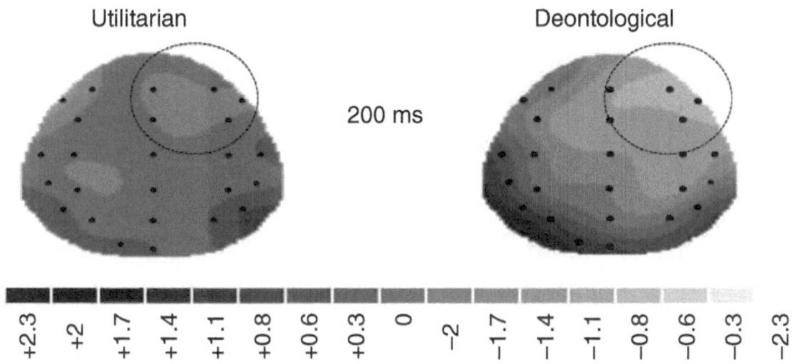

Figure 5.7 Cortical maps of N200 effect for utilitarian and deontological responses. The circle highlights the right-frontal area where the N200 effect is greater.

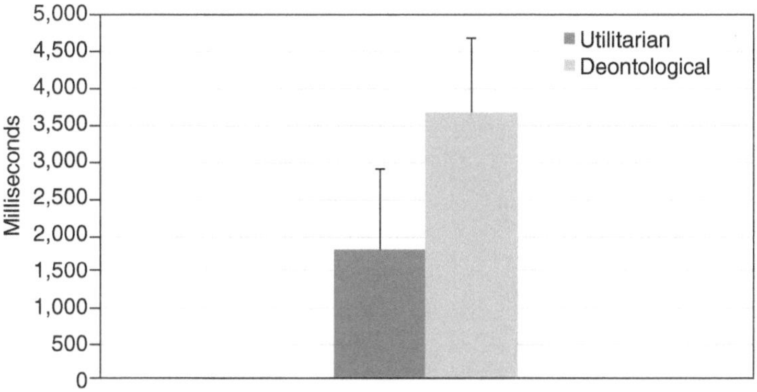

Figure 5.8 Reaction times detected during the moral dilemmas divided by utilitarian and deontological responses.

Successive ANOVAs were performed in order to verify the differences between groups for the autonomic behavior, in response to moral decisions. We reported only the significant results for the autonomic dependent measures. As shown, both deontological and utilitarian groups revealed an increased SCR, PULS, and BVP in comparison with the rest condition (before the experimental performance) (all $p \leq 0.01$), whereas no significant differences were found between the two groups (Figure 5.9).

IOWA Gambling Task

For the second task (IGT), distinct ANOVAs were performed for the following dependent variables: number of deck choices; RTs for deck choices; autonomic measures (only significant results reported). As showed by the ANOVA, the two groups did not show different behavior in terms of decks ($F(1, 24)=1.77$; $p=0.35$; $\eta^2=0.13$) since they more consistently opted for the more favorable decks (C and D). Nevertheless, it was observed that the utilitarian group chose more frequently for the unfavorable B deck in comparison with the other deck category.

In parallel, the RT measures were undifferentiated between the two groups for each type of deck (all $p>0.01$). Finally, autonomic measures revealed a significant increased psychophysiological activation (for the three measures of SCR, PULS, and BVP) during the decision-making in comparison with the rest condition for the two subject groups. Nevertheless, no differences were found between them for each autonomic measure and as a function of the deck type (all $p>0.01$) (Figure 5.10).

Correlational analysis between tasks

A final correlational analysis was performed between the autonomic measures into the two tasks (moral dilemma and IGT) in order to compare the autonomic

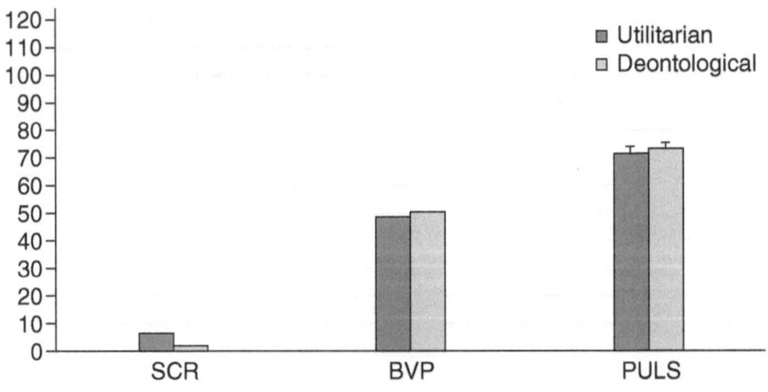

Figure 5.9 Average of the autonomic indices observed during the moral dilemmas, divided by utilitarian and deontological subjects (SCR in Hz, BVP in mmHg, PULS in h/m).

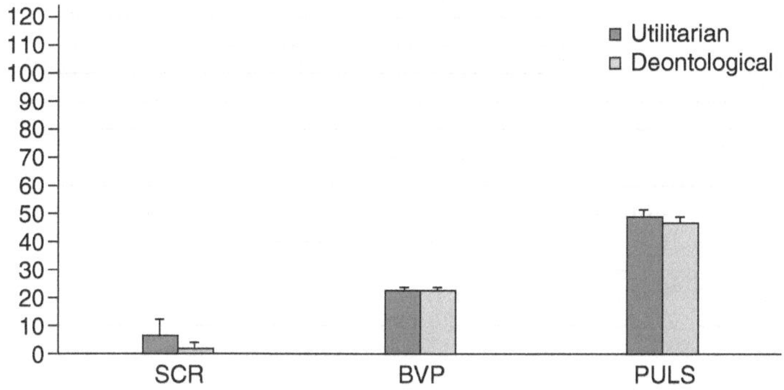

Figure 5.10 Average of the autonomic indices observed during the IGT, divided by utilitarian and deontological subjects (SCR in Hz, BVP in mmHg, PULS in h/m).

modulation across the task. Highly significant Pearson correlational values were observed between the moral and gain decisional processes for each of the autonomic measures (respectively SCR, PULS, and BVP; correlational values for all $p \leq 0.01$). Thus, an analogous emotional behavior may be supposed between the tasks, which reveals an automatic and unconscious contribution to the decisional processing that is similar across the two decisional tasks.

Discussion

Emotions in moral decisions

As observed in the present analysis, a significant N200 ERP deflection was revealed in response to the moral decisional processes. Second, both of the two categories of subject showed an analogous cortical response to their decisional choice, with an increased frontal (presumably ventromedial localized) responsiveness. In previous research the emotional significance of this ERP deflection was underlined. In fact, an increased N200 amplitude was found in response to situations where subjects were required to judge the emotional significance of the stimuli (Balconi and Mazza 2009) or when a conflictual emotional condition is present with an increased arousal (Balconi and Pozzoli 2007; Balconi and Lucchiari 2005; Krolak-Salmon *et al.* 2001; Sato *et al.* 2001; Streit *et al.* 2000). The N200 is a component used to recognize the emotive value of the stimulus. Also, the specific emotional content has an impact on the ERP variation (Balconi and Lucchiari 2006). Moreover, it was represented as a marker of a conflictual condition in which the subject is faced with an emotionally involving context that induces the subject to exclude one behavior in favor of another.

It is relevant that both utilitarian and deotological choice categories showed an increased N200 in comparison with a non-decisional condition, and thus an increased emotional behavior, when they have to decide within a moral context.

We may suppose that also the utilitarian choices require an emotional involvement, where the subject could "emotionally pay" for his/her decision to violate his/her moral value (to not kill a person) in favor of safeguarding other people (and their lives).

Previous studies focused on factors that elicit or suppress judgments consistent with utilitarianism, which mandates promoting "the greatest good for the greatest number," where goodness is assessed from an impersonal point of view, and each person's welfare counts equally. Because utilitarianism requires summing the degree of satisfaction of welfare interests (i.e., basic needs) across individuals, it mandates a process for the choices participants face in the current context: count the number of lives saved by each alternative and choose accordingly. Choices that maximize lives saved are consistent with utilitarianism. Otherwise, they are not. Previous models have supposed this process may avoid including emotional components, since it acts as a function of general cognitive pathways (Greene *et al.* 2001). A general disconfirmation of this model about the exclusive cognitive and rational feature of the utilitarian behavior was found in the present research. In fact, not only an emotional involvement was observed for the two types of choices, but also the utilitarian condition did not produce a higher cognitive cost, as supposed by Greene's model. RTs were in fact reduced in response to utilitarian choices, in opposition to the supposed greater cognitive effort due to the controlled reasoning and to the greater cognitive workload.

Emotional conscious and unconscious contribution in decision-making

A second important result of the present research points out that unconscious processes, in addition to the conscious ones, are active during both the moral and gain task, as shown by consistent responses by autonomic indices. Specifically, SCR, BVP, and PULS indices were increased during the decisional choices, with a specific autonomic modulation due to the contextual situations. We may conclude that utilitarian and deontological choices require, in addition to a central monitoring by cortical sites, also a simultaneous increased peripheral responsiveness.

It may be suggested that an increased arousal may have determined this responsiveness. In previous studies psychophysiological measures (SCR, cardiac frequency, and blood pressure) were used, taking into account the modulation in *arousal*. In fact, arousal is considered a fundamental feature of behavior and is defined as the neurophysiological basis underlying all the processes in the human organism. So, the emotional tasks could favor an arousal response in the subjects. Specifically, the psychophysiological index of SCR is a significant value for emotion discrimination. According to the literature, SCR is higher when the decisional process is associated with emotional conditions than neutral conditions.

At an autonomic level the subject responds automatically to the emotional context and this response might be unconsciousness. A great amount of research confirms that unconscious processes may elicit emotional responses by increasing the arousal level: for example, a larger SCR is observed when a more salient stimulus (e.g., a facial expression) is perceived without awareness (Dimberg *et al.* 2000). Moreover, all emotional conditions prompt larger increases in skin conductance than neutral conditions, since skin conductance change is a direct consequence of general activation of the autonomic nervous system (Cuthbert *et al.* 2000).

More generally, it was stated that the concept of choice included the convergence of different decisional systems, such as a *deliberative* (generally consciously mediated process) and an *intuitive* (mainly unconscious emotionally mediated process) *system* (Deppe *et al.* 2005; Kahneman and Tversky 1982; Loewenstein *et al.* 2001; Slovic *et al.* 2004). Specifically, the mechanism of decision-making should be considered by an affective (emotional response) and a cognitive (mental effort) point of view. Thus, the intrinsic relationship between cognition and emotion needs to be reconsidered (Elster 1998; Glimcher and Rustichini 2004; Loewenstein 2000). More specifically, regarding the dichotomy of *conscious vs. unconscious* contribution to decisional processes, it was demonstrated that the controlled processes are serial, deliberative, and often associated with a subjective perception of effort. On the contrary, the automatic processes are multi-tasking, they are unconsciousness, and they don't need a particular effort, so they are faster than the controlled processes. Moreover, LeDoux (1989) has argued that the emotional system gives an affective meaning to the stimuli and this brain mechanism operates unconsciously to generate the conscious experience of emotion.

Many studies have reported that emotions influence cognitive processes (Scott and Cervone 2002) because affective conditions are used by people as salient information ready to formulate evaluations and judgments (*affect as information*). The affective processes (Zajonc 1998) motivate approach or avoidance behavior, so they comprehend emotions, drives, and motivational situations, while the cognitive processes are related more to true-or-false issues. Among the recent theories about emotion, Russell's circumflex model proposes an *appraisal process* able to explain that each emotion represents a specific response to a particular kind of significant event, evaluated by the subject in line with its motivational significance. This appraisal process is governed by two criteria: the *arousing power* (high or low) and the *valence* (positive or negative) of the emotional stimulus (Balconi and Pozzoli 2007; Russell 2003). The affective dimension of valence, that is its hedonic quality, is related to the arousal dimension, because extremely pleasant or unpleasant stimuli are associated with increased arousal (Russell and Carroll 1999).

The best way to obtain a gain: what kind of relationship with the utilitarian and deontological distinction?

Some important points have been elucidated by the present results about the gambling task performance. First, autonomic responses were equally modulated by the four deck options, since an increased arousal may be suggested for the four conditions in comparison to the pre-experimental condition (resting). Second, this modulation was registered immediately before and after the decisional process. These facts may be a partial disconfirmation of the somatic marker hypothesis, which states the activation of an autonomic (specifically the SCR increasing) response only *before* an *unfavorable* response. In the present research we do not directly discuss the significance of our results for the somatic marker hypothesis. Nevertheless, the type of "autonomic marker" we have found may be useful in order to signal to the subject the emotional relevance of the incoming behavior, a functional strategy that was analogously applied by the utilitarian and the deontological category.

This emotional contribution may have favored the successive best strategy to opt for the gaining games more than the losing games. In fact, a second main result regards the observed effect for the best choice performed between the four decks. The two subject groups equally reported a functional behavior (more C and D choices), even if they diverge about the unfavorable decks (A and B), since the utilitarian group chose the unfavorable B deck a significant number of times, which was the deck that allowed a great number of loses but in a limited number of games. In this case, a generally less efficient behavior may be suggested for this subject group, with a possible reduction of the overall efficacy of their cognitive strategy. We suspect in this case the presence of an intervenient variable, for example related to some personality components, that should be better explained by future research. At present, we suggest a more consistent risk-seeking and less conservative strategy was adopted by utilitarian subjects, which may have produced a generally non-functional choice.

The third main point we found relates to the high consonance between moral choice and gain behavior with regard to autonomic modulation. That is, subjects showed an analogous unconscious response to the decisional conditions by increasing their physiological responsiveness to emotionally charged situations. This increased responsiveness was undifferentiated across deontological and utilitarian categories, with a consonant automatic reaction to the moral and gain-related decision.

Some conclusive remarks

The emerging insights from this research point toward a model in which automatic processing may act in parallel with central neural circuits, many of which are associated with social emotions, personality components, and contextual constraints (Figure 5.11).

Through various mechanisms of competition shown in Figure 5.11, only a subset of these circuits ultimately causes a decision or an action, mainly related to scenario, type of tasks, and personal attitude. This activity is primarily emotional (as evidenced by ERP measures) and acted unconsciously (as evidenced by autonomic measures), and secondarily experienced consciously as a subjective sense of choice that is moral, immoral, and efficient (gain) or not (loss).

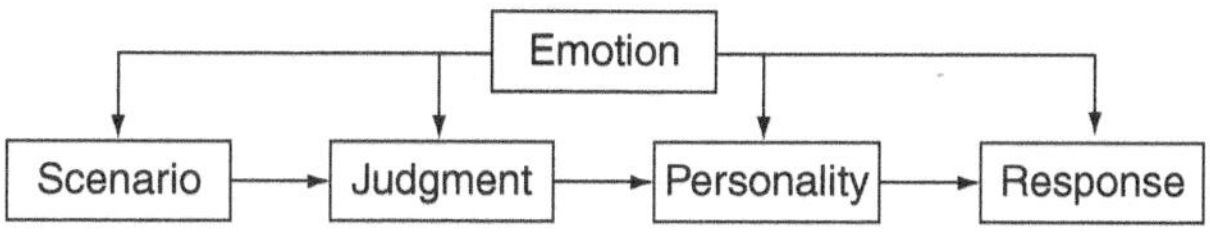

Figure 5.11 The possible influence of emotion during moral decision-making.

An interpretive process offers post-hoc explanations designed to link the social context with the subjective moral response using whatever explicit information is available. Specifically, the current study suggested decisional processes are influenced by (1) emotional reactions to decisional processes, and (2) conscious and unconscious processing able to incorporate emotional reactions in judgments.

More generally, there is a good reason to include emotion in the process of decisional reasoning. Rather than defeating the reasoning process, emotions can actually aid reasoning by acting as a centralizing agent, focusing our attention and our cognitive resource on the decisional topic. This characteristic of emotions makes them desirable for the process of moral decision-making and gain behavior. More generally we may use their influence to serve our high-order moral beliefs, as a remarkable source of moral judgment and action, as well as to coordinate the strategy to obtain a gain.

References

Anderson, S.W., Barrash, J., Bechara, A., and Tranel, D. (2006) "Impairments of emotion and real-world complex behavior following childhood- or adult-onset damage to ventromedial prefrontal cortex," *Journal of the International Neuropsychological Society*, 12: 224–235.

Balconi, M. (2008) *Neuropsicologia della comunicazione*, Milan: Springer Verlag.

Balconi, M. and Lucchiari, C. (2008) "Consciousness and arousal effects on emotional face processing as revealed by brain oscillations: a gamma band analysis," *International Journal of Psychophysiology*, 67: 41–46.

Balconi, M. and Mazza, G. (2009) "Consciousness and emotion: ERP modulation and attentive vs. pre-attentive elaboration of emotional facial expressions by backward masking," *Motivation and Emotion*, 33: 113–124.

Balconi, M. and Lucchiari, C. (2005) "Morphed facial expressions elicited a N400 ERP effect. A cerebral domain-specific semantic module," *Scandinavian Journal of Psychology*, 46: 467–474.

Balconi, M. and Pozzoli, U. (2007) "Event-related oscillations (ERO) and event-related potentials (ERP) comparison in facial expression recognition," *Journal of Neuropsychology*, 1: 283–294.

Balconi, M. and Pozzoli, U. (2008) "Consciousness and arousal effects on emotional face processing as revealed by brain oscillations: a gamma band analysis," *International Journal of Psychophysiology*, 67 (1): 41–46.

Balconi, M., Brambilla E., and Falbo, L. (2009) "Appetitive vs. defensive responses to emotional cues: autonomic measures and brain oscillation modulation," *Brain Research*, 1296: 72–84.

Bartels, D. (2008) "Principled moral sentiment and the flexibility of moral judgment and decision making," *Cognition*, 108: 381–417.

Bechara, A. and Damasio, A.R. (1997) "Deciding advantageously before knowing the advantageous strategy," *Science*, 275: 1293–1295.

Bechara, A., Damasio, A.R., Damasio, H., and Anderson, S.W. (1994) "Insensitivity to future consequences following damage to human prefrontal cortex," *Cognition*, 50: 7–15.

Blair, R.J. (1995) "A cognitive developmental approach to morality: investigating the psychopath," *Cognition*, 57: 1–29.

Botvinick, M.M., Braver, T.S., Barch, D.M., Carter, C.S., and Cohen, J.D. (2001) "Conflict monitoring and cognitive control," *Psychological Review*, 108: 624–652.

Cuthbert, B.N., Schupp, H.T., Bradley, M.M., Birbaumer, N., and Lang, P.J. (2000) "Brain potentials in affective picture processing: covariation with autonomic arousal and affective report," *Biological Psychology*, 52: 95–111.

Damasio, A.R. (1994) *Descartes Error*, New York: Harper Perennial.

Damasio, A.R., Tranel D., and Damasio, H. (1990) "Face agnosia and the neural substrates of memory," *Annual Review of Neuroscience*, 13: 89–109.

Dean, R. (2010) "Does neuroscience undermine deontological theory?," *Neuroethics*, 3: 43–60.

Deppe, M., Schwindt, W., Krämer, J., Kugel, H., Plassmann, H., Kenning, P., and Ringlestein, E.B. (2005) "Evidence for a neural correlate of framing effect: bias-specific activity in the ventromedial prefrontal cortex during credibility judgements," *Brain Research Bulletin*, 67: 413–421.

Dimberg, U., Elmehed, K., and Thunberg, M. (2000) "Unconscious facial reactions to emotional facial expressions," *Psychological Science*, 11: 86–89.

Elster, J. (1998) "Emotions in economic theory," *Journal of Economic Literature*, XXXVI: 47–74.

Forsyth, D.R. (1980) "A taxonomy of ethical ideologies," *Journal of Personality and Social Psychology*, 39: 175–184.

Fukui, H., Murai, T., Fukuyama, H., Hayashi, T., and Hanakawa, T. (2005) "Functional activity related to risk anticipation during performance of the Iowa Gambling Task," *Neuroimage*, 24: 253–259.

Gallese, V. (2003) "The roots of empathy: the shared manifold hypothesis and the neural basis of intersubjectivity," *Psychopathology*, 36: 171–180.

Glimcher, P.V. and Rustichini, A. (2004) "Neuroeconomics: the consilience of brain and decision," *Science*, 306: 447–451.

Greene, J.D. (2007) "Why are VMPFC patients more utilitarian? A dual-process theory of moral judgment explains," *Trends in Cognitive Sciences*, 11 (8): 322.

Greene, J.D. and Haidt, J. (2002) "How (and where) does moral judgment work?," *Trends in Cognitive Science*, 6: 517–523.

Greene, J.D., Sommerville, R.B., Nystrom, L.E., Darley, J.M., and Cohen, J.D. (2001) "An fMRI investigation of emotional engagement in moral judgment," *Science*, 293 (5537): 2105–2108.

Greene, J.D., Nystrom, L.E., Engell, A.D., Darley, J.M., and Cohen, J.D. (2004) "The neural bases of cognitive conflict and control in moral judgment," *Neuron*, 44 (2): 389–400.

Greene, J.D., Morelli, S.A., Lowenberg, K., Nystrom, L.E., and Cohen, J.D. (2008) "Cognitive load selectively interferes with utilitarian moral judgment," *Cognition*, 107: 1144–1154.

Grinband, J., Hirsch, J., and Ferrera, V.P. (2006) "A neural representation of categorization uncertainty in the human brain," *Neuron*, 49 (5): 757–763.

Haidt, J. (2001) "The emotional dog and its rational tail," *Psychological Review*, 108: 814–834.

Hauser, M.D. (2006) *Moral Minds: How Nature Designed our Universal Sense of Right and Wrong*, New York: Harper Collins.

Hoffman, M. (1982) "Development of prosocial motivation: empathy and guilt," in N. Eisenberg (ed.), *Development of Prosocial Behavior*, New York: Academic Press.

Hoffman, M. (2000) *Empathy and Moral Development: Implications for Caring and Justice*, Cambridge: Cambridge University Press.

Iidaka, T., Okada, T., Murata, T., Omori, M., Kosaka, H., Sadato, N., and Yonekura, Y. (2002) "Age-related differences in the medial temporal lobe responses to emotional faces as revealed by fMRI," *Hippocampus*, 12 (3): 352–362.

Kahneman, D. and Tversky, A. (1982) "Variants of uncertainty," *Cognition*, 11: 143–157.

Kelly, B. (1996) "Invest in yourself: speaking up: a moral obligation," *Nursing Forum*, 31: 31–34.

Koenigs, M., Young, L., Adolphs, R., Tranel, D., Cushman, F., Hauser, M., and Damasio, A.R. (2007) "Damage to the prefrontal cortex increases utilitarian moral judgments," *Nature*, 446: 908–911.

Krolak-Salmon, P., Fischer, C., Vighetto, A., and Mauguiere, F. (2001) "Processing of facial emotional expression: spatio-temporal data as assessed by scalp event related potentials," *European Journal of Neuroscience*, 13: 987–999.

LeDoux, J.E. (1989) "Cognitive-emotional interactions in the brain," *Cognitive Emotion*, 3: 267–290.

Liepelt, R., Von Cramon, D.Y., and Brass, M. (2008) "How do we infer others' goals from nonstereotypic actions? The outcome of context-sensitive inferential processing in right inferior parietal and posterior temporal cortex," *Neuroimage*, 43: 784–792.

Loewenstein, G.F. (2000) "Emotions in economic theory and economic behavior," *American Economic Review*, 90: 426–433.

Loewenstein, G., Weber, E.U., Hsee, C.K., and Welch, N. (2001) "Risk as feelings," *Psychological Bulletin*, 127 (2): 267–286.

McGuire, J., Langdon, R., Coltheart, M., and Mackenzie, C. (2009) "A reanalysis of the personal/impersonal distinction in moral psychology research," *Journal of Experimental Social Psychology*, 45 (3): 577–580.

Meltzoff, A.N. and Moore, M.K. (1977) "Imitation of facial and manual gestures by human neonates," *Science*, 198: 75–78.

Mendez, M.F., Anderson, E., and Shapira, J. (2005) "An investigation of moral judgment in frontotemporal dementia," *Cognitive and Behavioral Neurology*, 18: 193–197.

Mikhail, J. (2007) "Universal moral grammar: theory, evidence, and the future," *Trends in Cognitive Sciences*, 11: 143–152.

Miller, E. and Cohen, J.D. (2001) "An integrative theory of prefrontal cortex function," *Annual Review of Neuroscience*, 24, 167–202.

Moll, J., Oliveira-Souza, R., Eslinger, P.J., Bramati, I.E., Mourão-Miranda, J., Andreiuolo, P.A., and Luiz, P. (2002) "The neural correlates of moral sensitivity: a functional magnetic resonance imaging investigation of basic and moral emotions," *Journal of Neuroscience*, 22: 2730–2736.

Moll, J., Oliveira-Souza, R., and Eslinger, P.J. (2003) "Morals and the human brain: a working model," *Neuroreport*, 14: 299–305.

Prinz, J. (2006) "The emotional basis of moral judgment," *Philosophical Exploration*, 9: 29–43.

Rozin, P. (1997) "Moralization and becoming a vegetarian," *Psychological Science*, 8: 67–73.

Rozin, P., Lowery, L., Sumio, I., and Haidt, J. (1999) "The CAD triad hypothesis: a mapping between three moral emotions (contempt, anger, disgust) and three moral codes (community, autonomy, divinity)," *Journal of Personality and Social Psychology*, 76 (4): 574–586.

Russell, J.A. (2003) "Core affect and the psychological construction of emotion," *Psychological Review*, 110: 145–172.

Russell, J.A. and Carroll, J.M. (1999) "On the bipolarity of positive and negative affect," *Psychological Bulletin*, 125: 3–30.

Sato, W., Takanori, K., Sakiko, Y., and Michikazu, M. (2001) "Emotional expression boosts early visual processing of the face: ERP recording and its decomposition by independent component analysis," *Neuroreport*, 12: 709–714.

Scott, W.D. and Cervone, D. (2002) "The impact of negative affect on performance standards: evidence for an affect-as-information mechanism," *Cognitive Therapy and Research*, 26: 19–37.

Slovic, P.P., Finucane, M.L., Peters, E., and McGregor, D.D. (2004) "The affect heuristics," in T. Gilovich, D. Griffin, and D. Kahneman (eds.), *Intuitive Judgment: Heuristics and Biases*, Cambridge: Cambridge University Press.

Strawson, P. (1960) "Freedom and resentment," *Proceedings of the British Academy*, 47: 1–25.

Streit, M., Wolwer, W., Brinkmeyer, J., Ihl, R., and Gaebel, W. (2000) "Electrophysiological correlates of emotional and structural face processing in humans," *Neuroscience Letters*, 278: 13–16.

Young, L., Cushman, F., Hauser, M., and Saxe, R. (2007) "The neural basis of the interaction between theory of mind and moral judgment," *Proceedings of the National Academy of Science*, 104: 8235–8240.

Zajonc, R.B. (1998) "Emotions," in D. Gilbert, S. Fiske, and G. Lindzey (eds.), *The Handbook of Social Psychology*, New York: Oxford University Press.

6 Emotional decisions

The induction-of-intrinsic-desires theory

Christoph Lumer

Introduction: collocating the approach to be presented

There are several ways in which emotions or feelings in general can influence decisions; the following are among the most important (Rottenstreich and Shu 2004; Zeelenberg *et al.* 2008; Weber and Lindemann 2008).

1 In a first group of mechanisms the emotion precedes the deliberation:
   1.1 The emotion or feeling may induce a specific emotion-related aim or desire; e.g. if we feel compassion for someone we may be inclined to help him, without aiming at personal advantages for ourselves.
   1.2 A mood or emotion may alter our subjective probabilities; if we are quite happy we may be induced to believe that the world is on our side and hence that certain aspired events will likely occur, where the likelihood is higher than the one we would have expected without the emotion.
   1.3 The emotion or mood may change our risk behaviour: in good moods we tend to underrate risk, and in bad moods we tend to overrate risk – in part this may already be a consequence of the second effect mentioned, but only in part.

2 In the second group of mechanisms the emotion or feeling arises during the deliberation.
   2.1 In such a case we may use our emotional feeling about a certain option as a heuristic for the value of this option (affect heuristics); if, for example, we inspect an apartment as a possible candidate for rental, a good emotional state during the inspection may be taken as a heuristic that this apartment is attractive compared to other apartments.
   2.2 The emotion may arise from thinking about a certain consequence of an option and thus stress the respective importance of this consequence (Damasio's emotional markers); e.g. thinking of the possibility of a certain kind of accident that may occur as a consequence of one of our options may horrify us so that we become very careful in our planning to avoid this possible negative effect.
   2.3 The decision process itself may lead to certain feelings that influence

the process itself, e.g. difficult decisions may lead to avoidance behaviour, or nervous unrest about the decision may lead to an immediate choice of the last considered option.

3 Finally, emotions very often have a final(istic) 'influence' on our decisions: they are the aim of our decisions.

All these mechanisms exist, and they do not exclude each other.

The topic of this chapter is the very first mechanism mentioned: emotions and feelings in general often induce aims or desires, which may even lead to open the deliberation in the first place for realising this aim or desire. The induced aim or desire is not simply *triggered* by the emotion; but its specific content is determined by the emotion's content. For example, fear may induce a particular search for security; rage may induce the aim to hurt or kill the person one is furious with; sympathy may induce the aim to help the other person. In addition, the content of the induced aim or desire may completely depend on the inducing emotion in such a way that a desire or aim with this content would be impossible without the respective emotion. Emotions or feelings inducing aims or desires is the most specific way emotions causally influence decisions, because they determine the action's content so specifically.

The aim of this chapter is to sketch a general theory of emotion-induced desires, which resolves problems of some existing approaches to the phenomenon and provides a good explanation of acts committed in the heat of the moment, in particular elaborating the aims and desires underlying such actions (the induction-of-intrinsic-desires theory), as well as some reflections on the origin and value of this mechanism.

Some approaches to emotional decisions

Before presenting the induction-of-intrinsic-desires theory, some words about existing approaches to emotional decisions shall elucidate the problems and lacunae the theory has to respond to. Several approaches for explaining emotional decisions have been provided in the literature. First, there are some approaches that see emotions as special kinds of motivations (Frijda 1986: 460, 466, 469, 479; Izard 1977; Lang 1988: 186). However, this is simply ontologically impossible; emotions can have motivational influence and force – whose content and extent then have to be determined – but they *are* not motives. Then there are more sophisticated approaches like those of Heckhausen or Zeelenberg and others. Heckhausen assumes that emotions are a rudimentary motivational system with emotionally induced motives leading directly to decisions and actions without any expectancy-value elaboration (Heckhausen 1989: 71–76, esp. 74). Problems with this approach are, first, that Heckhausen did not elaborate an exhaustive and specific list of the motives induced and, a fortiori, he did not explain such a list. Second, the assumption that there are two motivational mechanisms does not explain how the two types of motives can be combined and contribute to one and the same decision – as they however do, for example when someone is acting out of revenge but carefully chooses his action so as to avoid damages to himself.

Zeelenberg and others instead propose that emotions lead to specific *aims* (Zeelenberg *et al.* 2008: 183), where they see the necessity and desirability of having a precise list of these aims, yet without providing it. This approach fares much better with respect to the second of Heckhausen's problems because it makes it possible to combine emotional and calm components into one decision; and it is quite close to my own. Therefore, I want to stress some critical points about it for motivating my own approach.

One main target of my critique is that in this approach *aims* or *goals* are the specific elements induced by emotions. Aims or, better, goal intentions are opposed to executive intentions. *Executive intentions* are (1) self-binding commitments to realise a certain behaviour, (2) where the action is subjectively described in a way understandable to the executive system (e.g. to write a specific word, to walk to the fridge), and (3) which can cause the respective behaviour via one's executive system. By comparison, *aim intentions* are (1) self-binding commitments to realise a certain behaviour as well, (2) however, where the behaviour to be executed is described by reference to a desired end (e.g. to have something fresh to drink, to pass an exam) and, therefore, is not understandable for the subject's executive system, (3) their function is to cause a deliberation during which an executive intention whose realisation leads to the desired end is formed.

What is particularly important here is that goal intentions are already self-binding commitments. That emotions – regularly, always? – induce goal intentions is a strong hypothesis because, usually, forming a goal intention is already the result of some deliberation during which several options and their most important consequences are considered and weighed against each other. If emotions induced aims this would imply that the deliberation and its weighing are skipped. I think this hypothesis is too strong. (1) Most of our emotions are weak. If they all induced some goal we would not have the time to do anything else than react to emotions. To avoid this probably false consequence one could introduce a cut-off mechanism into the model, i.e. a threshold of emotional intensity below which emotions would not influence our decisions. However, not even this is very convincing. (2) Strong-willed people often do not follow the indications given by their emotions. However, if the emotions already induce aims this is hardly possible. (3) Even not-so-strong-willed people have their other desires and aims, which often make them decide against the emotion-induced indication. So there must be a way to include these desires and aims even in cases of emotion-induced inclinations. (4) Goal intentions are not specified up to entailing an executable action description, but nonetheless they usually contain rather already specific aims; the emotional system alone, however, does not have the information to make such specific choices. For example, if one is in a rage, the ultimately resulting aim may vary from killing the person one is furious with to making a smug observation about that person to one's friends; inventing such (medium-specified) options and selecting from this spectrum is probably beyond the emotional system's capacities.

I think it is true that emotions influence our decisions quite specifically. But the upshot of the criticisms just raised is that the assumed place of influence is not the *aim* or *goal intention* but one or two steps before them, so that more flexible reactions to the emotion and its indications are possible.

Preliminaries to the induction-of-intrinsic-desires hypothesis

The hypotheses to be proposed in this chapter imply that the place where emotions bring in their indications for decisions are desires, or more specifically, *intrinsic desires*. I have developed these hypotheses in earlier publications as part of a more embracing theory about the content of intrinsic desires (Lumer 1997; [2000] 2009: 477–493). Here I want to re-propose and expand these hypotheses to a theory of emotional decisions.

The approach presupposes some expectancy-valence or desire-belief or decision-theoretic model of decision. This is a theory according to which actions are chosen on the basis of information about various possible consequences of several options, the (conditional) probabilities of these consequences and evaluations of these consequences and the options; all these elements are integrated to build an overall evaluation of the options; finally, the best option is chosen. Which form of expectancy-valence theory is the empirically right one (e.g. subjective expected utility theory (e.g. Davidson *et al.* [1957] 1977) or prospect theory (Tversky and Kahneman 1992) etc.) is not important to our present concern.[1] However, I will stick to a more action philosophical terminology. Hence the psychological 'valences' here will be called 'desires' or 'motivational value judgements'.

Desires and motivational value judgements may be intrinsic, extrinsic, total or prospect desires. In an *intrinsic desire* a certain state of affairs is valued in a certain way for its own sake, not for its consequences or other states of affairs implied by it. If subjects are asked why they (intrinsically) value this state of affairs in a certain way, they cannot give any further answer: 'There is no further reason or consequence why this is good (or bad); it is simply good, good in itself.' All the other desires are dependent on intrinsic desires. Someone *desires* something *p extrinsically* in some respect if he desires it in this respect because he thinks that *p* will have a specific intrinsically desirable consequence *c*. A person *desires* something *p totally* to a certain degree, if he thinks that the intrinsic desirability of *p* and all its extrinsic desirabilities add up to that degree. This does not imply that people valuing something as *totally* good in that moment must be *aware* of the intrinsic desires behind that value judgement. But on reflection they may work out their reasons. Finally, someone *desires* an object *p prospectively* (or has a *prospective desire* for *p*) if he integrates the intrinsic or extrinsic values of the consequences plus the information about the probability of these consequences into a comprehensive value judgement, which makes use of the probabilistic information. By convention, I will call also the total desires (impure) prospect desires. Most aims people are consciously striving for (rushing to work, having breakfast, washing their hands, earning money, etc.) are *not* intrinsically desired. Instead, such aims are rather directly accessible by well-known actions, and they are held to have a certain positive *prospect* desirability because their realisation does ensure some intrinsic ends. The criterion introduced above for intrinsic desires was that the respective subject desires the object for its own sake and cannot give any reason why he does so. Now people may simply forget these reasons – because they are too obvious. In this way what originally was a prospect desire turns into an intrinsic desire. For our purposes, only originally intrinsic desires are of interest and will be discussed in the following. However, I will mostly omit the qualification 'original'.

The just introduced usage of 'intrinsic' should not be confused with the psychological use of 'intrinsic motivation', whose most common meaning seems to be autotelic motivation, i.e. that someone is doing something with a motivation not aiming beyond the immediate situation, such as playing, humming, working with flow. However, according to the philosophical meaning, these activities are not intrinsically desired; what is intrinsically desired instead are the immediate consequences of these activities: the enjoyment during playing or working with flow.

What are the contents of intrinsic desires in the philosophical sense, i.e. which things are desired for their own sake? *Strong psychological hedonism* says that only the respective subject's own feelings, i.e. bodily feelings, emotions or moods, are intrinsically desired. Many authors (beginning with Plato (*Philebus*) and continuing e.g. with Joseph Butler (1726) and G.E. Moore (1912: ch. 7) as famous modern followers) have contested strong psychological hedonism and claimed that other things can also be intrinsically desired. But usually they do not criticise that we desire our own feelings according to their pleasantness; so they accept weak psychological hedonism. (Hedonic desires are very stable: we always desire our pleasant feelings *intrinsically* positively, independently of the time of their occurrence. So, today, I can desire not to have unpleasant feelings of hunger *tomorrow* and therefore today buy some food for tomorrow; tomorrow my respective desire has not changed, I am glad to have bought the food. This stability over time is a very important basis for rational planning.) The hypotheses to be presented now imply that emotion-induced intrinsic desires have a non-hedonic content. So the theory implies that strong psychological hedonism is false, but it is compatible with weak psychological hedonism.

The model of feeling-induced desires

Having presented the preliminaries, the topic of emotional desires can be resumed. A paradigm case may be this: a little girl of about three years old who has been provoked by her elder brother (who is around ten years old), and being really furious with him grabs his arm and bites his forearm, directly above his wristwatch with all her strength. Surely the girl knows what she is doing – biting her brother's forearm – and she will have known in advance that this action will 'damage' or 'destroy' the aggressor, perhaps even that it will injure him and that he will suffer. And she has chosen 'carefully' the point where to bite him – in a place where her mouth has enough grip, and not on the wristwatch which would hurt her. Damaging or destroying the aggressor seems to be the (desired) aim of that action, and there seems to be no other aim behind that; so she desires intrinsically to damage the aggressor. This is a non-hedonic intrinsic desire. Afterwards the girl will be satisfied in a crude moral way. But it seems to be too far-fetched to suppose that such a little girl already knows about such hedonic consequences of her acting out of rage; at least when she acts out of rage the first time she cannot have the empirical knowledge about these hedonic consequences, but must acquire this knowledge and perhaps some time, some years later may even have the intrinsic hedonic aim of being morally satisfied.

Such desires here are called 'feeling-induced', or in this case 'emotion-induced'. What is the general mechanism behind feeling-induced desires? (Table 6.1 summarises the various steps now to be explained.)

Phase I: first emotion. In the first phase an emotion occurs. Emotions themselves typically – but not always[2] – arise out of some *affective* valuation of a situation or thought: the subject considers some situation or has some thought and classifies this in a specific way, e.g. – in the case of what later will develop to be pride – as proof of his own strength or – in the case of developing into rage – as an (unjustified) aggression by someone against himself (with the other neither being too strong nor too insignificant). This classification is implicitly a valuation, i.e. the classificatory attributes are meant to be positive or negative attributes (Table 6.1, steps 1–2).

The next step is that the affective valuation causes the core of the appertaining emotion, i.e. its phenomenal, feeling part, such as pride or rage, with its hedonic component. The content of the affective valuation is the propositional content of the emotion (Table 6.1, step 3): in the examples, the subject will be proud of his strength, or furious at the aggressor and his aggression. The affective evaluation can also cause bodily phenomena, such as accelerated heartbeat, blushing or upset stomach, which may be subjectively felt in addition to the primary emotional feeling (Table 6.1, step 4).

Phase II: emotion-induced desire and action. Every type of emotion has its specific affective valuation like pride and rage (above and Table 6.1, step 2), e.g. fear rests on the classification and valuation that something rather harmful probably will happen (Solomon [1976] 1993: 220–310). Such classifications and valuations are not hedonic; but they are only *affective* in the sense that they cause certain emotions; they are *not* motivational, i.e. influencing (at least somewhat) our decisions. So this is not yet the non-hedonic intrinsic motivational desirability function we are looking for. However, every type of emotion is linked with another, satisfying type of emotion in the way that tokens of the first emotion seem to aim at tokens of this second emotion. Rage has (moral) satisfaction as its satisfying companion, happiness has attachment as its satisfying companion, fear has relief as its satisfying companion, etc. – see Table 6.2. This sort of companionship that every emotion is aiming at another emotion is not ordered in a circular way but points to ultimate emotions having themselves as their satisfying companion, e.g. aesthetic pleasure aims at further aesthetic pleasure, a feeling of power aims at more feelings of power, a feeling of security at more

Table 6.1 The succession of events belonging to emotion-induced desires

I First emotion e_1*
1 Thoughts or consideration of a situation
2 Affective valuation of that thought or situation (i.e. classification as being of a certain (positive or negative) type F_1)
3 Emotion e_1 (i.e. emotional feelings)
4 Accompanying bodily phenomena

II Emotion-induced desire and action
5 Consideration of some action *a* and of its consequences
6 Classification of one of the consequences *c* as F_2 (F_2 being the affective value criterion of the satisfying emotion type E_2 belonging to e_1, qua E_1)
7 Emotion-induced desire, i.e. intrinsic motivational appraisal of the consequences *c* being F_2 (as positive according to the criterion of emotion type E_2, with the absolute value being proportional to the intensity of emotion e_1)
8 Total appraisal of action *a* as being optimum
9 Action *a*
10 Occurring of consequence *c*

III Satisfying emotion e_2
11 Perception of *c*
12 Affective valuation of *c* as being F_2 (and, therefore, being positive)
13 Emotion e_2
14 Accompanying bodily phenomena

Note
* Capital letters here denote types or qualities, lower case letters denote tokens or individuals.
The table lists a complete sequence from the first emotion to the accompanying emotion. This sequence may be interrupted after nearly every step.

feelings of security, satisfaction at more satisfaction, positive self-esteem at higher positive self-esteem, positive sympathy at more positive sympathy. Such ultimate emotions are always some form of satisfaction.

This interrelation, in particular the non-hedonic *motivational* and originally intrinsic valuation, can be described somewhat more precisely in the following hypothesis:

Law of emotion-induced desires
1 If someone has a certain emotion e_1 (of type E_1) and
2 during his emotional arousal classifies some consequence *c* of a potential action *a* of himself as F_2 and
3 F_2 is the classificatory attribute of the (positive) *affective* valuations of the satisfying emotion type E_2 belonging to E_1, then
4 the state of affairs that *c* is F_2 is originally intrinsically (positively) desired proportional to the strength of the emotion e_1 (Table 6.1, steps 5–7).

Consider our little girl: the girl is furious with her brother (emotion e_1; Table 6.1, steps 1–4); the satisfying accompanying emotion type is (moral) satisfaction

Table 6.2 Emotions and their satisfying counterparts

First emotion E_1	*Satisfying emotion E_2*	*Value quality F_2 (core of induced intrinsic desire)*
Admiration	Positive self-esteem	I am valuable (by being near the admired object)
Aesthetic pleasure	Further aesthetic pleasure/positive sympathy	Others are enjoying the same aesthetic pleasure
Anger	Gratification/satisfaction	Cause destroyed, punished/just situation restored
Attachment	More attachment/positive sympathy	We are close(r) to each other/others are well off
Contempt	Feeling of security	Safety from the despised being
Curiosity	Satisfaction	Things (new knowledge) are as I have desired them
Depression	Joy, happiness	Desire (unexpectedly) fulfilled, i.e. lost things regained
Despair	Hope	Not too bad chance that the world changes to the better
Disappointment	Joy	Desire (unexpectedly) fulfilled
Disgust	Feeling of security	Safety from disgusting entity
Embarrassment	Feeling of being recognised	Others accept me or what I do
Envy	Gratification/satisfaction	Morally just situation restored (the other reduced)/desire fulfilled (myself elevated)
Fear	Relief	Danger vanished
Feeling of being recognised	Positive sympathy	The others are well off
Feeling of power	More feelings of power	I control still more important domains
Feeling of security	Further feelings of security	More safety from further danger, protection against everything
Feeling of senselessness	Satisfaction	Things (sense of life, of the world) are as I have desired them
Frustration	Joy	Desire (unexpectedly) fulfilled
Gloat	Gratification, moral satisfaction	Still more bad people punished
Gratification, moral satisfaction	More gratification, moral satisfaction	World morally still better
Gratitude	Feeling to be recognised/positive self-esteem	The other accepts me for my deeds/I am valuable
Guilt	Relief	Punishment is over or definitely will not happen
Happiness	Attachment/positive sympathy	We are close to each other/others are well off
Hate	Gratification	Cause destroyed, punished
Hope	Joy	Desire (= hoped-for state) (unexpectedly) fulfilled

Indignation	Gratification	Responsible entity punished; or morally just situation restored
Jealousy	Feeling of power/feeling of security	I (can) control the beings I am jealous of and about/safety from losing
Joy, happiness	Positive sympathy	Others are well off
Loving affection	Positive sympathy	The beloved is very well off
Pleasure of functioning	More pleasure of functioning	My doing is functioning smoothly
Pride	Positive self-esteem/pride	I am valuable, meet high standards
Rage	(Moral) satisfaction, gratification	Villain punished
Regret	Satisfaction	Damage repaired or compensated
Relief	Feeling of security	Safety, no need to worry, protection against everything
Respect	Feeling of security	Safety for the respected object
Sadness	Joy	Desire to regain the lost entity (unexpectedly) fulfilled
Satisfaction	Further satisfaction	Further desire fulfilled
Self-esteem, negative	Positive self-esteem/gratification (depending on the first emotion's intensity)	I have met the standards adopted by me/I have been punished (for not meeting the standards adopted by me)
Self-esteem, positive	Further, continuous, higher positive self-esteem	I have met the (higher) standards adopted by me
Shame	Feeling to be accepted, recognised	Others accept me
Sympathy, positive and negative	Positive sympathy	The other is (still) better off

Note
Rich material supporting several of the hypotheses in the third column of this table, i.e. on the cognitive origins of the various emotions, is provided by Solomon ([1976] 1993: 223–308).

(E_2); and the affective valuation causing this (moral) satisfaction rests on classifying that some villain or aggressor has gotten his just punishment or, a bit more primitively, is damaged or destroyed (F_2); now the girl considers the possibility that one of her actions will have the consequence that the brother will be hurt (*c*), which is classified as damaging the aggressor (F_2; Table 6.1, steps 5–6); this possible consequence then is motivationally (positively) intrinsically desired (Table 6.1, step 7); and the strength of that desire corresponds to the intensity of our girl's rage.

Such intrinsic desires are emotionally induced; i.e. being in a certain emotional state is the central and necessary cause of such desires, and if the emotion fades the desire fades too. So the dependency on the inducing emotion is responsible for a characteristic instability of such desires over time. This makes actions out of emotionally induced desires problematic and often irrational, because the subject not infrequently will soon regret the action committed. Their instability not withstanding, emotionally induced desires are full-fledged (intrinsic) motivational desires on a par with other desires – like intrinsic desires with a hedonic content or any other prospect desire which, in the end, can aggregate a multitude of other intrinsic desires. And as motivational desires, emotionally induced desires can enter into the valuation of actions and hence, according to the expectancy-valence model, into the decision about the action to do. So if the emotionally induced desire is strong enough or if it is accompanied by other desires fostering the same action, which taken alone may not be sufficiently strong for choosing this action, then it may cause the choice and hence the execution of the action that is thought to satisfy the emotionally induced desire (Table 6.1, steps 8–9). However, as the many conditions in the last sentences indicate (an action fulfilling the emotionally induced desire is contemplated, the emotionally induced desire in itself is sufficiently strong or accompanied by other desires, which then together are sufficiently strong (which implies that there are no sufficiently strong incompatible desires for other actions or for non-action), a decision is taken), there is no automatism leading from emotionally induced desires to affective action. This creates room e.g. for strength of will against affective action, which may take several forms: not considering actions at all, thereby ignoring the emotion-induced desire, bringing to mind incompatible desires, in particular regarding long-term consequences of the affective action, postponing the decision so that the emotion can cool down a bit and thus weaken the emotion-induced desire. The elbow-room opened by the conditions provides opportunities not only for blocking respective actions but also for improving one's actions, i.e. choosing variants of one's options that are more effective and have better collateral consequences. All this is what we experience every day. In other words, the integration of the law of emotion-induced desires into the decision-theoretic model explains the complexities of real life with respect to affective action.

One objection to the law of emotion-induced desires is that there are some emotions that may lead to inactivity instead of inducing motivation: depression, despair, feeling of futility, sadness. However, the fact that these emotions reduce our tendencies to act does not make it necessary to reduce the range of that law; the motivation, i.e. the intrinsic desire may be there, but it is part of the respective primary emotion that the subject believes that there are no actions available to fulfil the intrinsic desire. Another objection is that some emotions have only a consumptive function but do not induce new desires because the desires have just been fulfilled; this holds for all emotions of the satisfaction type. However, experience speaks against this objection; humans are too active for this kind of rest: happy people tend to make others happy as well (Table 6.2). In the end, the emotion-induced intrinsic desire may simply be to prolong or intensify this emotion or to cause a different emotion of the same type.

Phase III: satisfying emotion. If the affective action has been executed the intrinsically desired consequence may eventually occur (Table 6.1, step 10). This, by recognising this consequence and classifying it as before, may lead to the satisfying emotion – in our example: the girl hearing her brother howling with pain is deeply satisfied: 'This is what you deserve' (Table 6.1, steps 11–14). Of course, often things will not go that smoothly: the desired consequence does not occur (the bite was not strong enough, the brother was wearing sufficiently protective clothes, etc.), the consequence is not classified at all or unlike it was during the decision (the loud howling frightens the girl), or a corresponding classification is immediately overshadowed by other perceptions (the brother is starting a counter-attack, the mother comes in, guilty conscience comes up, etc.). However, because of the anticipated classification of the desired consequence with the emotion-triggering concept F_2, recognising the intended consequence will frequently stimulate exactly this classification and with it the satisfying emotion.

Emotion-induced desires in a certain sense rest on *anticipating* affective valuations. Our girl's (first) emotion rests on a first affective classification and valuation F_1 that she has been offended by her brother (Table 6.1, step 2); the content of the emotionally induced desire is instead that it is good that the consequence c is F_2: the offending brother will be hurt/punished (Table 6.1, step 7). This content of the emotionally induced desire is the same as that of the (possible) later *affective* valuation which actually causes satisfaction – apart from a different indexical time index: 'My offending brother *has been* hurt or punished' (Table 6.1, step 12). In this sense the emotionally induced motivational valuation is an *anticipating* affective valuation with motivational function. One may suspect that this anticipating affective valuation may immediately cause the pertinent emotion, i.e. in our example moral satisfaction, because mere *thoughts* of the specific content are sufficient for arousing emotions. This actually may happen but only if the subject *revels* in thoughts of that specific content, e.g. thoughts of revenge. Then, however, the subject's main concern changes, the first emotion temporarily makes room for the conjoined satisfying emotion, and so the emotionally induced motivation is diminished or even erased. But this is not the case we are considering; in our case there was only one short thought that a certain course of action will damage or hurt the aggressor (Table 6.1, step 6). Under the specific circumstances this is enough for (motivationally) desiring to hurt him (step 7), but it is not enough for causing moral satisfaction.

So far we have considered only *emotionally* induced desires. There seems to be a similar phenomenon in bodily feelings, which here I can only touch on. Having a strong positive bodily feeling, at least sometimes people desire the continuation of that feeling more intensely than would be adequate according to the normal anticipatory hedonic desirability function; and having a strong negative bodily feeling, they excessively desire its cessation (e.g. Brandt 1979: 39f.). People with high sexual lust might be prepared to pay a much higher price for the continuation of their pleasure and fulfilment of their lust than they would do in advance with a cool head – prostitutes know this; people suffering strong pain might be prepared to pay a much higher price for the cessation of their pain than they would do with a cool head – torturers exploit this mechanism. Such overvaluations are also feeling-induced, but they are somewhat less interesting than the emotion-induced desires because their content is still hedonistic: prolongation of pleasant and cessation of unpleasant bodily feelings. But they are not normal hedonic motivational desires because they are desires out of proportion. This may explain several cases of weakness of will. Finally, there may even be intrinsic desires induced by moods.

At least there are some well-known effects that might be interpreted in this way. First, in negative moods people are impatient in the sense that they are less willing to bear any kind of negative feeling: the more depressed they are, the further they postpone unpleasant tasks; they prefer smaller but immediate rewards to greater but later rewards.[3] Second, in positive moods people are much more willing to help others (Morris 1989: 100; Dovidio 1984). But one problem with these findings is that it is not always clear that the effect is due to *moods* and not to emotions. Another problem is that all these findings can be explained in a different way; e.g. the preference for the 'smaller' reward may in fact be a preference for a materially smaller reward, which however now has much greater hedonic effects in improving the negative mood than the materially bigger reward would have later on. A third problem is that we are always in a certain mood but there cannot be permanent distortion of normal desires; this is conceptually impossible. So if the mentioned effects are to be explained by mood-induced desires, this hypothesis has to be complemented by a threshold condition, according to which only moods of a certain intensity induce desires.

Theoretical conclusions

Feeling-induced desires are probably an evolutionary older motivational system than the normal hedonic motivational system because the former has less prerequisites and is much more primitive than the latter. First, emotionally induced intrinsic desires lead to aiming at rather immediate changes of the exterior situation. These changes often will be beneficial for the subject; otherwise this motivational system would not have survived evolution. But there is no room for changing these aims if they are not beneficial for the subject or if there are other possibilities of further advancing the (long-term) well-being of the subject. Second, feeling-induced desires are bound to current feelings so that they change rapidly over time. This implies that they are not suitable as a basis for long-term planning and long-term decisions: at the moment of a possible long-term decision, e.g. to hurt one month later a probable aggressor who will have revealed himself as such only that month later, the intrinsic desire simply does not yet exist; and if in rage one plans to hurt the aggressor only one week later when there will be a better opportunity for doing so then that week later, when the moment of action has come, often the emotion and with it the emotionally induced desire will be lacking – with the consequence that the agent will decide otherwise. In this respect, feeling-induced desires differ sharply from normal hedonic desires: if someone knows that she might suffer from hunger or anxiety one year later she intrinsically disapproves of such feelings now, one year later or whenever; the stability of such a valuation is the basis for the fact that she can now plan to avoid such feelings which otherwise will arise only very much later.

A theoretically important question is: where do the contents of the feeling-induced desires come from? Why do these desires have exactly these contents? Of course, a hypothesis of feeling-induced desires is not logically bound to the value closure assumption that the resulting intrinsic desires derive from satisfying feelings, in particular satisfying emotions E_2, taking up their criterion for affective valuations F_2 and making it a criterion of intrinsic motivational desirability too. First, however, examining the content of emotion-induced intrinsic desires and the content of affective valuations, the just stated overlap is simply an empirically striking result. Second, this prima facie somewhat complicated mechanism of primary and satisfying emotions has a clear function. Because of their immense practical importance, mentally present and fixed intrinsic desirability functions are not evolutionarily arbitrary and for reasons of parsimony must be selective. Emotions already imply such intrinsic desirability functions – but with an affective function. Why should the emotion-induced motivational desirability functions not take up these affective desirability functions? And what is more, pure emotions (the consequences of affective evaluations) would make little sense evolutionarily – in particular at evolutionary stages before the formation of the hedonic decision system, which aims at certain emotions. If they already express something which is important for survival and for our vital functions and if the emotions are integrated into a motivational system, this system should take up exactly the concerns inherent in the emotions; i.e. it should make the emotionally positively valued and actively realisable states into aims of our actions or – later, having reached the flexibility of the expectancy-valence system of decision – at least to also *motivationally* positively desired states. In short, the contents of affective desirability functions should reappear in the motivational desirability function. Third, to this fundamental reason one may add a more trivial one: further desirability functions require further contents and brain systems to represent them. By not assuming too many desirability functions, theoretical parsimony reflects evolutionary parsimony and robustness. The discrepancy and tension between hedonic and feeling-induced desires is already problematic; introducing further values would increase the problems of the motivational system even more. With the value closure of the emotional-motivational system obtained by making the satisfying emotions' value criteria motivationally effective as well and, additionally, by taking up these values in a secondary form in the hedonic motivational system – for having our hedonic desires regarding certain emotions fulfilled, the states that are positively valued in these emotions have to be realised first (for making us happy we have to realise the happy-making states first) – these tensions are considerably reduced.

Emotion-induced desires are theoretically, and in particular philosophically, interesting because they successfully challenge strong psychological hedonism so that only weak psychological hedonism may be true. A theory of intrinsic desires that takes feeling-induced desires into account might be acceptable for those with reservations with respect to strong psychological hedonism. On the other hand, the instability over time of feeling-induced intrinsic desires makes them unsuitable as a basis for *rational* desirability functions. One aim of rational desirability functions is to permit long-term planning for taking advantage of good opportunities and for cheaper satisfaction of desires in the long run; this is not possible if desirability changes over time (Lumer 1998: 41, 52–55; Lumer [2000] 2009: 340–346, 484–489, 521f.). From this point of view, quickly changing desirabilities seem to be quite irrational. And for this reason, too, we often regard acts committed in the heat of passion as irrational: directly after having reached his aim the agent may already regret his deed; this does not look like rational behaviour. These rational considerations notwithstanding, we may be uneasy about excluding this feeling-induced part of our motivational intrinsic desirability function from our rational desirability function. However, there is no reason to worry much about this: because of the value closure of the system of emotion-induced desires, all the just-dismissed irrational intrinsic desires have their extrinsic counterparts in the – rational – hedonic desirability function where the same object now is extrinsically desirable. If we, unlike the little girl in our example, know that punishment of the aggressor will make us feel gratified we may aim at the punishment also for hedonic reasons. However, these extrinsic desirabilities are rationally redimensioned as compared to the irrational emotion-induced intrinsic desire.

Taking into account also these theoretical implications, what has been achieved by the theory of emotion-induced desires? First, assuming that emotions induce intrinsic desires, on the one hand – and unlike a mere arousal theory – explains the specificity of our emotional decisions; on the other, it leaves considerable room for explaining the flexibility of emotional decisions and their adaptation to the respective circumstances – in contrast to the aim-induction hypothesis. Second, the hypothesis of emotion-induced intrinsic desires permits integrating the model of emotional decisions into the general decision-theoretical model of decisions and explaining the combination of both types of considerations as well as flexible reactions to our emotions – from impulsive action to reflective exertion of strength of will. It explains how an older and newer motivational system can cooperate. Third, the closure hypothesis, according to which the induced motivational intrinsic desires take up the concern of specific satisfying emotions, does not only provide a general approach to the specific content of emotion-induced desires, it is also theoretically parsimonious and explains the motivational effectiveness of the affective desirability function and hence a big part of the evolutionary function of emotions.

Acknowledgements

I want to thank Rowland Stout, Marcel Zeelenberg and the participants of the LabSi conference for the discussion of a previous version of this chapter.

Notes

1 I have developed my own approach in Lumer (2005).
2 Exceptions are e.g. fear induced by unexpected loss of ground or quickly approaching big objects.
3 Morris (1989: 109f.) gives a list of confirmations for these effects.

References

Brandt, R.B. (1979) *A Theory of the Good and the Right*, Oxford: Clarendon.

Butler, J. ([1726] 1896) 'Fifteen sermons', in W.E. Gladstone (ed.), *The Works. Vol. II: Sermons*, Oxford: Clarendon.

Davidson, D. and Suppes, P., in collaboration with Segal, S. ([1957] 1977) *Decision Making: An Experimental Approach*, Stanford, CA: Stanford University Press, 1957, Reprint: Westport, CT: Greenwood Press; Chicago, IL: University of Chicago Press.

Dovidio, J.F. (1984) 'Helping behavior and altruism: an empirical and conceptual overview', in L. Berkowitz (ed.), *Advances in Experimental Social Psychology. Vol. 17*, New York: Academic Press.

Frijda, N.H. (1986) *The Emotions*, Cambridge: Cambridge University Press; Paris: Editions de la Maison des Sciences de l'Homme.

Heckhausen, H. (1989) *Motivation und Handeln*, 2nd revised edn, Berlin: Springer.

Izard, C.E. (1977) *Human Emotions*, New York and London: Plenum Press.

Lang, P.J. (1988) 'What are the data of emotion?', in V. Hamilton, G.H. Bower and N.H. Frijda (eds), *Cognitive Perspectives on Emotion and Motivation*, Dordrecht, Boston and London: Kluwer.

Lumer, C. (1997) 'The content of originally intrinsic desires and of intrinsic motivation', *Acta Analytica*, 18: 107–121.

Lumer, C. (1998) 'Which preferences shall be the basis of rational decision?', in C. Fehige and U. Wessels (eds), *Preferences*, Berlin and New York: De Gruyter.

Lumer, C. ([2000] 2009) *Rationaler Altruismus: Eine prudentielle Theorie der Rationalität und des Altruismus*, 2nd revised edn, Paderborn: Mentis.

Lumer, C. (2005) 'Intentions are optimality beliefs: but optimizing what?', *Erkenntnis*, 62: 235–262.

Moore, G.E. ([1912] 1966) *Ethics*, 2nd edn, London: Oxford University Press.

Morris, W.N. (1989) *Mood: The Frame of the Mind*, New York, Berlin and Heidelberg: Springer.

Plato (1997) 'Philebus', in J.M. Cooper (ed.), *Complete Works*, Indianapolis, IN: Hackett.

Rottenstreich, Y. and Shu, S. (2004) 'The connections between affect and decision making: nine resulting phenomena', in D.J. Koehler and N. Harvey (eds), *Blackwell Handbook of Judgment and Decision Making*, Oxford: Blackwell.

Solomon, R.C. ([1976] 1993) *The Passions: Emotions and the Meaning of Life*, revised edn, Indianapolis, IN and Cambridge: Hackett.

Tversky, A. and Kahneman, D. (1992) 'Advances in prospect theory: cumulative representation of uncertainty', *Journal of Risk and Uncertainty*, 5: 297–323.

Weber, E.U. and Lindemann, P. (2008) 'From intuition to analysis: making decisions with your head, your heart, or by the book', in H. Plessner, C. Betsch and T. Betsch (eds), *Intuition in Judgment and Decision Making*, New York: Lawrence Erlbaum Associates.

Zeelenberg, M., Nelissen, R. and Pieters, R. (2008) 'Emotion, motivation, and decision making: a feeling-is-for-doing approach', in H. Plessner, C. Betsch and T. Betsch (eds), *Intuition in Judgment and Decision Making*, New York: Lawrence Erlbaum Associates.

Part III

Learning and risk attitude in decision-making

Part III

7 From habit to addiction

A study in online gambling behavior

D. William Jolley and Deborah N. Black

Introduction

Why do some individuals lose control over their gambling habit and continue to gamble despite heavy losses? Notwithstanding progress in understanding why a person might begin to gamble and in some cases continue (Raichlin 1990), we still lack an adequate understanding of the factors that govern the transition from a gambling habit to a behavior that bears the hallmarks of a behavioral addiction (Holden 2001).

Starting with the premise that addiction is a pathological form of habit, we address the question: How does a good habit go bad? We combine insights from neurobiology with decision science to study the factors leading from volitional (habit) to involuntary (addiction) gambling behavior. Understanding the factors that govern the progression from occasional, to habitual, to addictive behavior has important implications for the study of consumer behavior, addictive psychology, and public health policy.

The evolving construct of habit

Habits are "sequential, repetitive, motor, or cognitive behaviors elicited by external or internal triggers that, once released, can go to completion without constant conscious oversight" (Graybiel 2008). In the 1940s and 1950s behavioral theorists used classical and operant conditioning to explain the formation of habits based on reinforcement of physiological (Hull 1943) or emotionally based drives (Spence 1956). Triandis' (1980) attitude-behavior model defined habits as "situation specific sequences that are or have become automatic." Posner and Snyder (1975), and later Ajzen (2002), recognized the automaticity of habits, meaning that the process that initiates and controls the habitual response is performed quickly and with minimal conscious oversight. Later researchers operationalized habit as the frequency of past behavior. Bettman *et al.* (1991) defined habit as a choose-what-one-chose-last-time heuristic. Triandis' (1980) construct of habit strength was defined as "the number of times the act has already been performed by the person." Ajzen (2002) hypothesized that if a weak habit is the subject's random choice among several options, a strong habit could be defined by the frequency with which a subject repeatedly selects the same response option in a stable environment. Wood *et al.* (2005) concluded that "To the extent that behaviors and contexts are linked, simple frequency measures may be sufficient to assess habit strength." Collins *et al.* (1987), Orford (1985), and Kanvil and Umeh (2000) found that previous behavior accounted for 70 percent of the variation in the motivation to continue to smoke, while health cognitions explained only a marginal 3 percent. With respect to gambling, playing frequency is a more powerful indicator of potential gambling addiction than the structural characteristics of the game, its atmospherics, or its accessibility (AELLE 1999; Livingstone and Woolley 2008).

Once formed, habits are relatively impervious to cognitive control. Individuals with strong habits are not likely to attend to new information or respond favorably to interventions aimed at altering beliefs and attitudes toward the habitual behavior (Verplanken and Aarts 1999). Oh and Hsu (2001) applied Ajzen's (1991) theory of planned behavior to the survey responses of 226 habitual gamblers and concluded that "gambling possesses to some degree, a routine behavioral or habitual component." Dickerson *et al.* (1992) demonstrated that gambling behavior very quickly stabilizes. Beliefs and attitudes are no longer operative once strongly conditioned behavior is established. Furthering the evidence that high-frequency gamblers discount cognitive intervention, Jolley *et al.* (2006) observed that online gamblers who received strong harm warning statements not only continued to play, but rationalized that the warning statements were intended to protect them (Harinck *et al.* 2007).

In summary, cognitions are insufficient to modify behavior once it has become habitual (Albarracin and Wyner 2000; Eagly and Chaiken 1993). In fact, habit as measured by past behavior has been modeled as a stochastic process without any cognitive component (Ehrenberg 1988; Livingstone and Woolley 2007; Mizerski *et al.* 2001). Neither automaticity theory nor reinforcement theory, however, provides a satisfactory explanation of why some habits are practiced more frequently than others and, for a small fraction of the population, become addictions. In these individuals, modification of their environment is ineffective in reducing the incidence of harmful behaviors. Indeed, the incidence of harmful behaviors has stayed constant or increased over the past several decades and across several consumption venues (Lemonick and Park 2007).

The neurobiological basis of habit

The neurobiology of drug addiction provides a model for the development and persistence of gambling behavior. Both drug addiction and pathological gambling may proceed from recreational, to habitual, to addictive. Like the drug addict, the addicted gambler may experience craving, tolerance, withdrawal, and major occupational, interpersonal, and financial impairment (Holden 2001; Grant *et al.* 2006).

The initial events in the development of a drug habit involve the release of dopamine in the nucleus accumbens core in the ventral striatum, which is a critical node in the brain's reward system (Everitt *et al.* 2008). Dopamine encodes the motivational significance ("salience") of a pleasurable event and facilitates the acquisition of memory connected to its fulfillment (Volkow and Baler 2007). At this stage, drug taking is governed by a conscious, effortful "action–outcome" (A–O) system that regulates instrumental responses designed to achieve a goal (Yin and Knowlton 2006). A critical factor in the transition from conscious to automatic behavior is the frequency with which the behavior is practiced (Yin and Knowlton 2006). The transition from voluntary to automatic, stimulus-driven behavior is associated with a shift in locus of behavioral control from the ventral to the dorsal striatum (Graybiel 2008; Everitt *et al.* 2008). At the same time, there is a marked decline in dopamine in the reward circuit and a need for increasing amounts of the abused substance in order to maintain baseline dopamine homeostasis (Volkow and Baler 2007). Sensitivity to natural reinforcers such as food, money, or friendship is decreased. Addictions can be said to subvert the brain's natural reward system (Volkow and Baler 2007; Helmuth 2001) such that, over time, obtaining and consuming the abused substance becomes an overwhelming preoccupation akin to a compulsion (Volkow and Baler 2007; Nestler 2005).

Once established, the dopamine-mediated stimulus–response pathway is highly resistant to "reinforcer devaluation," meaning that the habitual behavior is impervious to negative or adverse outcomes. The shift toward dorsal striatal dominance in the addicted individual is among widespread neuroplastic changes involving the striatum, amygdala, hippocampus, orbitofrontal and anterior cingulate cortex, and insula. These brain regions constitute a network involved in learning and memory, regulation of drive, motivation, and behavioral control (Graybiel 2008; Volkow and Baler 2007; Nestler 1997).

Addiction is thus an extreme learned response to a reward stimulus under minimal conscious control. Studies of cocaine addicts viewing drug paraphernalia show marked activation in nucleus accumbens dopamine pathways and also in basal ganglia motor circuits, confirming the pathological link between reward-dominated motivated behavior and stimulus-driven repetitive behavior (Graybiel 2008; Yin and Knowlton 2006).

In addition to the role of dopamine in mediating the pleasurable, or reinforcing, qualities of addiction, serotonin in the frontal cortex, as well as the brain's endogenous opiate system, are involved in regulating addictive behavior. Converging evidence shows deficits in decision-making and judgment and decreased frontal serotonin in addicted individuals (Grant *et al.* 2006; Volkow and Baler 2007; LeMarquand *et al.* 1999). Functional neuroimaging of addicted individuals, including pathological gamblers, shows decreased activity in the anterior cingulate and orbitofrontal cortex, brain regions responsible for self-monitoring, behavioral inhibition and self-control (Grant *et al.* 2006; Peoples 2002). The intense motivational value of the reward, and inadequate capacity to regulate the consequences of reward-seeking behavior, combine in a catastrophic cycle of compulsive drug seeking (Grant *et al.* 2006; Volkow and Baler 2007; Helmuth 2001).

Impulsivity and addiction

Why don't all individuals progress from an occasional behavior to a pathological habit? Fewer than 20 percent of individuals exposed to a potentially addictive substance become addicted (Anthony *et al.* 1994). Genetic factors govern 30–60 percent of the vulnerability to addiction (Kreek *et al.* 2005). Impulsivity and sensation-seeking are endophenotypes, or inherited biological markers, of vulnerability to substance addiction (Belin *et al.* 2008; Ersche *et al.* 2010). Impulsivity is operationally defined as a tendency to choose immediate over deferred rewards, and is both a risk factor for and a consequence of addiction (Dalley *et al.* 2007; Verdejo-García *et al.* 2008). Impulsivity is associated with a wide range of personality traits – impatience, carelessness, sensation-seeking, and extroversion. The behavioral spectrum of impulse dyscontrol includes substance abuse, kleptomania, bulimia, unprotected sex, intermittent explosive disorder, fire-setting, behavioral addictions (e.g., gambling, internet, sex, shopping), anti-social personality disorder, and poor treatment outcome (Grant *et al.* 2006; Verdejo-García *et al.* 2008; Forbush *et al.* 2008; Hollander and Evers 2001; Skitch and Hodgins 2004; Steel and Blaszczynski 1998). In a group of frequent college-student gamblers, personality measures of impulsivity and compulsivity were positively correlated with pathological gambling (Skitch and Hodgins 2004). Forbush *et al.* (2008) found impulsivity to be more significant than neurocognitive measures in predicting the variance in pathological gambling behavior. Acceptance of risk accounts for a significant proportion of the variance in gambling and in anti-social behavior (Mishra *et al.* 2011). Impulsivity is the common thread binding impulse control disorders and substance abuse (Grant *et al.* 2006).

Impulsivity and addiction-proneness have been linked both to low and high dopaminergic tone in the ventral striatum. Some addiction-prone individuals show lower than normal brain and cerebrospinal levels of dopamine (Dackis 2005; Volkow 2005). The "reward deficiency syndrome" (Blum *et al.* 2000) proposes that abuse of euphoriant drugs and repetitive sensation-seeking may be a means of restoring homeostatic equilibrium in a sluggish dopaminergic reward system (Koob and Le Moal 2005; Paulus 2007). These individuals are poorly responsive to punishment or negative feedback (Dagher and Robbins 2009). Other addiction-prone individuals show an exaggerated dopamine response to reward and an increased density of D2 dopamine receptors in the ventral striatum. These individuals attribute exaggerated importance to reward cues and show preserved ability to learn from negative feedback (Dagher and Robbins 2009; Bechara 2005).

Individuals with either abnormally low or abnormally elevated striatal dopaminergic tone share a dysregulated state of drive, impaired processing of reward, and defective willed control of behavior, even in the face of persistent adversity (Grant *et al.* 2006; Hollander and Evers 2001). The addict repeatedly makes choices that may result in financial ruin, loss of relationships, and social failure (Shaw *et al.* 2007). Both the addict and the frontally damaged patient are unable to exert conscious control over their behavior despite recurrent adverse consequences (Goodman 2005). Both substance abusers and pathological gamblers are impaired on cognitive tasks involving response inhibition, working memory, and decision-making, and both groups show impaired response reversal – that is, a tendency to perseverate on tasks that require a shift of cognitive set (Forbush *et al.* 2008). This perseverative response style is present both during periods of substance abuse and after prolonged abstinence (Verdejo-García *et al.* 2008; Barry and Petry 2008). Functional brain imaging and neuropsychological studies of addicts consistently show abnormalities in prefrontal cortex, insula, and somatosensory cortex, which have been called "a neural system for willpower" (Bechara 2005).

Disorders of impulse control are costly. Disruption of families, job failure, accidents, violence, suicide, and criminality severely tax public health, legal, and financial resources (Hollander and Evers 2001; Shaffer and Korn 2002). Incorporating the neurobiological trait of impulsivity into the study of pathological habit opens a new track of consumer behavior investigation. This study of online gambling in a cohort of 155 university undergraduates tests our hypothesis that impulsivity moderates the relationship between gambling habit and gambling addiction. A moderator is a "variable that affects the direction and/or strength of the relation between an independent or predictor variable and a dependent or criterion variable" (Baron and Kenny 1986). Restated, gambling habit moderated by impulsivity leads to addictive gambling behavior (Figure 7.1).

Figure 7.1 shows the hypothesized constructs and their relationships. The direct path between *gambling habit* and *addictive gambling behavior* reflects the hypothesis that habit has a significant positive relationship with addiction. The heavy dashed line from *impulsivity* to the path between habit and addiction indicates the hypothesized moderating effect of impulsivity; that is, the strength of the relationship between gambling habit and addictive behavior will be stronger, but still positive, at higher levels of impulsivity.

Definitions of constructs

Impulsivity: total net score on the Iowa Gambling Task (IGT). A positive net score on the IGT indicates advantageous choice, and a negative net score indicates disadvantageous choice or higher levels of impulsivity.

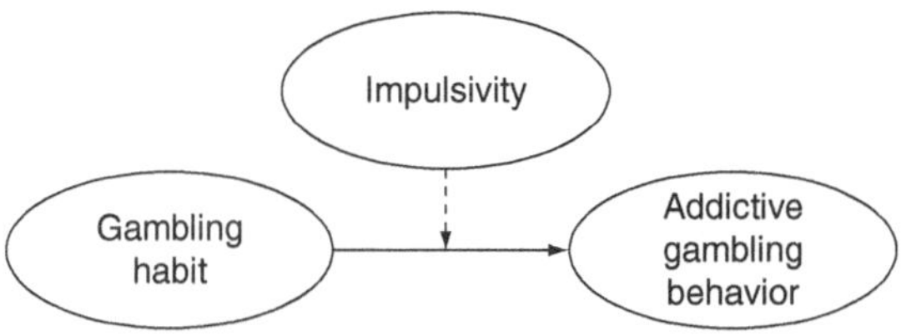

Figure 7.1 Hypothesized relationships between gambling habit and addictive gambling.

Gambling habit: frequency (number of bets) and average amount bet per betting occasion (buy-in).

Addictive gambling behavior: amount won/lost, amount bet, and duration of play. These variables reflect sensitivity to the stimulating effects of reward versus the punishing effects of risk (AELLE 1999; Barr and Dubach 2008) and are a function of the volatility of the slot game (Lucas and Singh 2008).

Measuring impulsivity

The IGT (Bechara *et al.* 1994) is a computerized card game that measures sensitivity to the consequences of risk. The task consists of 100 consecutive choices from four decks. Decks A and B are risky: they yield higher financial rewards but also greater losses (punishments), so that repeatedly choosing from these decks results in net financial loss. Decks C and D offer lower rewards but also lower losses, so that choosing from these decks results in a net gain. Even if they can't explicitly identify the risky decks, most normal subjects shift their pattern of response toward the less risky decks (C and D), suggesting that non-conscious, or "somatic markers," bias normal individuals away from disadvantageous outcomes under situations of risk (Bechara *et al.* 1997). Individuals with damage to the orbitofrontal cortex, anti-social personality disorder, pathological gambling, drug abuse, and other impulse control disorders are pulled toward the high-stakes risky decks, incurring substantial losses by the end of the game (Barry *et al.* 2008; Goudriaan *et al.* 2004). Losing players in the IGT show "myopia for the future" – they are unable to override the tendency to seek immediate reward and avoid future negative consequences.

Most cocaine addicts tested on the IGT (67 percent) by Barry and Petry (2008) performed like patients with frontal lobe damage – that is, they were unable to stop choosing from punishing card decks despite incurring financial losses (Bechara 2005). A smaller group of addicts seemed "stuck on reward" – their attraction to the risky decks overwhelmed their knowledge of future losses, and they showed exaggerated autonomic reactivity to the immediately rewarding decks (Bechara *et al.* 1994). An even smaller minority of addicts performed like normal controls. These findings underscore the heterogeneity of addiction. Nevertheless, the IGT most consistently taps the decision-making deficits in addicts across the behavioral spectrum.

Research procedure

A total of 155 university undergraduates registered for eCasinoland, a virtual online casino, and 118 completed the study. To play on the site visitors had to have a verified age of 18 years or older and be a current student. The mean age was 19.7 and 81 percent of participants were male. Before playing, participants completed the IGT. Players were then randomly assigned to a test cell with a predefined slot machine game configuration and 500 virtual credits in their account. Game stimuli were manipulated by experimentally varying the return to player (RTP), the payout ratio, the hit rate, and responsible gambling warning levels (Cochran and Cox 1957). These variables constitute the volatility (or coefficient of variation) of the reinforcement schedule designed to affect the level of excitement or entertainment value, measured by duration and autonomic arousal (Lucas and Singh 2008; Dumont and Ladouceur 1990; Moodle and Finnigan 2005). These game parameters address individual differences in the processing of risk and reward (Xue *et al.* 2008). Players stayed in their originally assigned test cell throughout the study. They could continue to play as long as their credit balance was sufficient to cover their bets or for the three-month duration of the study. Each player saw their credit balance displayed in the "credits" window. Players could borrow in increments of $250 in virtual credits in exchange for committing to two hours of volunteer work for the university. Based on the rank order net winnings (total won minus total bet), a player could win from $10 to a maximum of $500. By clicking on a link on the game page, players could see a "leader board" that displayed their ranking and prize level relative to other players. Upon cashing out players completed an online attitude survey about their game experience. The survey included the DSM-IV-TR Screening Questionnaire for Pathological Gambling (DSM-IV 1994). No actual money was placed at risk by study participants. At any time a player could terminate their participation in the study without penalty. The research design was approved by the university's Institutional Review Board. A more detailed description of the research procedures can be found in supplemental materials available on request.

Results

An insufficient number of players completed the DSM-IV-TR Screening Questionnaire for Pathological Gambling, so results are not included in our analysis.

IGT results

Mean IGT score was 0.25; median –2.0; range –44 to 90. Mean IGT net value was –$1035.08; median –$1115.0; range –$2875.0 to $3480.0. The distributions of IGT net scores and net values met the Kolmogorov–Smimov test for normality ($\alpha=0.039$). Dichotomization of the sample based on a median split produced two subgroups. Median low versus high impulsivity IGT scores were 14.0 and –12.0, respectively. Median low versus high IGT values were –$480 and –$1,635, respectively.

Differences in gambling behavior between low and high impulsivity groups

To determine whether players with higher levels of impulsivity as measured by net IGT score exhibited higher levels of addictive gambling behavior, Mann–Whitney U-tests were conducted on the distributions of the indicators for the latent variable, *addictive gambling behavior*, between two sample groups based

Table 7.1 Median values of the indicators of addictive gambling behavior for the two impulsivity groups

	Bet	*Won*	*Lost*	*Duration (min)*
Median low impulsivity group	\$9.30	\$7.31	\$1.98	1,670.0
Median high impulsivity group	\$7.95	\$8.00	\$1.22	1,634.0

on the median value of –2.0. The median values of the indicators of addictive gambling behavior for the two impulsivity groups are shown in Table 7.1.

There were no significant differences in the distribution of addictive gambling behavior indicators between the low impulsivity group compared to the high impulsivity group. A significant difference between low and high impulsivity groups' addictive gambling behaviors would have provided behavioral markers of the threshold where frequent gambling transitions to addictive gambling as a result of the moderating effect of impulsivity.

Partial least squares path modeling

Partial least squares (PLS) path modeling was used to test our hypothesis that *impulsivity* moderates the relationship between *gambling habit* and *addictive gambling behavior*. We conducted an a priori three-factor analysis using varimax rotation to identify the indicators for the hypothesized latent variables, *gambling habit*, *addictive gambling behavior*, and *impulsivity*. The three-factor solution explained 57.6 percent of the variance in the data with several cross loadings greater than 0.5. This solution was compared with an exploratory factor analysis that resulted in a six-factor solution explaining 77.7 percent of the variance, still with several cross loadings greater than 0.5. A final four-factor solution with a 65.4 percent explained variance and no cross loadings greater than 0.5 was used to develop the measurement model. Confirmatory factor analysis using PLS structural equation modeling showed the four-factor solution to have strong reliability and validity (factor analysis and PLS output can be found in the supplemental materials). The final measurement model used to test the moderation effect of *impulsivity* is shown in Figure 7.2.

We tested an interaction construct to represent *gambling habit* as the combined effect of betting frequency and buy-in, or the amount bet per betting occasion. First we tested the significance of this interaction term by introducing it into the main effects global model before dichotomization of the sample into high and low impulsivity groups based on the median split criteria. The effect of *gambling habit* was found to be significant (*t*-statistic 2.89), and the effect size of introducing the interaction term for *gambling habit* into the main effects model was strong (0.496) and was thus retained in testing the moderating effects of *impulsivity* (Cohen 1988). The model's standardized path coefficients show that a 1.0 standard deviation (SD) increase in buy-in resulted in a 1.27 (0.587 + 0.681) SD increase in *addictive gambling behaviors*. In the full global

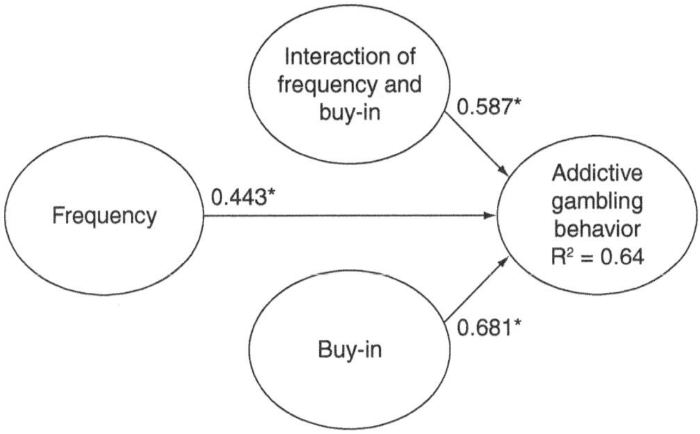

Figure 7.2 Full global models.

Note: * Significant at p=0.05.

model with the interaction term (Figure 7.2), *gambling habit* explained 64 percent of the variation in *addictive gambling behaviors*. Thus the model was carried forward to test the moderating effects of *impulsivity* on *addictive gambling behaviors*.

Results of the PLS output after dichotomization of IGT scores into lowest and highest *impulsivity* players based on IGT median scores (–2.0) are illustrated in Figures 7.3 and 7.4. Analyses showed the model to exceed the minimum criteria for reliability and validity (Henseler and Fassott 2009). Detailed tables of the factor analysis and PLS output can be found in the supplemental materials.

Since there is not as yet a uniformly accepted method for goodness of fit for PLS path models (Henseler *et al.* 2009; Vinzi *et al.* 2009), differences in the

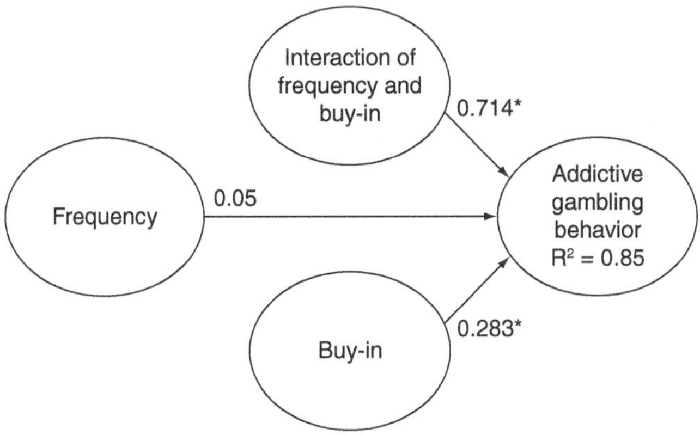

Figure 7.3 PLS model for low impulsivity group.

Note: * Significant at p=0.05.

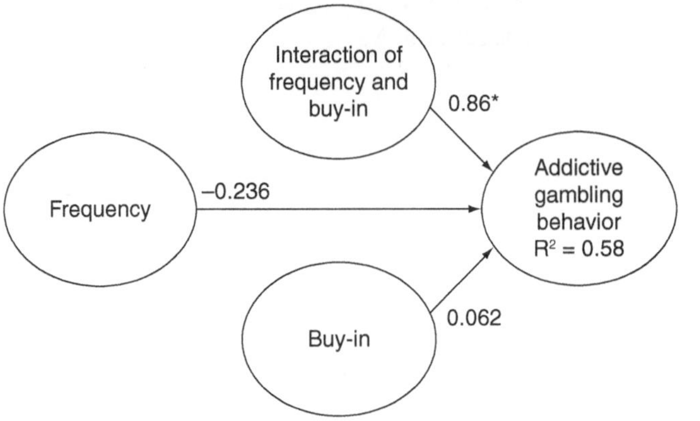

Figure 7.4 PLS model for high impulsivity group.

Note: * Significant at $p = 0.05$.

significance, strength, and direction of the path coefficients plus the prediction quality of the models were used to evaluate the moderating effect of impulsivity on the relationship between *gambling habit* and *addictive gambling behaviors*. The significantly lower prediction strength among highly impulsive gamblers suggests a significant moderating effect of impulsivity. The effect size of the R^2 is strong (0.641), further supporting the hypothesis of moderation (Cohen 1988). The most notable effect of the moderating effect of *impulsivity* is to reduce the ability of *gambling habit* to predict *addictive gambling behaviors* among high impulsivity players ($R^2 = 0.58$ compared to 0.85).

Discussion

Many cognitive and psychological factors have been studied with regard to their effects on addiction (Patterson *et al.* 2006). Even at high gambling rates, many individuals do not report gambling-related problems (Chipman *et al.* 2006). Not all highly impulsive persons become problem gamblers (Kreek *et al.* 2005). In the population of recreational and even habitual gamblers, gambling habit and characterological impulsivity are thought to be independent, as shown in Figure 7.5. It is our premise that what uniquely identifies problem gamblers is the interaction between impulsivity and gambling habit, and this interaction moderates the relationship between habitual and problem gambling.

In our population of college-age online gamblers we found that the neurobiological trait of impulsivity, as measured by IGT net score, moderated the relationship between *gambling habit* and *addictive gambling behaviors*. Surprisingly, for the more impulsive players the amount of variance in their addictive gambling behaviors explained by their gambling habits was significantly lower compared to normal or low impulsivity players. However, there were no significant

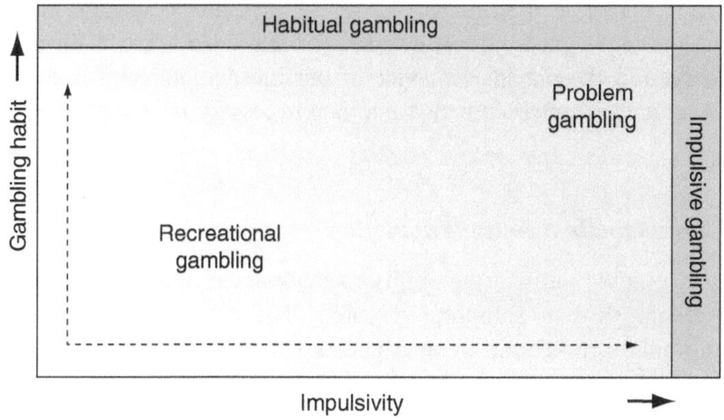

Figure 7.5 The relationship between gambling habit and neurobiological markers.

differences in the indicators of *addictive gambling behavior* between the two impulsivity groups. Thus, the models that explained their behavior were different, but their outcomes were not!

Our findings support our hypothesis that impulsivity moderates the transition from habitual to pathological gambling; however, *addictive gambling behaviors* were not higher for more impulsive players. One possible explanation is that, unlike substance addictions, impulsivity does not confer vulnerability to gambling addiction. However, studies of pathological gamblers consistently identify impulsivity as a significant vulnerability factor for gambling (Forbush *et al.* 2008; Goudriaan *et al.* 2008; McDaniel and Zuckerman 2003).

The "reward deficiency" hypothesis (Blum *et al.* 2000) may account for our paradoxical findings. All addictive drugs, and pleasurable stimuli in general, release dopamine in the nucleus accumbens. Individuals with lower dopaminergic tone in the brain's reward pathways may require higher levels of stimulation in order to obtain a comparable level of satisfaction. Individuals with a blunted reward system indulge in activities or use substances in order to restore normal hedonic tone. Recent studies are beginning to identify constitutional deficiency in the dopamine D2 receptor in individuals with different addictions, including obesity, alcoholism, smoking, drug abuse, and compulsive gambling, and also depression, which is frequently comorbid (Dalley *et al.* 2007; Dackis 2005; Comings and Blum 2000; Geiger *et al.* 2009; Johnson and Kenny 2010; Kamarajan *et al.* 2010). A direct link between reduced striatal dopamine receptor availability and impulsivity has recently been reported in methamphetamine users (Lee *et al.* 2009). Disordered dopamine neurotransmission may alter the ability to maintain reward expectation across a time delay ("temporal discounting"), which is the hallmark of impulsive choice (Pine *et al.* 2010).

The reward deficiency hypothesis suggests that the most impulsive individuals in our study may have required a more potent online gambling experience than eCasinoland in order to manifest addictive behavior. In other words, our game stimuli may not have delivered a sufficient "dose" of pleasure to engage their brains' reward systems. A sluggish response to reward may also account for the variability we observed in the playing behavior of our most impulsive subjects. Including games with greater entertainment value is a necessary next step in this research.

Advantages of eCasinoland in a college population

Shaffer *et al.* (2010) pointed out that the ability to track actual online gambling behavior is a paradigm shift in gambling research. The naturalistic study of online gambling eliminates potential inconsistencies between self-reported and actual behavior and allows prospective identification of factors that precede and foster pathological gambling. Our internet laboratory has similar ecological validity. We can unobtrusively collect data on actual gambling behavior in a naturalistic environment 24 hours per day. Our ability to manipulate experimental variables such as reward dose and frequency and harm-minimization strategies allows us to take a step beyond naturalistic observation to dissect characteristics of the game that interact with neurobiological variables to influence behavioral outcomes. To our knowledge, this is the first study to use the IGT in a prospective, real-time environment to study the moderating effect of impulsivity on gambling addiction. Our use of the IGT allows us to supplement purely behavioral descriptions of pathological gambling with a quantifiable, neurobiologically based marker at the interface between habit and addiction.

Global internet gambling revenues are growing by 10–20 percent annually and are expected to reach $24.5 billion in 2010 (Monaghan 2005). Internet gamblers are more likely to have a gambling problem than non-internet gamblers (Wood and Williams 2007). These factors make internet gambling an ideal model for testing hypotheses relating to the relationships between habit, impulsivity, and addiction.

Our population of university students is well suited for this research. The prevalence of problem gambling among college students is higher than in the general adult population (Wood and Williams 2007; Browne and Brown 1993; Griffiths and Barnes 2008). In a national survey of college students, LaBrie *et al.* (2003) reported that 39.9–43.8 percent of survey respondents had participated in some form of gambling in the previous school year. LaBrie *et al.* (2003) estimated the maximum prevalence of "compulsive" or "problem" gambling to be 2.6 percent based on the percentage of students who said they gambled weekly or more often. College students are both more impulsive and sensation seeking than the general population (McDaniel and Zuckerman 2003), and "top-down" control mechanisms dependent on the integrity of the dorsolateral prefrontal cortex and anterior cingulate are not yet fully developed (Prencipe *et al.* 2011). Consistent with these observations, the median IGT score of –2.0 in our student sample is well below the general population mean of 10, and considered to be in the pathological range (Bechara and Martin 2004).

Limitations

Our use of the IGT to measure impulsivity may not capture the heterogeneity of impulsivity, which includes distinct constructs such as reward dependence, boredom proneness, lack of forethought, impatience, underestimation of harm, and poor behavioral inhibition (Hollander and Evers 2001; Arce 2006; Holub 2008). Although impulsivity and sensation seeking often coexist, these traits may confer different vulnerabilities to addiction (Belin *et al.* 2008; Parke *et al.* 2004). The majority of addicts studied by Bechara (2005) performed like patients with frontal lobe damage – that is, they were unable to stop choosing from punishing card decks despite incurring financial losses. A smaller group of addicts seemed "stuck on reward" and showed exaggerated autonomic reactivity to the immediately rewarding decks. Although deficient frontal control and hypersensitivity to reward are both likely present in our population of young, predominantly male college students, biological heterogeneity may have blurred critical behavioral differences in response to eCasinoland.

Net IGT score may not be a sufficient measure of impulsivity. It may be more pertinent to look at the pattern of choices across the 100 trials on this task (Buelow and Suhr 2009). The "ecological validity" of the IGT is unknown with respect to risky decision-making in the real world (Buelow and Suhr 2009). Our characterization of impulsivity could have benefitted from the incorporation of additional measures such as the Barrett Impulsivity Scale (Patton *et al.* 1995), or other measures of gambling addiction such as the DSM-IV Gambling Questionnaire (1994) or the South Oaks Gambling Screen (Lesieur and Blume 1997). Although we were able to detect an effect size of sufficient strength to support a moderation hypothesis, our sample of highly impulsive players may have been insufficient to produce pathological levels of playing behavior (Chin *et al.* 2003).

Future research

How much of addiction is related to game versus player variables? In the next phase of this research we expect to increase the entertainment value of eCasinoland by incorporating commercial gambling site graphics, card-based games, and facilitating social networking among players. Virtual currency that players deposit into their eCasinoland accounts to transact bets, wins, and losses will more closely approximate conditions of real-life online gaming. We will add non-behavioral measures of impulsivity such as the Barratt Impulsivity Scale (Barratt and Patton 1983) and measures of cognitive control such as the Stroop test (Lamm *et al.* 2006). The impact of different harm-minimization methods will be tested in relation to the reward properties of the games and the discounting of consequences by individual players.

Using an online research model to explore the role of impulsive choice in gambling behavior is a critical methodological advance in understanding, and ultimately preventing, excessive gambling and other addictive behaviors (Shaffer *et al.* 2010; Griffiths 2006; Schmitz 2005; Treuer *et al.* 2001). Our model is relevant to other frequent-choice behavior (Kau *et al.* 2003), to other gambling venues such as state lotteries, and to other disorders of impulse control, including substance abuse (Schmitz 2005). Our goal is to wed insights from consumer behavior and neuroscience in a cross-disciplinary collaboration to understand the process by which behavior that starts out as reasoned and controlled becomes compulsive, uncontrolled, and destructive. Understanding the critical variables in the progression from habit to addiction allows intervention to start before denial begins (Krych 1989).

References

AELLE (1999) *Lottery Gambling and Addiction: An Overview of European Research.* Report compiled for the Association of European National Lotteries (AELLE), Lausanne, Switzerland. Nottingham Trent University Psychology Division (accessed at www.europeanlotteries.org).

Ajzen, I. (1991) "The theory of planned behavior," *Organizational Behavior and Human Decision Processes*, 50: 179–211.

Ajzen, I. (2002) "Residual effects of past on later behavior: habituation and reasoned action perspectives," *Personality and Social Psychology Review*, 6: 107–122.

Albarracin, D. and Wyner Jr., R.S. (2000) "The cognitive impact of past behavior: influences on beliefs, attitudes, and future behavioral decisions," *Journal of Personality & Social Psychology*, 79: 2–22.

Anthony, J.C., Warner, L.A., and Kessler, R.C. (1994) "Comparative epidemiology of dependence on tobacco, alcohol, controlled substances, and inhalants: basic findings from the National Comorbidity Survey," *Experimental and Clinical Psychopharmacology*, 2: 244–268.

Arce, E. and Santisteban, C. (2006) "Impulsivity: a review," *Psicothema*, 18: 213–220.

Baron, R.M. and Kenny, D.A.K. (1986) "The moderator-mediator variable distinction in social psychological research: conceptual, strategic, and statistical considerations," *Journal of Personality and Social Psychology*, 51: 1173–1182.

Barr, G.D.I. and Durbach, I.N. (2008) "A Monte Carlo analysis of hypothetical multi-line slot machine play," *International Gambling Studies*, 8: 265–280.

Barratt, E.S. and Patton, J.H. (1983) "Impulsivity: cognitive, behavioral, and psychophysiological correlates," in M. Zuckerman (ed.), *Biological Bases of Sensation Seeking, Impulsivity, and Anxiety*, Hillsdale, NJ: Lawrence Erlbaum Associates.

Barry, D. and Petry, N.M. (2008) "Predictors of decision-making on the Iowa Gambling Task: independent effects of lifetime history of substance use disorders and performance on the Trail Making Test," *Brain and Cognition*, 66: 243–252.

Bechara, A. (2005) "Decision making, impulse control and loss of willpower to resist drugs: a neurocognitive perspective," *Nature Neuroscience*, 8: 1458–1463.

Bechara, A. and Martin, E.M. (2004) "Impaired decision making related to working memory deficits in individuals with substance addictions," *Neuropsychology*, 18: 152–162.

Bechara, A., Damasio, A.R., Damasio, H., and Anderson, S.W. (1994) "Insensitivity to future consequences following damage to human prefrontal cortex," *Cognition*, 50: 7–15.

Bechara, A., Damasio, H., Tranel, D., and Damasio, A.R. (1997) "Deciding advantageously before knowing the advantageous strategy," *Science*, 275: 1293–1295.

Belin, D., Mar, A.C., Dalley, J.W., Robbins, T.W., and Everitt, B.J. (2008) "High impulsivity predicts the switch to compulsive cocaine-taking," *Science*, 320: 1352–1355.

Bettman, J.R., Johnson, E.J., and Payne, J.W.P. (1991) "Consumer decision making," in T.S. Robertson and H.H. Kassarjian (eds.), *Handbook of Consumer Behavior*, Englewood Cliffs, NJ: Prentice Hall.

Blum, K., Braverman, E.R., Holder, J.M. *et al.* (2000) "Reward deficiency syndrome: a biogenetic model for the diagnosis and treatment of impulsive, addictive, and compulsive behaviors," *Journal of Psychoactive Drugs*, 32 (Suppl.): 1–112.

Browne, B.A. and Brown, D.J. (1993) "Using students as subjects in research on state lottery gambling," *Psychological Reports*, 72: 1295–1298.

Buelow, M.T. and Suhr, J.A. (2009) "Construct validity of the Iowa Gambling Task," *Neuropsychology Review*, 19: 102–114.

Chin, W.W., Marcolin, B.L., and Newsted, P.R. (2003) "A partial least squares latent variable modeling approach for measuring interaction effects: results from a Monte Carlo simulation study and an electronic-mail emotion/adoption study," *Information Systems Research*, 14: 189–217.

Chipman, M., Govoni, R., and Roerecke, M. (2006) *The Distribution of Consumption Model: An Evaluation of its Applicability to Gambling Behaviour*, Final report prepared for the Ontario Gambling Center.

Cochran, W.G. and Cox, G.M. (1957) *Experimental Designs*, 2nd edn, New York: John Wiley & Sons.

Cohen, J. (1998) *Statistical Power Analysis for the Social Sciences*, Hillsdale, NJ: Lawrence Erlbaum Associates.

Collins, L.M., Sussman S., Rauch, J.M. (1987) "Psychosocial predictors of young adolescent cigarette smoking: a sixteen-month, three-wave longitudinal study," *Journal of Applied Social Psychology*, 17: 554–573.

Comings, D.E. and Blum, K. (2000) "Reward deficiency syndrome: genetic aspects of behavioral disorders," *Progress in Brain Research*, 126: 325–341.

Dackis, C. (2005) "Neurobiology of addiction: treatment and public policy ramifications," *Nature Neuroscience*, 8: 1431–1436.

Dagher, A. and Robbins, T.W. (2009) "Personality, addiction, dopamine: insights from Parkinson's disease," *Neuron*, 61: 501–510.

Dalley, J.W., Fryer, T.D., Brichard L., *et al.* (2007) "Nucleus accumbens D2/3 receptors predict trait impulsivity and cocaine reinforcement," *Science*, 315: 1267–1270.

Dickerson, M.J.H., England, S.L., Fabre, J., and Cunningham, R. (1992) "On the determinants of persistent gambling behaviour: I. High-frequency poker machine players," *British Journal of Psychology*, 83: 237–248.

DSM-IV. (1994) *Pathological Gambling Diagnostic Form* (accessed at www.oasas.state.ny.us/gambling/documents/822dsmivforweb.pdf).

Dumont, M. and Ladouceur, R. (1990) "Evaluation of motivation among video poker players," *Psychological Reports*, 66: 95–98.

Eagly, A.H. and Chaiken, S. (1993) *The Psychology of Attitudes*, Fort Worth, TX: Harcourt Brace.

Ehrenberg, A.S.C. (1988) *Repeat-buying: Facts, Theory, and Applications*, London: Griffin.

Ersche, K.D., Turton, A.J., Pradhan, S., Bullmore, E.T., and Robbins, T.W. (2010) "Drug addiction endophenotypes: impulsive versus sensation-seeking personality traits," *Biological Psychiatry*, 68: 770–773.

Everitt, B.J., Belin, D., Economidou, D., Pelloux, Y., Dalley, J.W., and Robbins, T.W.

(2008) "Neural mechanisms underlying the vulnerability to develop compulsive drug-seeking habits and addiction," *Philosophical Transactions of the Royal Society B*, 363: 3125–3135.

Forbush, K.T., Shaw, M., Graeber, M.A., *et al.* (2008) "Neuropsychological characteristics and personality traits in pathological gambling," *CNS Spectrums*, 13: 306–315.

Geiger, B.M., Haburcak, M., Avena, N.M., Moyer, M.C., Hoebel, B.G., and Pothos, E.N. (2009) "Deficits of mesolimbic dopamine neurotransmission in rat dietary obesity," *Neuroscience*, 159: 1193–1199.

Goodman, J. (2005) "Faulty reasoning and gambling behavior: special session summary," in G. Menon and A.R. Rao (eds.), *Advances in Consumer Research XXXII*, Duluth, MN: Association for Consumer Research.

Goudriaan, A.E., Oosterlaan, J., de Beurs, E., and Van Den Brink, W. (2004) "Pathological gambling: a comprehensive review of biobehavioral findings," *Neuroscience & Biobehavioral Reviews*, 28: 123–141.

Goudriaan, A.E., Oosterlaan, J., De Beurs, E., and Van Den Brink, W. (2008) "The role of self-reported impulsivity and reward sensitivity versus neurocognitive measures of disinhibition and decision-making in the prediction of relapse in pathological gamblers," *Psychological Medicine*, 38: 41–50.

Grant, J.E., Brewer, J.A., and Potenza, M.N. (2006) "The neurobiology of substance and behavioral addictions," *CNS Spectrums*, 11: 924–930.

Graybiel, A.M. (2008) "Habits, rituals, and the evaluative brain," *Annual Review of Neuroscience*, 31: 359–387.

Griffiths, M. (2006) "Internet addiction: a critical review," *International Journal of Mental Health and Addiction*, 4: 31–51.

Griffiths, M. and Barnes, A. (2008) "Internet gambling: an online empirical study among student gamblers," *International Journal of Mental Health and Addiction*, 6: 194–204.

Harinck, F., Dijk, E.V., Beest I.V., and Mersmann, P. (2007) "When gains loom larger than losses: reversed loss aversion for small amounts of money," *Psychological Science*, 18: 1099–1105.

Helmuth, L. (2001) "Addiction: beyond the pleasure principle," *Science*, 294: 983–984.

Henseler, J. and Fassott, G. (2009) "Testing moderating effects in PLS Path models: an illustration of available procedures," in V.E. Vinzi, W.W. Chin, J. Henseler, and H. Wang (eds.), *Handbook of Partial Least Squares: Concepts, Methods and Applications*, Heidelberg: Springer.

Henseler, J., Ringle, C., and Sinkovics, R. (2009), "The use of partial least squares path modeling in international marketing," *Advances in International Marketing*, 20: 277–319.

Holden, C. (2001) "'Behavioral' addictions: do they exist?," *Science*, 294: 980–982.

Hollander, E. and Evers, M. (2001) "New developments in impulsivity," *Lancet*, 358: 949–950.

Holub, A. (2008) *The Structure of Impulsivity in Pathological Gambling*, Calgary, AB: University of Calgary.

Hull, C.L. (1943) *Principles of Behavior: An Introduction to Behavior Theory*, New York: Appleton-Century-Crofts.

Johnson, P.M. and Kenny, P.J. (2010) "Dopamine D2 receptors in addiction-like reward dysfunction and compulsive eating in obese rats," *Nature Neuroscience*, 13: 635–641.

Jolley, B., Mizerski, R., and Olaru, D. (2006) "How habit and satisfaction affects player retention for online gambling," *Journal of Business Research*, 59: 770–777.

Kamarajan, C., Rangaswamy, M., Tang, Y., *et al.* (2010) "Dysfunctional reward processing in male alcoholics: an ERP study during a gambling task," *Journal of Psychiatric Research*, 44: 576–590.

Kanvil, N. and Umeh, K.F. (2000) "Lung cancer and cigarette use: cognitive factors, protection motivation and past behaviour," *British Journal of Health Psychology*, 5: 235–248.

Kau, A.K., Tang, Y.E., and Ghose, S. (2003) "Typology of online shoppers," *Journal of Consumer Marketing*, 20: 139–156.

Koob, G.F. and Le Moal, M. (2005) "Plasticity of reward neurocircuitry and the 'dark side' of drug addiction," *Nature Neuroscience*, 8: 1442–1444.

Kreek, M.J., Nielsen, D.A., Butelman, E.R., and LaForge, K.S. (2005) "Genetic influences on impulsivity, risk taking, stress responsivity and vulnerability to drug abuse and addiction," *Nature Neuroscience*, 8: 1450–1457.

Krych, R. (1989) "Abnormal consumer behavior: a model of addictive behaviors," in T.K. Srull (ed.), *Advances in Consumer Research*, Provo, UT: Association for Consumer Research.

LaBrie, R.A., Shaffer, H.J., LaPlante, D.A., and Wechsler, H. (2003) "Correlates of college student gambling in the United States," *Journal of American College Health*, 52: 53–62.

Lamm, C., Zelazo, P.D., and Lewis, M.D. (2006) "Neural correlates of cognitive control in childhood and adolescence: disentangling the contributions of age and executive function," *Neuropsychologia*, 44: 2139–2148.

Lee, B., London, E.D., Poldrack, R.A., *et al.* (2009) "Striatal dopamine d2/d3 receptor availability is reduced in methamphetamine dependence and is linked to impulsivity," *Journal of Neuroscience*, 29: 14734–14740.

LeMarquand, D.G., Benkelfat, C., Pihl, R.O., Palmour, R.M., and Young, S.N. (1999) "Behavioral disinhibition induced by tryptophan depletion in nonalcoholic young men with multigenerational family histories of paternal alcoholism," *American Journal of* Psychiatry, 156: 1771–1779.

Lemonick, M.D. and Park, A. (2007) "The science of addiction," *Time*, July 16: 42–48.

Lesieur, H. and Blume, S. (1997) "The South Oaks Gambling Screen (SOGS): a new instrument for the identification of pathological gamblers," *American Journal of Psychiatry*, 144: 1184–1188.

Livingstone, C, and Woolley, R. (2007) "Risky business: a few provocations on the regulation of electronic gaming machines," *International Gambling Studies*, 7: 361–376.

Livingstone, C. and Woolley, R. (2008) *The Relevance and Role of Gaming Machine Games and Game Features on the Play of Problem Gamblers*. Report prepared for the Independent Gambling Authority, South Australia.

Lucas, A. and Singh, A.K. (2008) "Decreases in a slot machine's coefficient of variation lead to increases in customer play time," *Cornell University Quarterly*, 49: 122–133.

McDaniel, S.R. and Zuckerman, M. (2003) "The relationship of impulsive sensation seeking and gender to interest and participation in gambling activities," *Personality and Individual Differences*, 35: 1385–1400.

Mishra, S., Lalumière, M.L., Morgan, M., and Williams, R.J. (2011) "An examination of the relationship between gambling and antisocial behavior," *Journal of Gambling Studies*, 27 (3): 409–426.

Mizerski, R., Jolley, D., and Mizerski, K. (2001) "Are electronic gaming machines the 'crack cocaine' of gambling?," in *ANZMAC 2001 National Conference*, Auckland.

Monaghan, S. (2005) *A Critical Review of the Impact of Internet Gambling*. A report submitted to the Australasian Gaming Council.

Moodle, C. and Finnigan, F. (2005) "A comparison of the autonomic arousal of frequent, infrequent and non-gamblers while playing fruit machines," *Addiction*, 100: 51–59.

Nestler, E.J. (1997) "Schizophrenia: an emerging pathophysiology," *Nature*, 385: 578–579.

Nestler, E.J. (2005) "Is there a common molecular pathway for addiction?," *Nature Neuroscience*, 8: 1445–1449.

Oh, H. and Hsu, C. (2001) "Volitional degrees of gambling behaviors," *Annals of Tourism Research*, 28: 618–637.

Orford, J. (1985) *Excessive Appetites: A Psychological View of Addictions*, New York: John Wiley & Sons.

Parke, A., Griffiths, M., and Irwing, P. (2004) "Personality traits in pathological gambling: sensation seeking, deferment of gratification and competitiveness as risk factors," *Addiction Research & Theory*, 12: 201–212.

Patterson, J.C.I., Holland, J., and Middleton, R. (2006) "Neuropsychological performance, impulsivity, and comorbid psychiatric illness in patients with pathological gambling undergoing treatment at the CORE Inpatient Treatment Center," *Southern Medical Journal*, 99: 36–43.

Patton, J.H., Stanford, M.S., and Barratt, E.S. (1995) "Factor structure of the Barratt impulsiveness scale," *Journal of Clinical Psychology*, 51: 768–774.

Paulus, M.P. (2007) "Decision-making dysfunctions in psychiatry: altered homeostatic processing?," *Science*, 318: 602–606.

Peoples, L.L. (2002) "Will, anterior cingulate cortex, and addiction," *Science*, 296: 1623–1624.

Pine, A., Shiner, T., Seymour, B., and Dolan, R.J. (2010) "Dopamine, time, and impulsivity in humans," *Journal of Neuroscience*, 30 (26): 8888–8896.

Posner, M.I. and Snyder, C.R.R. (1975) "Attention and cognitive control," in R.L. Solso (ed.), *Information Processing and Cognition: The Loyola Symposium*, Hillsdale, NJ: Lawrence Erlbaum Associates.

Prencipe, A., Kesek, A., Cohen, J., *et al.* (2011) "Development of hot and cool executive function during the transition to adolescence," *Journal of Experimental Child Psychology*, in press.

Rachlin, H. (1990) "Why do people gamble and keep gambling despite heavy losses?," *Psychological Science*, 1: 294–297.

Schmitz, J. (2005) "The interface between impulse-control disorders and addictions: are pleasure pathway responses shared neurobiological substrates?," *Sexual Addiction and Compulsivity*, 12: 149–168.

Shaffer, H.J. and Korn, D.A. (2002) "Gambling and related mental disorders: a public health analysis," *Annual Review of Public Health*, 23: 171–212.

Shaffer, H.J., Peller, A.J., LaPlante, D.A., Nelson, S.E., and LaBrie, R.A. (2010) "Toward a paradigm shift in internet gambling research: from opinion and self-report to actual behavior," *Addiction Research and Theory*, 18: 270–283.

Shaw, M.C., Forbush, K.T., Schlinder, J., Rosenman, E., and Black, D.W. (2007) "The effect of pathological gambling on families, marriages, and children," *CNS Spectrums*, 12: 615–622.

Skitch, S. and Hodgins, D. (2004) "Impulsivity, compulsivity and pathological gambling: an exploratory study of pathological gambling as an impulsivity–compulsivity spectrum disorder," *International Gambling Studies*, 4: 175–188.

Spence, K.W. (1956) *Behavior Theory and Conditioning*, New Haven, CT: Yale University Press.

Steel, Z. and Blaszczynski, A. (1998) "Impulsivity, personality disorders and pathological gambling severity," *Addiction*, 93: 895–905.

Treuer, T., Fabian, Z., and Furedi, J. (2001) "Internet addiction associated with features of impulse-control disorder: is it a real psychiatric disorder?," *Journal of Affective Disorders*, 66: 267–282.

Triandis, H.C. (1980) "Values, attitudes, and interpersonal behavior," *Nebraska Symposium on Motivation*, 27: 195–259.

Verdejo-García, A., Lawrence, A.J., and Clark, L. (2008) "Impulsivity as a vulnerability marker for substance-use disorders: review of findings from high-risk research, problem gamblers and genetic association studies," *Neuroscience & Biobehavioral Reviews*, 32: 777–810.

Verplanken, B. and Aarts, H. (1999) "Habit, attitude, and planned behavior: is habit an empty construct or an interesting case of goal-directed automaticity?," *European Review of Social Psychology*, 10: 101–134.

Vinzi, V.E., Chin, W.W, Henseler, J., and Wang, H. (eds.) (2009) *Handbook of Partial Least Squares: Concepts, Methods and Applications*, Heidelberg: Springer.

Volkow, N.D. (2005) "The neuroscience of addiction," *Nature Neuroscience*, 8: 1429–1430.

Volkow, N.D. and Baler, R.D. (2007) "The neural substrates of addiction," *Psychiatric Times*, 24: 66–69.

Wood, R.T. and Williams, R.J. (2007) "Problem gambling on the internet: implications for internet gambling policy in North America," *New Media & Society*, 9: 520–542.

Wood, W., Tam, L., and Witt, M.G. (2005) "Changing circumstances, disrupting habits," *Journal of Personality and Social Psychology*, 88: 918–933.

Xue, G., Lu, Z., Levin, I.P., Weller, J.A., Li, X., and Bechara, A. (2008) "Functional dissociations of risk and reward processing in the medial prefrontal cortex," *Cerebral Cortex*, 19: 1019–1027.

Yin, H.H. and Knowlton, B.J. (2006) "The role of the basal ganglia in habit formation," *Nature Reviews Neuroscience*, 7: 464–476.

8 Gains and losses in intertemporal preferences

A behavioural study

Valeria Faralla, Francesca Benuzzi, Paolo Nichelli and Nicola Dimitri

Introduction

Time preference is a concept originally introduced by Rae (1834) in his study on differences of wealth among nations. According to Rae, time preference is determined by four different factors, which may positively or negatively affect the desire of accumulation: the bequest motive, the propensity to self-restraints, uncertainty of human life and the gratification derived from immediate consumption. Time preference is also described as an intertemporal allocation of consumption by Fisher (1930), who enriched Rae's view with two additional personal factors: foresight and fashion. All these factors were later integrated into the discount rate of the discounted utility (DU) model (Samuelson 1937). The DU model is based on various assumptions including stationary instantaneous utility, independence of discounting from consumption, diminishing marginal utility, positive time preference and, in particular, constant discounting, which implies time-consistent preferences. Time consistency means that later preferences are in line with earlier preferences – namely, preferences are constant across time. Individual time preferences are time-consistent if 'for any two consumption profiles $(c_t, \ldots, c_T)$ and $(c'_t, \ldots, c'_T)$, with $c_t = c'_t$, $U^t(c_t, c_{t+1}, \ldots, c_T) \geq U^t(c'_t, c'_{t+1}, \ldots, c'_T)$ if and only if $U^{t+1}(c_t, c_t+1, \ldots, c_T) \geq U^{t+1}(c'_t, c'_{t+1}, \ldots, c'_T)$' (Frederick *et al.* 2002: 358).

Although this model has been widely accepted and applied to the study of intertemporal choice, according to recent evidence (Frederick *et al.* 2002; Read 2004) the classical DU model has a limited ability to describe realistic behaviour. Particularly, while DU assumes that the discount rate is the same for all time periods and different types of outcomes, there are several documented empirical regularities that seem to contradict this statement, both with certainty and uncertainty conditions. The present study focuses on *sign effect* or *gain–loss asymmetry* (Frederick *et al.* 2002; Loewenstein and Prelec 1992; Read 2004), which implies that gains are discounted more than losses. Specifically, subjects usually prefer to expedite, rather than delay, negative outcomes as depicted by classical theory. It is not yet evident whether to consider the sign effect and other empirical regularities – such as magnitude effect, preference for improving sequences, or delay–speed-up asymmetry – as subjects' errors in performing the task or, instead, as real anomalies of the classical DU model. In fact, in their study on workers' preferences for increasing wage profiles, Loewenstein and Sicherman write, 'Respondents do not see themselves as violating any such fundamental property because they see no contradiction in deriving satisfaction from increasing payments, despite the effect on total consumption' (Loewenstein and Sicherman 1991: 82). Nevertheless, this behavioural pattern is observed not only for monetary choices, but also for non-monetary gains and losses.

Literature review

The empirical study of intertemporal gains and losses under certainty may be considered to have its roots in experimental psychology and, in particular, in the works by Mischel and colleagues, originally conducted on both adults and children in the 1960s. In Mischel *et al.* (1969), effects of expected time delay on the subjective value of monetary and non-monetary rewards and punishments were investigated. The study presented the results obtained in four different experiments. In the first, children were asked to indicate their preferences for four different types of rewards – 50 cents, a notepad, six packs of chewing gum or 80 cents – and punishments – eat a can of unpleasant-tasting food, listen to a noise for 15 minutes, spend 30 minutes with an unpleasant teacher or do four difficult tasks in front of the class – available immediately or after a delay of one day, one week or three weeks. Data from this first experiment showed that subjective values of children for positive outcomes decreased with time delay and also that immediate rewards were preferred to delayed ones, at all delay levels. Nevertheless, this was not true for immediate punishments and, indeed, immediate negative outcomes were neither more nor less preferred as delayed ones.

These results were confirmed in the second experiment in which the two alternatives were both delayed (immediate options were no longer available). The third experiment of the study was conducted on adults. Although the researchers applied similar experimental procedures, rewards and punishments were slightly modified in order to be more suitable for older subjects. Data were consistent with the findings for children's positive outcomes. For losses, instead, adults preferred immediate punishments to delayed ones, indicating a preference for anticipating losses. Since the effect was not so significant, however, Mischel *et al.* carried out a final experiment in which they asked participants – adults – to choose between different electric shocks. In particular, the electric shock was higher in voltage and time duration for one group and lower for a second group. These differences were applied in order to investigate the relative importance of punishment intensity. As a result, Mischel *et al.* found that the stronger shocks were less preferred. Moreover, subjects tended to choose the more immediate shock irrespective of the intensity and the duration, confirming previous results. Note that Mischel *et al.* also found no correlation between the state of anxiety and the results obtained in this fourth experiment. The general findings by Mischel *et al.* were consistent with experimental research on children (Grusec 1968), adults (Hare *et al.* 1966) and with shorter time delays (Cook and Barnes 1964; Hare 1966).

The work by Mischel *et al.* inspired a subsequent experiment on monetary losses, realized by the psychologists Yates and Watts (1975). In their study, participants had to choose between two monetary options that they would prefer to pay. Each binary option was represented by a pie and was different in the monetary amount to be repaid (–\$1 and –\$2) and time delay (15, 35 or 75 days). They also introduced an element of uncertainty, which was indicated by a slight ($p=0.6$) or complete ($p=1$) darkening of the pie. Binary choice with identical net amounts was also presented under controlled conditions in which other participants were invited to select one of two positive monetary options. Yates and Watts classified their subjects as 'deferrers' or 'advancers'. Deferrers tended to procrastinate over the outcome, whereas advancers generally preferred the more immediate option. As a result, they found that the number of advancers and deferrers under the two conditions was completely different. In the experimental condition – negative amounts – they found an equal number of advancers and deferrers (eight each), while in the control condition – positive amounts – they found a large prevalence of advancers (18 out of 19). Since the two groups obtained comparable scores in the anxiety test, this was not due to a possible state of anxiety. Given these facts, their data analysis supported the hypothesis that people were typically inclined to expedite monetary gains but not losses, as in Mischel *et al.* (1969). Yates and Watts attributed this kind of result to the possibility that Mischel *et al.* were unsuccessful in separating, in the subject's perception, compensation for participation and real outcome for preferred choice. As a matter of fact, punishments were not perceived as real negative outcomes by subjects.

As for economists, some years later, Thaler (1981) continued to investigate the issue of gains and losses in intertemporal choice in the framework of dynamic consistency (Strotz 1955–1956). In his study, participants were asked to complete four different forms. For each form three immediate monetary amounts were given: \$15, \$250 or \$3,000 in the first; \$75, \$250 or \$1,200 in the second; and \$15, \$250 or \$3,000 in the third. Different time delays for these three monetary values were given: three months, one year, or three years in the first form; six months, one year, and five years in the second form; one month, one year, and ten years in the third form. The fourth form was characterized instead by three negative dollar amounts: –\$15, –\$100 and –\$250. Time delays were, in this case, three months, one year and three years. Data revealed very high implicit discount rates, negatively correlated with both size of the outcome, for gains and losses, and time delay, for gains only. Most important, these rates were smaller for losses than for gains. Compared with the previous studies of Mischel *et al.* and Yates and Watts, Thaler introduced longer time delays – years instead of days. Nonetheless, he also provided evidence for sign effect, confirming that intertemporal preferences for gains and losses are not the same.

Later, Loewenstein (1988) and Benzion *et al.* (1989) applied Thaler's method of implicit discount rates in other experiments on intertemporal preferences for monetary gains and losses, obtaining similar results. In particular, Loewenstein (1988) investigated the frame effect in intertemporal choice of monetary rewards and punishments; that is, how different questionnaire formats influenced the weighting of waiting and, in general, intertemporal choice (the connections between question frame and discount rates for gains and losses have also been investigated by Shelley (1993)). Loewenstein also found higher discount rates for gains than for losses, confirming previous findings by Thaler (1981). Loewenstein suggested that waiting for a punishment is generally unpleasant. Consequently, waiting for a negative outcome introduces an additional cost which could be responsible for lower discount rates. In contrast, waiting for a reward could be pleasant or frustrating, depending on the outcome. In particular, waiting is frustrating for people with impulsivity and self-control problems. This is especially true when the delay is initially unexpected or when both the amount of the outcome and the time delay are high.

Benzion *et al.* (1989) proposed a questionnaire to participants with items from four different scenarios: (1) postpone a receipt, (2) postpone a payment, (3) expedite a receipt and (4) expedite a payment. As a matter of fact, one could consider scenarios 1 and 3 as gain frames, and 2 and 4 as loss frames. Data analysis confirmed the previous results of Thaler (1981). Benzion *et al.* found, in fact, that implicit discount rates were decreasing as time delay and monetary amount increased and, in particular, such rates were smaller for losses (scenarios 2 and 4) than for gains (scenarios 1 and 3). Although the findings of Benzion *et al.* supported the hypothesis of sign effect, implicit discount rates were smaller than in Thaler and, moreover, differed widely across participants. Benzion *et al.* underlined that this last result could be determined by inter- and intra-individual differences in economic knowledge or approach regarding the future. Note that in this experiment the immediate option was not available and, in fact, time delays were six months (the more immediate option), one, two or four years.

As noted earlier, gain–loss asymmetry has been investigated not only for monetary outcomes, but also for non-monetary gains and losses. In particular, Loewenstein (1987) reported the results of a study in which participants were asked to indicate the amount they would pay immediately to have $4 or a kiss from their favourite movie star, for gains, and avoiding to lose $4, $1,000 or receiving an electric shock, for punishments. These rewards and punishments were immediately available (three hours) or could be delayed for 24 hours, three days, one year, or ten years. Data revealed that implicit discount rates were higher for non-monetary rather than for monetary items. Moreover, subjects were willing to pay more for a non-monetary reward – the kiss – which was not immediately available and for avoiding a non-monetary punishment – the electric shock – which was delivered with long time delays, that is one or three days.

Preference for anticipating aversive events was also demonstrated to be a very robust preference pattern by Prelec and Loewenstein (1998). In their study, Prelec and Loewenstein presented a ‘double-entry mental accounting model’ which took into account both the pleasure of consumption and the pain of paying, which could adversely affect consumption itself, considering the payment as a potential loss. To test the model, Prelec and Loewenstein conducted an experiment in which participants were asked to plan a vacation in a luxury apartment. Considering that the apartment cost them $3,000 for three weeks, participants were also required to rate different hypothetical situations. Indeed, different combinations for vacation time and payment for consumption were given. As a result, Prelec and Loewenstein found that the majority of people actually preferred prepayment or, at least, to alternate consumption with payment for the vacation. In any case, however, participants mainly avoided situations in which the vacation payment was entirely delayed. These findings not only refuted the statement that the discount rate should be constant for all time periods and different types of outcomes, but also confirmed the hypothesis that people prefer to expedite payments, which was in line with previous studies with monetary and non-monetary punishments, as previously mentioned. This particular pattern of choice could be connected with the need to be free of payment concerns – during or after consumption – and likely derived from a strong debt aversion.

Based on the state-of-the-art found in the literature, the present study analysed individual behaviour in choosing symmetric monetary gains and losses under certain conditions (Dimitri 2007) in order, primarily, to provide test evidence for sign effect or other empirical anomalies (Frederick *et al.* 2002). Moreover, a statistical analysis was realized in order to identify significant variables in the choice between short- and long-term positive and negative outcomes: monetary value, time delay and proportional difference between the two alternatives of choice. Gender and schooling effects were also evaluated.

Methods

Participants

Twenty-five students were recruited to participate in the study, comprising 13 females and 12 males, with a mean age of 25.5 years (standard deviation (SD) 5). Each subject took about 21 minutes to complete the task (SD=7).

Materials and procedures

Before the experiment, subjects were told that they were participating in a study concerning the theory of cognitive processes in decision-making. They were instructed that there were no correct answers, but that they were required to state their preferences in a series of positive and negative choice tasks. Subjects were informed that at the end of the experiment they would be paid €5 in cash as a participation fee and told they could receive an additional reward which would be paid in the form of a mobile phone top-up. Specifically, the final reward given to each subject would be determined by randomly extracting – the uniform distribution was applied – one of the positive and negative choices they made. The choices selected were added and approximated to the nearest mobile phone top-up's size for a minimum of €8 and a maximum of €15. The top-up would be made on the day calculated as the mean between the time delays of the selected preferences. Given this, subjects were explicitly told that because of this payment scheme they would make choices as if it were the one they were actually going to receive. This method of reward was thought of in order to tie the monetary incentive to the performance task.

Stimulus presentation and behavioural response collection were controlled by the software Superlab (4.0, Cedrus Corporation, Inc.). Stimuli were adapted from the experimental paradigm used by McClure *et al.* (2004) on immediate and delayed monetary rewards. The first two questions were fixed to allow subjects to acquire familiarity with the task and the experimental tools. Each subject completed a task comprising 240 positive and negative monetary choices (120 gains and 120 losses) displayed as a pair of sentences. Choices were generated by combining three different variables: size of the outcome, time delay and proportional difference. Three different smaller, earlier monetary values were used as possible outcomes: small (€5), medium (€15) and large (€30) for gains; symmetric small (–€5), medium (–€15) and large (–€30) for losses. For both gains and losses, there were five possible time delays between the late and the early monetary value: today–two weeks, today–one month, two weeks–one month, two weeks–one month plus two weeks, and one month–one month plus two weeks. The proportional differences in euros between the two alternative of choice were 1 per cent, 3 per cent, 5 per cent, 10 per cent, 15 per cent, 25 per cent, 35 per cent or 50 per cent. The smaller, earlier gain/loss was always presented on the left side of the computer screen and the sequence of choices were randomly generated by Superlab. The choice between the early and the late amount was always for the same type of monetary outcome (gain or loss), and each stimulus was presented only once.

Each experiment was conducted in only one session. Subjects were sitting in front of a computer screen on which the task was presented. For each choice subjects were asked to select the key A or L on the keyboard for respectively selecting the smaller, earlier alternative or the larger, later outcome. No time limits were given for the experiment. Once the subject made the choice, the screen remained white for 500 ms to signal the presentation of the new stimulus. Each choice was made with the event editor of Superlab using black Geneva 72 pt fonts on white screen, colour (R=250; G=250; B=250) (Figure 8.1).

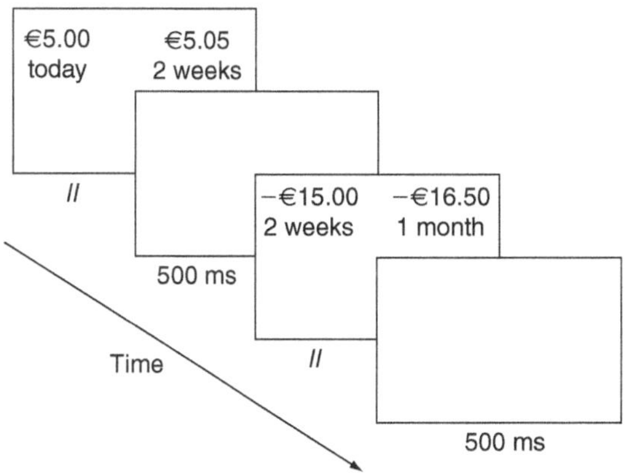

Figure 8.1 Temporal sequence of events during trials of the experimental session (gain and loss, respectively).

Data were analysed using software R (2.7.2, R Foundation for Statistical Computing, Inc.).

Results

Descriptive analysis of the data revealed that subjects preferred the smaller, earlier alternative for gains (61.50 per cent) with a percentage that was decreasing with the value of the monetary amount. For losses, instead, even if there was not a clear pattern of preference for one of the two options – and indeed the difference between the preference for the smaller, earlier loss and the larger, later one was only 4.8 per cent (Figure 8.2) – outcomes were typically delayed for small outcomes (–€5) but expedited for intermediate and large ones (–€15 and –€30). Considering gender, moreover, males showed a little more preference for the larger, later option for losses (52.56 per cent) and smaller, earlier one for gains (60.96 per cent), whereas females tended to choose the smaller, earlier alternative for both losses and gains (57.78 per cent and 62.08 per cent, respectively), yielding results in the opposite direction. These results were reasonably consistent between both graduates and undergraduates, even if the first group seemed to be more undecided than the second one between smaller (earlier) and larger (later) alternatives.

Analysis of the variable time delay revealed that preferences were rather swinging. This is especially true for losses. From the point of view of proportional difference between the two alternatives of choice, instead, it was possible to discern a particular pattern of choice. Indeed, the percentage of responses for early losses was increasing with the proportional difference between the smaller, earlier and the larger, later outcome (Figure 8.3). The higher increment was observed between 5 per cent and 10 per cent (13.33 per cent) and 15 per cent and 25 per cent (13.60 per cent). Inversely, considering choices that involved gains, the pattern of choice was decreasing. Nevertheless, the higher percentage of responses continued to be between 5 per cent and 10 per cent (–16 per cent). As a matter of fact, subjects expedited gains and delayed losses when the proportional difference between the two alternatives was low (up to 5 per cent). In contrast, they delayed gains and expedited losses when the percentage was large

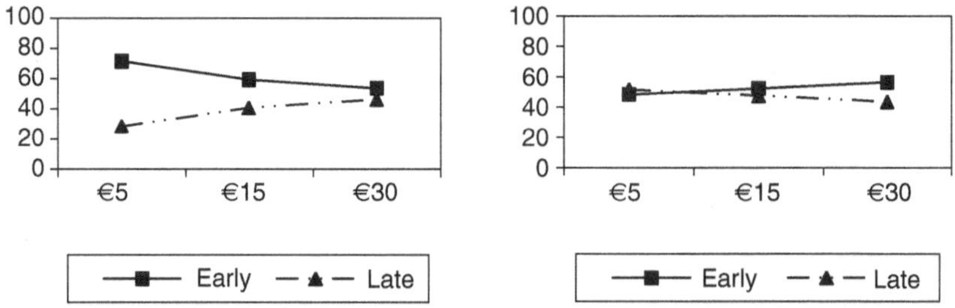

Figure 8.2 Percentage of responses for gains (on the left) and losses (on the right).

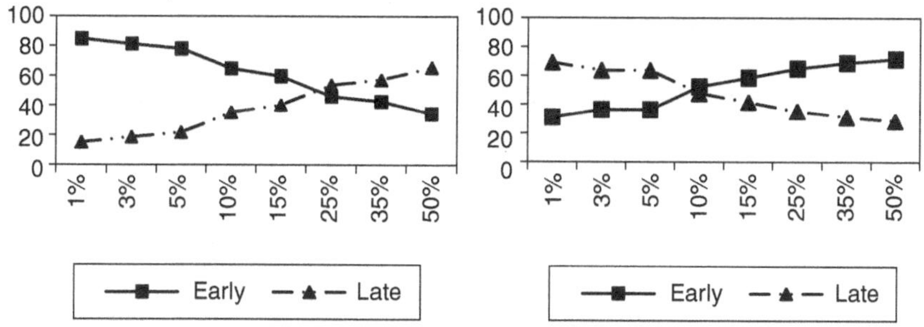

Figure 8.3 Percentage of responses for gains (on the left) and losses (on the right) for proportional difference between the smaller, earlier and the larger, later outcome.

(25–50 per cent). For intermediate proportional differences (10 per cent and 15 per cent), subjects preferred the early alternative irrespective of the sign of the payoff. These findings were consistent for both gender and schooling.

For completeness and accuracy, data were also analysed with the analysis of variance (ANOVA) for multiple regression analysis. Because of the complexity of the experimental paradigm, however, the significance of the variables was also valued with a logistic-normal model for binary data (Agresti 2002), obtaining quite similar results. As a result, for positive choices, the analysis yielded a significant effect on different variables: monetary value ($p<0.001$), time delay ($p<0.001$), proportional difference ($p<0.001$), schooling ($p<0.01$) and age ($p<0.001$). The analysis completed for negative choices yielded a significant effect for all variables: monetary value ($p<0.001$), time delay ($p<0.001$), proportional difference ($p<0.001$), gender ($p<0.001$), schooling ($p<0.05$) and age ($p<0.001$). Combining positive and negative choices, the analysis yielded significant effect for monetary value ($p<0.001$), gender ($p<0.001$) and schooling ($p<0.001$).

Matching analysis

The data from the study were also modelled and interpreted by matching subjects' answers for symmetric gains and losses. So, we can refer to this additional behavioural result as *matching analysis*. For simplicity, a specific code was assigned to the possible combinations of matching: code 0 if the subject preferred the earlier alternative for symmetric gain and loss; code 1 if the subject preferred the later alternative for symmetric gain and loss; code 2 if the subject preferred the earlier gain but the later symmetric loss; code 3 if the subjects preferred the later gain but the earlier symmetric loss. In accordance with the pattern of choice, code 0 and code 1 were defined as *concordant*, whereas code 2 and code 3 were *discordant*. The aim of the matching analysis was to verify if subjects were time-consistent. As noted earlier, time consistency means that later preferences are in line with earlier preferences – namely, preferences are constant across time. Considering both gains and losses, in particular, a person is dynamically consistent if she prefers a larger, later gain and a smaller, earlier loss or vice versa (Dimitri 2007). As a result, only codes 2 and 3 could be considered as time-consistent. Matching results for the behavioural study are summarized in Figure 8.4.

As Figure 8.4 shows, code 2 was the most preferred, with 37.17 per cent, followed by code 3 (28.07 per cent), code 0 (24.33 per cent) and code 1 (10.43 per cent). As a matter of fact, subjects preferred the smaller, earlier gain but the larger, later symmetric loss, even if the gap between the two most preferred codes was not really large (9.1 per cent). The pattern of choice described by code 2 continued to be consistent across all the variables investigated (monetary value, time delay, and proportional difference between earlier and later outcomes); even if code 3 was chosen when the monetary value and the proportional difference between the smaller, earlier and the larger, later outcome were high (€30 and 25 per cent, 35 per cent, or 50 per cent) or when the time delay was long (one month–one month plus two weeks). Note that although they cannot be considered as consistent intertemporal preferences, the percentage of responses for discordant codes, especially code 0, was high. In reference to the

Code	Total	Total (%)
0	730	24.33
1	313	10.43
2	1,115	37.17
3	842	28.07
Total	3,000	100

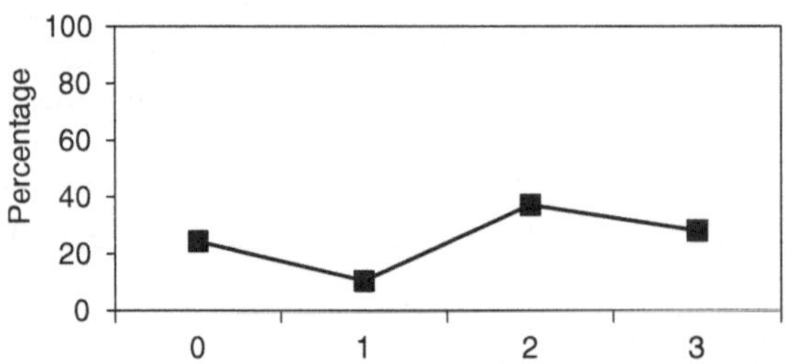

Figure 8.4 Matching results (number and percentage of responses) and percentage of responses for matching.

Table 8.1 Matching by sex and schooling (percentage of responses)

Code	Undergraduate		Graduate		Total (%)
	Male	Female	Male	Female	
0 (%)	20.74	30.37	14.38	30.28	24.33
1 (%)	8.43	9.07	14.79	14.72	10.43
2 (%)	45.28	29.63	35.21	38.06	37.17
3 (%)	25.56	30.93	35.63	16.94	28.07
Total (%)	100	100	100	100	100

matching analysis, males and females were quite different in their preferences according to their level of education. Specifically, with higher levels of schooling, females tended to move from code 3 (30.93 per cent) and 0 (30.37 per cent) to code 2 (38.06 per cent). Inversely, males increased their capacity of long-term planning, moving from code 2 (45.28 per cent) to 3 (35.63 per cent), even if the percentage assigned to code 3 was not far from code 2 (35.21 per cent). We have to notice that the female pattern did not seem to be influenced by instinct as suggested by reaction time. These switching effects are displayed in Table 8.1.

The analysis of variance yielded a significant effect for monetary value ($p<0.001$), proportional difference ($p<0.05$), schooling ($p<0.01$) and gender ($p<0.001$), for gains, and monetary value ($p<0.001$), time delay ($p<0.001$), proportional difference ($p<0.001$), gender ($p<0.01$) and age ($p<0.001$), for losses.

Discussion and conclusions

The aim of this study was to investigate individual behaviour in choosing symmetric monetary gains and losses under certainty. We also evaluated the effect of monetary amount, time delay, proportional difference, gender and schooling. As in previous research, results showed that gains and losses are not equal and seem to be drawn by different internal principles of choice. First, according to previous findings (Frederick *et al.* 2002), we found evidence that subjects preferred to lose sooner in time against average or high losses. Specifically, despite that there was not a distinct pattern of preference for one of the two given losses at a general level, subjects expedited negative outcomes when the loss was €15 and €30. Instead, for gains, we found a preference for earlier, smaller alternatives, independently of the size of the outcome. Note that in previous studies (Bickel and Madden 1999; Kirby *et al.* 1999; Madden *et al.* 1997) people who preferred short-term rewards were found to show impulse and addictive behaviours and lack of self-control. Second, considering the proportional difference between short and long-term alternatives of choice, the percentage of responses for early outcomes was increasing for losses and decreasing for gains, as the proportional difference variable rose. In fact, subjects expedited gains and delayed losses when the proportional difference between the two alternatives was low (up to 5 per cent) but, inversely, they delayed gains and expedited losses when this percentage was high (25–50 per cent). As a result, the present findings also suggested that magnitude effect, another empirical regularity that contradicts the classical DU model, played here a specific role in intertemporal choice, at least for losses. Third, preferences among different time delays were swinging, especially for losses; therefore, we could not identify a particular pattern of choice. Fourth, switching effects were revealed for both males and females with increasing level of education and, indeed, females reversed their choices from code 3 to code 2, whereas males moved precisely in the opposite direction (from code 2 to code 3). Note that gender differences in preferences were also found in Croson and Gneezy (2009). Finally, according to the statistical analysis, we found significant p-values, especially for monetary value, gender and schooling.

As stated in the literature reviewed, sign effect is not new in empirical research, and indeed gain–loss asymmetry was found both for monetary and non-monetary gains and losses. Particularly, most previous studies found that gains are discounted more than losses (Benzion *et al.* 1989; Loewenstein 1988; Thaler 1981) and non-monetary losses have been found to be preferred sooner rather than later (Loewenstein 1987; Mischel *et al.* 1969). The question of sign effect, however, is still open and indeed there are also other empirical studies highlighting that people do not overwhelmingly prefer to anticipate losses (Yates and Watts 1975), which is also summarized in Read (2004).

In light of these findings and for better understanding of gain–loss asymmetry, we suggest directing further research on gains and losses in intertemporal preferences towards new empirical directions as the result of a multiple-motive approach. The paper by McClure *et al.* (2004) represented an important step in the neuroeconomics of intertemporal choice; however, their study considered only monetary rewards. It could be of interest to realize additional studies with both positive and negative alternatives of choice (Xu *et al.* 2009). This kind of study could verify the possibility of different neural circuits in the processing of immediate and delayed losses as well, and it can also verify if these activations are the same as those that emerged for gains. A similar project could contribute to cognitive economics, considering intertemporal preferences with more detail, and to neuroscience by deepening the interaction among neural systems. This new direction is obviously filled with critical aspects, but thanks to neuroscience tools it is now possible to proceed in this worthwhile direction.

Acknowledgements

The authors thank Alessandro Innocenti (Dip. Politica Economica, Finanza e Sviluppo, Università di Siena, Italy) and Francesco Fallucchi (University of Texas at Austin) for their valuable help. A special thank you also goes to Lucio Barabesi and Luigi Greco (Dip. Metodi Quantitativi, Università di Siena, Italy), Andrea Cerioli (Dip. di Economia, Università di Parma, Italy) and Arsenio Stabile (Dip. Politica Economica, Finanza e Sviluppo, Università di Siena, Italy) for statistical advice.

Appendix

Table 8.2 Stimuli list

	Gains	*Losses*
1	€5.00 today vs €5.05 2 weeks	–€5.00 today vs –€5.05 2 weeks
2	€5.00 today vs €5.05 1 month	–€5.00 today vs –€5.05 1 month
3	€5.00 2 weeks vs €5.05 1 month	–€5.00 2 weeks vs –€5.05 1 month
4	€5.00 2 weeks vs €5.05 1 month and 2 weeks	–€5.00 2 weeks vs –€5.05 1 month and 2 weeks
5	€5.00 1 month vs €5.05 1 month and 2 weeks	–€5.00 1 month vs –€5.05 1 month and 2 weeks
6	€15.00 today vs €15.15 2 weeks	–€15.00 today vs –€15.15 2 weeks
7	€15.00 today vs €15.15 1 month	–€15.00 today vs –€15.15 1 month
8	€15.00 2 weeks vs €15.15 1 month	–€15.00 2 weeks vs –€15.15 1 month
9	€15.00 2 weeks vs €15.15 1 month and 2 weeks	–€15.00 2 weeks vs –€15.15 1 month and 2 weeks
10	€15.00 1 month vs €15.15 1 month and 2 weeks	–€15.00 1 month vs –€15.15 1 month and 2 weeks
11	€30.00 today vs €30.30 2 weeks	–€30.00 today vs –€30.30 2 weeks
12	€30.00 today vs €30.30 1 month	–€30.00 today vs –€30.30 1 month
13	€30.00 2 weeks vs €30.30 1 month	–€30.00 2 weeks vs –€30.30 1 month
14	€30.00 2 weeks vs €30.30 1 month and 2 weeks	–€30.00 2 weeks vs –€30.30 1 month and 2 weeks
15	€30.00 1 month vs €30.30 1 month and 2 weeks	–€30.00 1 month vs –€30.30 1 month and 2 weeks
16	€5.00 today vs €5.15 2 weeks	–€5.00 today vs –€5.15 2 weeks
17	€5.00 today vs €5.15 1 month	–€5.00 today vs –€5.15 1 month
18	€5.00 2 weeks vs €5.15 1 month	–€5.00 2 weeks vs –€5.15 1 month
19	€5.00 2 weeks vs €5.15 1 month and 2 weeks	–€5.00 2 weeks vs –€5.15 1 month and 2 weeks
20	€5.00 1 month vs €5.15 1 month and 2 weeks	–€5.00 1 month vs –€5.15 1 month and 2 weeks
21	€15.00 today vs €15.45 2 weeks	–€15.00 today vs –€15.45 2 weeks
22	€15.00 today vs €15.45 1 month	–€15.00 today vs –€15.45 1 month
23	€15.00 2 weeks vs €15.45 1 month	–€15.00 2 weeks vs –€15.45 1 month
24	€15.00 2 weeks vs €15.45 1 month and 2 weeks	–€15.00 2 weeks vs –€15.45 1 month and 2 weeks
25	€15.00 1 month vs €15.45 1 month and 2 weeks	–€15.00 1 month vs –€15.45 1 month and 2 weeks
26	€30.00 today vs €30.90 2 weeks	–€30.00 today vs –€30.90 2 weeks
27	€30.00 today vs €30.90 1 month	–€30.00 today vs –€30.90 1 month
28	€30.00 2 weeks vs €30.90 1 month	–€30.00 2 weeks vs –€30.90 1 month
29	€30.00 2 weeks vs €30.90 1 month and 2 weeks	–€30.00 2 weeks vs –€30.90 1 month and 2 weeks
30	€30.00 1 month vs €30.90 1 month and 2 weeks	–€30.00 1 month vs –€30.90 1 month and 2 weeks
31	€5.00 today vs €5.25 2 weeks	–€5.00 today vs –€5.25 2 weeks

	Gains	*Losses*
32	€5.00 today vs €5.25 1 month	–€5.00 today vs –€5.25 1 month
33	€5.00 2 weeks vs €5.25 1 month	–€5.00 2 weeks vs –€5.25 1 month
34	€5.00 2 weeks vs €5.25 1 month and 2 weeks	–€5.00 2 weeks vs –€5.25 1 month and 2 weeks
35	€5.00 1 month vs €5.25 1 month and 2 weeks	–€5.00 1 month vs –€5.25 1 month and 2 weeks
36	€15.00 today vs €15.75 2 weeks	–€15.00 today vs –€15.75 2 weeks
37	€15.00 today vs €15.75 1 month	–€15.00 today vs –€15.75 1 month
38	€15.00 2 weeks vs €15.75 1 month	–€15.00 2 weeks vs –€15.75 1 month
39	€15.00 2 weeks vs €15.75 1 month and 2 weeks	–€15.00 2 weeks vs –€15.75 1 month and 2 weeks
40	€15.00 1 month vs €15.75 1 month and 2 weeks	–€15.00 1 month vs –€15.75 1 month and 2 weeks
41	€30.00 today vs €31.50 2 weeks	–€30.00 today vs –€31.50 2 weeks
42	€30.00 today vs €31.50 1 month	–€30.00 today vs –€31.50 1 month
43	€30.00 2 weeks vs €31.50 1 month	–€30.00 2 weeks vs –€31.50 1 month
44	€30.00 2 weeks vs €31.50 1 month and 2 weeks	–€30.00 2 weeks vs –€31.50 1 month and 2 weeks
45	€30.00 1 month vs €31.50 1 month and 2 weeks	–€30.00 1 month vs –€31.50 1 month and 2 weeks
46	€5.00 today vs €5.50 2 weeks	–€5.00 today vs –€5.50 2 weeks
47	€5.00 today vs €5.50 1 month	–€5.00 today vs –€5.50 1 month
48	€5.00 2 weeks vs €5.50 1 month	–€5.00 2 weeks vs –€5.50 1 month
49	€5.00 2 weeks vs €5.50 1 month and 2 weeks	–€5.00 2 weeks vs –€5.50 1 month and 2 weeks
50	€5.00 1 month vs €5.50 1 month and 2 weeks	–€5.00 1 month vs –€5.50 1 month and 2 weeks
51	€15.00 today vs €16.50 2 weeks	–€15.00 today vs –€16.50 2 weeks
52	€15.00 today vs €16.50 1 month	–€15.00 today vs –€16.50 1 month
53	€15.00 2 weeks vs €16.50 1 month	–€15.00 2 weeks vs –€16.50 1 month
54	€15.00 2 weeks vs €16.50 1 month and 2 weeks	–€15.00 2 weeks vs –€16.50 1 month and 2 weeks
55	€15.00 1 month vs €16.50 1 month and 2 weeks	–€15.00 1 month vs –€16.50 1 month and 2 weeks
56	€30.00 today vs €33.00 2 weeks	–€30.00 today vs –€33.00 2 weeks
57	€30.00 today vs €33.00 1 month	–€30.00 today vs –€33.00 1 month
58	€30.00 2 weeks vs €33.00 1 month €5.75 and –€5.75	–€30.00 2 weeks vs –€33.00 1 month
59	€30.00 2 weeks vs €33.00 1 month and 2 weeks	–€30.00 2 weeks vs –€33.00 1 month and 2 weeks
60	€30.00 1 month vs €33.00 1 month and 2 weeks	–€30.00 1 month vs –€33.00 1 month and 2 weeks
61	€5.00 today vs €5.75 2 weeks	–€5.00 today vs –€5.75 2 weeks
62	€5.00 today vs €5.75 1 month	–€5.00 today vs –€5.75 1 month
63	€5.00 2 weeks vs €5.75 1 month	–€5.00 2 weeks vs –€5.75 1 month
64	€5.00 2 weeks vs €5.75 1 month and 2 weeks	–€5.00 2 weeks vs –€5.75 1 month and 2 weeks
65	€5.00 1 month vs €5.75 1 month and 2 weeks	–€5.00 1 month vs –€5.75 1 month and 2 weeks

	Gains	*Losses*
66	€15.00 today vs €17.25 2 weeks	−€15.00 today vs −€17.25 2 weeks
67	€15.00 today vs €17.25 1 month	−€15.00 today vs −€17.25 1 month
68	€15.00 2 weeks vs €17.25 1 month	−€15.00 2 weeks vs −€17.25 1 month
69	€15.00 2 weeks vs €17.25 1 month and 2 weeks	−€15.00 2 weeks vs −€17.25 1 month and 2 weeks
70	€15.00 1 month vs €17.25 1 month and 2 weeks	−€15.00 1 month vs −€17.25 1 month and 2 weeks
71	€30.00 today vs €34.50 2 weeks	−€30.00 today vs −€34.50 2 weeks
72	€30.00 today vs €34.50 1 month	−€30.00 today vs −€34.50 1 month
73	€30.00 2 weeks vs €34.50 1 month	−€30.00 2 weeks vs −€34.50 1 month
74	€30.00 2 weeks vs €34.50 1 month and 2 weeks	−€30.00 2 weeks vs −€34.50 1 month and 2 weeks
75	€30.00 1 month vs €34.50 1 month and 2 weeks	−€30.00 1 month vs −€34.50 1 month and 2 weeks
76	€5.00 today vs €6.25 2 weeks	−€5.00 today vs −€6.25 2 weeks
77	€5.00 today vs €6.25 1 month	−€5.00 today vs −€6.25 1 month
78	€5.00 2 weeks vs €6.25 1 month	−€5.00 2 weeks vs −€6.25 1 month
79	€5.00 2 weeks vs €6.25 1 month and 2 weeks	−€5.00 2 weeks vs −€6.25 1 month and 2 weeks
80	€5.00 1 month vs €6.25 1 month and 2 weeks	−€5.00 1 month vs −€6.25 1 month and 2 weeks
81	€15.00 today vs €18.75 2 weeks	−€15.00 today vs −€18.75 2 weeks
82	€15.00 today vs €18.75 1 month	−€15.00 today vs −€18.75 1 month
83	€15.00 2 weeks vs €18.75 1 month	−€15.00 2 weeks vs −€18.75 1 month
84	€15.00 2 weeks vs €18.75 1 month and 2 weeks	−€15.00 2 weeks vs −€18.75 1 month and 2 weeks
85	€15.00 1 month vs €18.75 1 month and 2 weeks	−€15.00 1 month vs −€18.75 1 month and 2 weeks
86	€30.00 today vs €37.50 2 weeks	−€30.00 today vs −€37.50 2 weeks
87	€30.00 today vs €37.50 1 month	−€30.00 today vs −€37.50 1 month
88	€30.00 2 weeks vs €37.50 1 month	−€30.00 2 weeks vs −€37.50 1 month
89	€30.00 2 weeks vs €37.50 1 month and 2 weeks	−€30.00 2 weeks vs −€37.50 1 month and 2 weeks
90	€30.00 1 month vs €37.50 1 month and 2 weeks	−€30.00 1 month vs −€37.50 1 month and 2 weeks
91	€5.00 today vs €6.75 2 weeks	−€5.00 today vs −€6.75 2 weeks
92	€5.00 today vs €6.75 1 month	−€5.00 today vs −€6.75 1 month
93	€5.00 2 weeks vs €6.75 1 month	−€5.00 2 weeks vs −€6.75 1 month
94	€5.00 2 weeks vs €6.75 1 month and 2 weeks	−€5.00 2 weeks vs −€6.75 1 month and 2 weeks
95	€5.00 1 month vs €6.75 1 month and 2 weeks	−€5.00 1 month vs −€6.75 1 month and 2 weeks
96	€15.00 today vs €20.25 2 weeks	−€15.00 today vs −€20.25 2 weeks
97	€15.00 today vs €20.25 1 month	−€15.00 today vs −€20.25 1 month
98	€15.00 2 weeks vs €20.25 1 month	−€15.00 2 weeks vs −€20.25 1 month
99	€15.00 2 weeks vs €20.25 1 month and 2 weeks	−€15.00 2 weeks vs −€20.25 1 month and 2 weeks

	Gains	*Losses*
100	€15.00 1 month vs €20.25 1 month and 2 weeks	–€15.00 1 month vs –€20.25 1 month and 2 weeks
101	€30.00 today vs €40.50 2 weeks	–€30.00 today vs –€40.50 2 weeks
102	€30.00 today vs €40.50 1 month	–€30.00 today vs –€40.50 1 month
103	€30.00 2 weeks vs €40.50 1 month	–€30.00 2 weeks vs –€40.50 1 month
104	€30.00 2 weeks vs €40.50 1 month and 2 weeks	–€30.00 2 weeks vs –€40.50 1 month and 2 weeks
105	€30.00 1 month vs €40.50 1 month and 2 weeks	–€30.00 1 month vs –€40.50 1 month and 2 weeks
106	€5.00 today vs €7.50 2 weeks	–€5.00 today vs –€7.50 2 weeks
107	€5.00 today vs €7.50 1 month	–€5.00 today vs –€7.50 1 month
108	€5.00 2 weeks vs €7.50 1 month	–€5.00 2 weeks vs –€7.50 1 month
109	€5.00 2 weeks vs €7.50 1 month and 2 weeks	–€5.00 2 weeks vs –€7.50 1 month and 2 weeks
110	€5.00 1 month vs €7.50 1 month and 2 weeks	–€5.00 1 month vs –€7.50 1 month and 2 weeks
111	€15.00 today vs €22.50 2 weeks	–€15.00 today vs –€22.50 2 weeks
112	€15.00 today vs €22.50 1 month	–€15.00 today vs –€22.50 1 month
113	€15.00 2 weeks vs €22.50 1 month	–€15.00 2 weeks vs –€22.50 1 month
114	€15.00 2 weeks vs €22.50 1 month and 2 weeks	–€15.00 2 weeks vs –€22.50 1 month and 2 weeks
115	€15.00 1 month vs €22.50 1 month and 2 weeks	–€15.00 1 month vs –€22.50 1 month and 2 weeks
116	€30.00 today vs €45.00 2 weeks	–€30.00 today vs –€45.00 2 weeks
117	€30.00 today vs €45.00 1 month	–€30.00 today vs –€45.00 1 month
118	€30.00 2 weeks vs €45.00 1 month	–€30.00 2 weeks vs –€45.00 1 month
119	€30.00 2 weeks vs €45.00 1 month and 2 weeks	–€30.00 2 weeks vs –€45.00 1 month and 2 weeks
120	€30.00 1 month vs €45.00 1 month and 2 weeks	–€30.00 1 month vs –€45.00 1 month and 2 weeks

References

Agresti, A. (2002) *Categorical Data Analysis*, Hoboken, NJ: John Wiley & Sons.

Benzion, U., Rapoport, A. and Yagil, J. (1989) 'Discount rates inferred from decisions: an experimental study', *Management Science*, 35: 270–284.

Bickel, W.K. and Madden, G.J. (1999) 'A comparison of measures of relative reinforcing efficacy and behavioral economics: cigarettes and money in smokers', *Behavioural Pharmacology*, 10: 627–637.

Cook, J.O. and Barnes, L.W. (1964) 'Choice of delay of inevitable shock', *Journal of Abnormal Psychology*, 68: 669–672.

Croson, R. and Gneezy, U. (2009) 'Gender differences in preferences', *Journal of Economic Literature*, 47: 448–474.

Dimitri, N. (2007) *A Note on the Reward–Loss Duality in Time Consistent Decisions*, Working Paper 8, Department of Economic Policy, Finance and Development, University of Siena, Siena, Italy. Retrieved from www.depfid.unisi.it/images/pdf/text8.pdf.

Fisher, I. (1930) *The Theory of Interest*, New York: MacMillan.

Frederick, S., Loewenstein, G. and O'Donoghue, T. (2002) 'Time discounting and time preference: a critical review', *Journal of Economic Literature*, 40: 351–401.

Grusec, J.E. (1968) 'Waiting for rewards and punishments: effects of reinforcement value on choice', *Journal of Personality and Social Psychology*, 9: 85–89.

Hare, R.D. (1966) 'Preference for delay of shock as a function of its intensity and probability', *Psychonomic Science*, 5: 393–394.

Hare, R.D., Krebs, D.L., Creighton, T.D. and Petrusic, W.M. (1966) 'Latency of self-administered shock as a function of its intensity and probability', *Psychonomic Science*, 6: 79–80.

Kirby, K.N., Petry, N.M. and Bickel, W.K. (1999) 'Heroin addicts have higher discount rates for delayed rewards than non-drug-using controls', *Journal of Experimental Psychology: General*, 128: 78–87.

Loewenstein, G. (1987) 'Anticipation and the valuation of delayed consumption', *The Economic Journal*, 97: 666–684.

Loewenstein, G. (1988) *The Weighting of Waiting: Response Mode Effects in Intertemporal Choice*, Working paper, Center for Decision Research, University of Chicago.

Loewenstein, G. and Prelec, D. (1992) 'Anomalies in intertemporal choice: evidence and interpretation', *Quarterly Journal of Economics*, 107: 573–597.

Loewenstein, G. and Sicherman, N. (1991) 'Do workers prefer increasing wage profiles?', *Journal of Labor Economics*, 9: 67–84.

McClure, S.M., Laibson, D.I., Loewenstein, G. and Cohen, J.D. (2004) 'Separate neural systems value immediate and delayed monetary rewards', *Science*, 306: 503–507.

Madden, G.J., Petry, N.M., Badger, G.J. and Bickel, W.K. (1997) 'Impulsive and self-control choices in opioid-dependent patients and non-drug-using control participants: drug and monetary rewards', *Experimental and Clinical Psychopharmacology*, 5: 256–262.

Mischel, W., Grusec, J. and Masters, J.C. (1969) 'Effects of expected delay time on the subjective value of rewards and punishments', *Journal of Personality and Social Psychology*, 11: 363–373.

Prelec, D. and Loewenstein, G. (1998) 'The red and the black: mental accounting of savings and debt', *Marketing Science*, 17: 4–28.

Rae, J. (1834) *The Social Theory of Capital*, London: MacMillan.

Read, D. (2004) 'Intertemporal choice', in D. Koehler and N. Harvey (eds), *Blackwell Handbook of Judgment and Decision Making*, Oxford: Blackwell.

Samuelson, P.A. (1937) 'A note on measurement of utility', *Review of Economic Studies*, 4: 155–161.

Shelley, M.K. (1993) 'Outcome signs, question frames and discount rates', *Management Science*, 39: 806–815.

Strotz, R. (1955–1956) 'Myopia and inconsistency in dynamic utility maximization', *Review of Economic Studies*, 23: 165–180.

Thaler, R.H. (1981) 'Some empirical evidence on dynamic inconsistency', *Economic Letters*, 8: 201–207.

Xu, L., Liang, Z.Y., Wang, K., Li, S. and Jiang, T. (2009) 'Neural mechanism of intertemporal choice: from discounting future gains to future losses', *Brain Research*, 1261: 65–74.

Yates, J.F. and Watts, R.A. (1975) 'Preferences for deferred losses', *Organizational Behavior and Human Performances*, 13: 294–306.

Part IV

Probability and judgment in decision-making

9 Cognitive and affective responses to schema-incongruent brand messages

An empirical investigation

Georgios Halkias and Flora Kokkinaki

Introduction

It is common ground in marketing communications that consistent and relevant brand messages appeal to consumers and increase brand equity over time (Aaker 1991; Keller 2003; Percy and Elliott 2005). This view has been widely documented through the various positioning and advertising models found in the literature, which emphasize the importance of identifying and managing consumers' brand and product schemata in order to develop effective persuasive communication (Gutman 1982; Reynolds and Gutman 1984; Ratchford 1987; Rossiter *et al.* 1991). The underlying premise is that consumers generally react more favorably to brand communication that is congruent with the associations tied to the specific product. By definition, congruent brand information fits product associations in an obvious and meaningful manner that is supposed to be later translated into greater liking of the communication content. In other words, traditional approaches to marketing communication propose that persuasive messages that correspond to consumers' knowledge and perceptions are more likely to be relevant, comprehensible, and appealing (Rossiter *et al.* 1991; Keller 2003; Brannon and Brock 2006; Petty and Wegener 1998). In essence, any persuasion situation can be thought of as consisting of three main components: (1) the recipient (e.g., the consumer); (2) the attitude object (e.g., the brand); and (3) the content of communication (e.g., the advertising) (Brannon and Brock 2006). Message persuasiveness is believed to be an increasing function of the fit between the attributes of these three components (Brannon and Brock 1994, 2006).

Despite its intuitive appeal, however, a number of studies in cognitive psychology challenge the above proposition, suggesting that schema-incongruent information may lead to a more positive outcome (Mandler 1982; Fiske 1982; Fiske and Pavelchak 1986). Schema-based research indicates that incongruent stimuli may attract more of the recipients' attention, increase their cognitive arousal, and may finally elicit more positive judgments (Mandler 1982; Thompson and Hamilton 2006; Fiske *et al.* 1987; Meyers-Levy *et al.* 1994; Meyers-Levy and Tybout 1989). This phenomenon has been observed in a variety of social domains, such as in people's interpersonal relations, preferences for musical compositions, or infants' preferences for objects (Meyers-Levy *et al.* 1994). In the consumer context, a number of studies have examined information incongruity under various marketing situations, providing insightful, yet inconclusive, findings (Lee and Mason 1999; Goodstein 1993; Wansink and Ray 1996). Most importantly, with a very few exceptions (Lange and Dahlén 2003; Dahlén *et al.* 2005), only limited attention has been given by researchers to the investigation of brand schemata incongruity. Drawing on schema research in cognitive psychology, we present an empirical study that builds upon existing literature by exploring cognitive and affective responses to brand communication that varies in terms of incongruity (i.e., *congruent*, *moderately incongruent*, and *extremely incongruent*) with consumers' established brand schemata.

Conceptual background

Schema theory

Schema theory has its foundations in cognitive psychology (Crockett 1988) and assumes that cognitive processing is guided by prior knowledge and experiences (Fiske and Linville 1980). As Fiske and Taylor (1991) argue, instead of storing one-by-one every individual experience and piece of information in its raw form, people tend to simplify reality by organizing and storing all available knowledge about their social surroundings in memory-based cognitive structures called *schemata.* In essence, a cognitive schema represents people's accumulated knowledge about an attitude object, including its attributes and the interrelations among these attributes (Fiske and Taylor 1991). Over time, people develop sets of expectations about the social stimuli encountered (Sujan 1985). These expectations depend on a number of assumptions and hypotheses about the attributes of these stimuli as specified by their relevant schema (Sujan and Bettman 1989; Fiske and Taylor 1991). Thus, schemata can be alternatively viewed as organized patterns of expectations about the social phenomena (Sujan *et al.* 1986). In social and cognitive psychology, the schema concept has been employed to study memory processes, objects/instances categorization, and to explain how people organize past experiences into patterns that facilitate understanding of subsequent behaviors and phenomena (Crockett 1988; Fiske and Taylor 1991). In reality, a cognitive schema can be viewed as an example of how prior information and memory can influence the perception of a current experience. Through the various mental schemata, memories can determine the interpretation of a present event by affecting how individual neurons encode the incoming information (Braun 1999). These schema effects have been manifested in behavioral experiments showing that even the interpretation of real sensory experiences may be affected by schematic knowledge (Braun 1999). Cohen (as cited in Braun 1999: 332) describes this by saying that perception is not a unidimensional process where stimuli cause brain events that are consequently transformed into an internal experience of an external occurrence. Stimuli cause brain events, but the way in which those events are coded depends on what the brain expects and remembers. Overall, it has been demonstrated that schematic knowledge provides cognitive economy, guides the perception of information, and allows us some sense of prediction and control that is essential to cope with the environment (Fiske and Taylor 1991). Smith and Medin (1981) point out that if people did not have cognitive schemata, many environments would be perceived as complex and chaotic.

Given that consumers' knowledge about the market can also be perceived through relevant cognitive structures (e.g., product schema, brand schema, advert schema), schema theory has been applied in marketing research, to study several aspects of consumer behavior (Sujan 1985; Stayman *et al.* 1992; Goodstein 1993; Boush and Loken 1991; Park *et al.* 1991). Regardless of the perspective followed, it has been revealed that consumers' schemata greatly affect the way they process product information and respond to persuasive communication (Sujan and Bettman 1989; Meyers-Levy and Tybout 1989; Goodstein 1993). In a highly competitive market environment, replete with advertising and brand messages, consumers use their schemata to integrate incoming with existing data, retrieve information from memory, draw inferences, and facilitate purchase decisions (Sujan and Bettman 1989). Out of the wide repertoire of consumers' schemata, the brand schema has been identified as the most relevant schema for the processing and the evaluation of persuasive communication (Rossiter *et al.* 1991; Gutman 1982; Sjödin and Törn 2006; Boush and Loken 1991). Brand schemata mediate both product and advert schemata and incorporate the most essential information for consumers' final choice (Gutman 1982; Sjödin and Törn 2006; Boush and Loken 1991). They represent knowledge about all the brand attributes, functional as well as symbolic, in relation to their ability to satisfy various consumer needs (Wansink and Ray 1996; Brannon and Brock 1994, 2006). In essence, the brand schema is an organized network of all the beliefs, emotions, and associations consumers attach to a specific brand and its attributes (Aaker 1991; Brannon and Brock 2006; Sjödin and Törn 2006).

Conceptualizing schema incongruity

Schema incongruity theory (also referred to as congruity theory) looks into the effects of information that is incompatible with existing knowledge and does not conform to some predefined pattern (Stayman *et al.* 1992). Alternatively, it can be perceived as trying to describe how confirmation or disconfirmation of expectations influences individual responses (Fiske and Taylor 1991; Stayman *et al.* 1992; Mandler 1982). Schema incongruity is defined as the extent to which semantic correspondence is achieved between the attributes of a stimulus object and the attributes specified by its relevant schema (Areni and Cox 1994; Halkias and Kokkinaki 2010). Heckler and Childers (1992) suggested a two-dimensional conceptualization of schema incongruity, in which the *relevancy* and the *expectancy* of the stimulus' content are hypothesized to determine the presence and the degree of incongruity. Relevancy refers to the degree to which a piece of information is useful to produce meaning and contributes to the identification of the primary message communicated by the stimulus object. Expectancy, on the other hand, refers to the degree to which a piece of information conforms to expectations and falls into some predefined pattern evoked by the stimulus object (Heckler and Childers 1992; Lee and Mason 1999). Following Heckler and Childers' (1992) approach, schema incongruity is this chapter refers to brand information and cues that conflict with what is expected and what is perceived as relevant by consumers with regard to their experience with the brand. In more detail, brand schema congruity is represented by a match, in terms of relevancy and expectancy, between the content of an advertisement and the content of consumers' schema for the advertised brand, whereas brand schema incongruity involves some degree of mismatch (Sujan 1985; Meyers *et al.* 1989).

In relation to research on information incongruity at present, Mandler (1982) has offered one of the most insightful theoretical frameworks to understand the effect of schema incongruity (Meyers-Levy *et al.* 1994; Peracchio and Tybout 1996; Lee and Schumann 2004). Mandler (1982) postulates that increases in the level of incongruity between a stimulus and a predefined schema leads to heightened cognitive arousal that in turn increases the extremity of evaluations. Whether an evaluation becomes relatively more or less favorable depends on how easily the receiver can process the incoming data and satisfactorily resolve the incongruities. Therefore, evaluative responses are influenced by the resolution of incongruity and not by the mere presence of it (Meyers-Levy and Tybout 1989). More specifically, Mandler (1982) suggests that congruent stimuli bear a high degree of familiarity and acceptability that is positively valued by recipients. Yet, being easily predictable they do not stimulate some further interest and tend to result in mildly favorable responses. In contrast, schema-incongruent stimuli attract attention and increase the cognitive arousal as people attempt to resolve discrepancies and produce meaning. According to Mandler (1982), people are likely to resolve moderate incongruities by implementing relatively minor revisions of existing knowledge (Meyers-Levy *et al.* 1994). The increased cognitive stimulation as well as the psychological reward produced by successfully resolving the incongruity is predicted to result in considerably more favorable responses than those produced by congruent information. Finally, Mandler (1982) proposes that extreme incongruity will initially stimulate almost the same amount of processing as moderate incongruity. However, contrary to moderate incongruity, extreme incongruity is unlikely to be successfully accommodated. People are typically not willing to invest the significant amount of psychological resources necessary to accommodate extremely inconsistent pieces of information. Given that, processing is more likely abandoned and the favorability of evaluations is limited. If processing is not abandoned and people persist in spending time and effort seeking resolution, responses will be considerably more negatively influenced as a function of the increased frustration produced by the futile attempts and the inability to appropriately interpret information.

Research hypotheses

Previous research suggests that novel and unexpected information stimulates people's cognitive processing (Lee and Schumann 2004; Törn and Dahlén 2008). Consistent with MacInnis *et al.*'s (1991) approach, cognitive processing in this study refers to the extent to which a consumer allocates attention and processing resources to comprehend and elaborate on the incoming information in an advert. Among the few empirical studies that have investigated this proposition, Goodstein (1993) has demonstrated that consumers generally attend more to atypical than typical adverts, while Törn and Dahlén (2008) showed that consumers pay more attention, in terms of longer viewing time, to adverts that mismatch with established brand beliefs. In a similar sense, Pieters *et al.* (2002) employed an eye-tracking technique and found that novelty and originality in the advert execution increases attention to the advert's elements, as indicated by an increased frequency of eye fixations, compared to typical and familiar adverts. Following a three-fold operationalization of incongruity, Ozzane *et al.* (1992) found support for a non-monotonic relationship between the degree of incongruity and consumers' information processing. They demonstrated that consumers exposed to products moderately incongruent with their associated category schema engage in deeper and more effortful processing of the available information than those exposed to either congruent or extremely incongruent new products. Along these lines, a non-monotonic relationship between the degree of incongruity and consumers' advert processing is anticipated. As incongruity increases, consumers are expected to attend more to the advert trying to reconcile discrepant information. However, as discrepancies become extreme and the resolution of incongruity highly uncertain, consumers are more likely to ignore incompatible information and curtail the amount of attention paid to the advert. In summary, it is expected that:

> **H1:** Consumers will pay more attention to adverts featuring moderately incongruent brand information, compared to advertisements featuring either congruent or extremely incongruent brand information.

A long-standing finding in psychology research is that increased processing and attention to a stimulus leads to better memory performance (Mick 1992; Hastie 1980; Friedman 1979). This is based on the idea that deeper and more extensive processing causes the creation of additional associative paths between original and new information (Mick 1992). From a schema-incongruity perspective, completely congruent information is assumed to receive only limited encoding, since it can be readily and effortlessly integrated into existing knowledge. In contrast, a greater amount of cognitive resources is required when people deal with schema-incongruent stimuli. As people engage in more extensive encoding trying to accommodate incongruent pieces of information into the activated schema, a larger number of associative linkages between the stimulus content and the knowledge stored in memory is developed (Houston *et al.* 1987; Hastie 1980). This is assumed to make new information more retrievable and easier to recall (Heckler and Childers 1992; Houston *et al.* 1987; Lange and Dahlén 2003). In addition, attending to a particular stimulus for a longer period of time results in a more detailed representation of the stimulus material available in working memory, thus increasing the probability of recognizing specific features of its content (Goodman 1980; Houston *et al.* 1987). A different effect is hypothesized for memory under extreme schema incongruity. As mentioned above, extremely discrepant information cannot be successfully linked to schematic knowledge and so discourage processing. As a consequence, both retrieval and discrimination processes are hindered, reducing the overall memory of the information presented. Overall, the following hypotheses are suggested.

H2: Adverts featuring moderately incongruent brand information lead to better advert recall, compared to adverts featuring either congruent or extremely incongruent brand information.

H3: Adverts featuring moderately incongruent brand information result in better advert recognition, compared to adverts featuring either congruent or extremely incongruent brand information.

Research in aesthetics and rhetoric has suggested that an "artful" deviation from the norm can produce a pleasurable degree of arousal (McQuarrie and Mick 1996). In fact, there seems to be an intrinsically rewarding value in interpreting some deviant configuration of signs (McQuarrie and Mick 1996). Following a similar logic, Mandler (1982) argues that the process of resolving incongruity is rewarding and may increase the favorability of final judgments. This hypothesis has received only mixed support in consumer research (Goodstein 1993; Lee and Mason 1999). For instance, Lange and Dahlén (2003) did not identify significant differences in attitude toward the brand between congruent and incongruent with the brand schema adverts, while Goodstein (1993) showed that adverts that do not match the typical advert schema lead to a lower advert and brand attitude than schema-congruent adverts. Similarly, Dahlén and colleagues (2005) found that adverts incongruent with consumers' brand perceptions result in a lower advert attitude and credibility compared to congruent advertisements. Interestingly, though, their study revealed a significant effect to the opposite direction for brand attitude that was enhanced under advert–brand incongruity. Lee and Mason (1999) followed Mandler's (1982) conceptualization and added an intermediate level (i.e., moderate incongruity) between congruity and incongruity. Their findings supported the positive effect of moderate incongruity on attitude toward the advert. The mean scores for attitude toward the brand also followed the predicted directionality, yet no significant differences between congruity and moderate incongruity were obtained (Lee and Mason 1999). Nonetheless, in line with Mandler's (1982) reasoning, a number of studies have provided full support to the inverted-U relationship between information incongruity and consumer evaluations. Meyers-Levy and Tybout (1989), for example, showed that when a new product proposition is moderately incongruent with the product category to which it supposedly belongs, it is evaluated more favorably than either congruent or extremely incongruent products (see also Peracchio and Tybout 1996). The same pattern has been evident in cases of incongruity between a parent brand and a brand extension (Meyers-Levy *et al.* 1994) or when product taste does not match with consumers' expectations (Stayman *et al.* 1992). We expect the same pattern to occur for advert and brand evaluations across the degrees of schema incongruity. The arousal stimulated by ambiguous and unexpected, yet resolvable, brand information will produce additional affect toward the stimulus advert compared to congruent information. However, this affect will disappear as information becomes extremely discrepant and people cannot make sense of the advert. The same relationship is predicted for brand attitudes, with the most favorable effect being expected in response to moderately incongruent adverts. In detail, it is predicted that:

> **H4:** Adverts featuring moderately incongruent brand information result in higher attitude toward the advert (A_{ad}), compared to adverts featuring either congruent or extremely incongruent brand information.

> **H5:** Adverts featuring moderately incongruent brand information result in higher attitude toward the brand (A_b), compared to advertisements featuring either congruent or extremely incongruent brand information.

Method

An experimental study was conducted to investigate the above hypotheses. Advertising incongruity with consumers' schema for a real brand was operationalized as a between-subjects factor, analyzed at three levels, that is, congruity, moderate incongruity, and extreme incongruity. More specifically, the degree of brand schema incongruity was manipulated through the pictorial component of a print advert by means of information *expectancy* and *relevancy* with the associated brand schema (Heckler and Childers 1992; Halkias and Kokkinaki 2010, 2011). The advert format and verbal elements were held constant across conditions. Print adverts are reader-paced, allowing for differences in attention among participants and are thus appropriate for the research purposes (Lange and Dahlén 2003). Fifty-four undergraduate business students participated in the main study in exchange for extra course credit. Cell sizes were equally distributed across the experimental conditions. The hypothesized relationships were tested through analysis of variance (ANOVA) and covariance (ANCOVA) with polynomial trend analysis.

Pretest

In order to determine the product category from which the final brand would be selected, the first pretest ($n_1 = 9$) involved a consumer focus group session. The product category of "chocolate bars" was proven to be sufficiently familiar and relevant to the sample population and was therefore chosen for the main study.

The second pretest (n_2=34) was conducted to identify consumers' brand schemata within the selected product category. Participants were asked to indicate their level of knowledge (1 = not knowledgeable at all, 7 = very knowledgeable) for a series of chocolate brands (Sujan and Bettman 1989) as well as to list every association they held for each brand (Aaker and Keller 1990; Ratneshwar and Shocker 1991). The brand that met the requirements of the research was "Lacta," the leading chocolate brand in the market. Brand awareness was 100 percent and participants were knowledgeable enough (M=6.18, SD=0.87) to have established a discrete schema for the brand. A frequency analysis of participants' associations was realized to reveal the most typical attributes of the brand schema. Individual brand associations representing the same concept (e.g., *"a sweet little treat for my boyfriend or girlfriend"* and *"it's a chocolate for couples in love"*) were collapsed under the same schema attribute, while idiosyncratic associations, i.e., associations listed by a single participant that could not be collapsed, were eliminated. In addition to the researchers, two independent coders categorized the same consumer associations to ensure reliability (inter-coder reliability above 85 percent). The most frequently mentioned brand associations, listed by at least 76 percent of respondents, pertained to the attributes of *love*, *romance*, and *passion*.

Following this, 37 new participants were recruited in a third pretest to confirm the configuration of the Lacta brand schema. The three most typical brand attributes above were quantified using nine-point, Likert-type scales. Respondents were asked to indicate how representative each attribute is with regard to their impression of the brand. The scale was anchored by 1 (not representative at all) and 9 (very representative). Attributes not mentioned to be part of the brand schema were used as control attributes. According to the results, schema attributes received consistently higher scores (mean ratings ranged from 7.03 to 7.49) than did control attributes (mean ratings ranged from 3.14 to 3.70). The least possible difference between schema and control attributes was statistically significant (*mean difference*=3.32, $t(36)=8.79$, $p<0.001$). Therefore the main theme of the brand schema was confirmed.

Stimulus development

Based on pretest findings, 20 pictures were selected with the intention to be either congruent, moderately incongruent, or extremely incongruent with the Lacta brand schema. In a fourth pretest (n_4=26) respondents were asked to rate each picture in terms of matching their impression of the brand along a nine-point scale (1 = mismatch, 9 = match). The pictures were also tested for likeability (1 = dislike, 9 = like) to ensure that the affect produced in the main study was attributed to differences in the degree of schema incongruity and not to differences in picture liking. The order of the pictures was counterbalanced to avoid possible carryover and fatigue effects. Based on the mean ratings, we selected the three pictures that seemed to best represent the three levels of incongruity and that were similarly rated in terms of likeability. These were submitted to separate one-way repeated measures ANOVAs with picture matching and likeability being operationalized as within-subjects variables. The results provided a significant effect of the three pictures on perceived match ($F(2, 50)=36.38$, $p<0.001$) and a non-significant effect on likeability ($F(2, 50)=2.78$, *NS*), indicating that the pictures correspond to a different degree of schema incongruity and are equally liked. These three pictures were used as the pictorial component of the final stimulus adverts. The same brand logo, tagline, and format were used across all advert versions. An advertising agency was utilized for the design of the experimental adverts to ensure they approximated real commercial print adverts.

Experimental procedure

The study took place in a laboratory setting. Upon arrival, participants were randomly assigned to one of the three experimental conditions and were given a questionnaire that contained all the necessary manipulations and dependent measures. Initially, subjects provided their evaluations for several brands across different product categories to familiarize themselves with the answering process. Evaluations for the brand Lacta were also included to control for differences in prior affect toward the brand. Following this, participants were told a brief cover story about the purposes of the study and were given additional guidelines on how to proceed. Immediately after, participants were exposed to two filler adverts followed by the experimental advert. When finished, they completed the advert and brand evaluation scales as well as the manipulation checks. A 15-minute filler task followed to clear short-term memory and then participants completed the recall and the recognition test. After completing a short section of demographic questions, participants were debriefed and thanked for their participation.

Dependent measures

Attention. The time consumers spent watching the advert was used to indicate the amount of attention (Goodstein 1993). A timer running on a computer screen was set at the beginning of each exposure. Participants were instructed to watch the adverts at their own pace and record the number appearing on the screen after they had formed their overall impression.

Recall. Recall was measured with an open-ended question asking participants to write down as many of the features they could remember from the advert within a two-minute time limit. Recall protocols were coded so that each correct mention of a distinct advert item represented a hit. The total number of hits was summed up to form the overall recall score for each respondent.

Recognition. Recognition was measured using 12 advert-related statements for which participants were asked to state whether they were true or false. The total number of correct answers formed the overall score for recognition.

Advert and brand evaluations. Attitude toward the advert (A_{ad}) and the brand (A_b) were measured on three nine-point semantic differential scales anchored by dislike and like, bad and good, and unfavorable and favorable (Goodstein 1993). The Cronbach's α coefficient for the averaged index of A_b prior and after the exposure was 0.95 and 0.94, respectively, while for A_{ad} was 0.96.

Results

Manipulation check

The effectiveness of the manipulation was checked using the same perceived match scale reported for the stimulus pretest. In addition, participants were asked to rate the adverts in terms of relevancy and expectancy with regard to their impression of the brand (Heckler and Childers 1992) on a nine-point scale anchored by irrelevant/unexpected and relevant/expected. The average ratings for perceived match, relevancy, and expectancy were analyzed with a one-way ANOVA in a single factor, between-subjects design. According to results, statistically significant main effects were obtained for perceived match ($F(2,51)=33.97$, $p<0.001$), relevancy ($F(2,51)=25.52$, $p<0.001$), and expectancy ($F(2,51)=19.86$, $p<0.001$). Mean ratings for all three dependent measures differed significantly across the three experimental conditions (see Table 9.1), indicating that the manipulation of schema incongruity is successful.

Hypotheses testing

Analysis of variance revealed a significant main effect of the degree of schema incongruity on attention ($F(2,51)=23.68$, $p<0.001$). Participants spent significantly more time watching the moderately incongruent advert than the congruent (*mean* difference 8.83 seconds, $p<0.001$) or the extremely incongruent advert (*mean* difference 7.16 seconds, $p<0.001$). Trend analysis showed a highly significant quadratic trend for attention (*quadratic component*; $F(1,51)=45.87$, $p<0.001$), showing that attention follows an inverted-U across the experimental conditions. The mean values for recall and recognition were also proven to follow the inverted-U pattern, and significant main effects were obtained in both cases (see Table 9.2). In more detail, consistent with the second hypothesis,

Table 9.1 Summary of results for manipulation check

Experimental condition	*Perceived match*	*Relevancy*	*Expectancy*
Congruity	7.61 (1.14)	7.38 (1.46)	7.88 (1.32)
Moderate incongruity	5.66 (1.57)	4.66 (2.08)	4.94 (2.18)
Extreme incongruity	3.05 (2.12)	3.16 (1.79)	3.66 (2.49)
F-value	33.97*	25.52*	19.86*

Notes
* $p<0.001$.
Standard deviations in parentheses.

Table 9.2 Cell means, standard deviations, and main effects for attention and memory

Dependent variables	*Degree of schema incongruity*			
	Congruity	*Moderate incongruity*	*Extreme incongruity*	*F-value*
Attention (H1)	8.56 (3.50)	17.39 (5.04)	10.22 (3.54)	23.68*
Quadratic component				*45.87**
Recall (H2)	2.61 (0.98)	6.11 (2.63)	2.94 (1.89)	17.57*
Quadratic component				*34.87**
Recognition (H3)	5.33 (1.45)	7.50 (1.58)	5.00 (1.37)	15.31*
Quadratic component				*30.15**

Notes
* $p<0.001$.
Standard deviations in parentheses.

participants recalled more advert features for the moderately incongruent advert (M=6.11, SD=2.63), compared to the congruent (M=2.61, SD=0.98) and the extremely incongruent (M=2.94, SD=1.89) advert version ($F(2,51)=17.57$, $p<0.001$). Similarly, a significant effect supported our prediction on recognition memory ($F(2,51)=15.31$, $p<0.001$), with participants demonstrating a much greater ability to successfully discriminate the content of the advert that is moderately incongruent with their brand schema. Mean differences in recognition between moderate schema incongruity and the two other conditions (*mean difference* 2.16 and 2.50 for congruity and extreme incongruity, respectively) were significant at the 0.001 level.

Preliminary data analyses detected significant differences in respondents' prior brand attitude ($F(2,53)=9.78$, $p<0.001$), with those participating in the extreme incongruity condition having more positive prior attitudes toward the experimental brand Lacta than those in the congruity (*mean difference* 1.85, $p<0.01$) or the moderate incongruity condition (*mean difference* 1.91, $p<0.001$). These differences would obscure the predicted effects related to the dependent variables of advert and brand evaluations. To eliminate this confounding factor and control for individual differences in prior affect stored in participants' brand schema, prior brand attitude was used as a covariate in the investigation of A_{ad} and A_b. According to the ANCOVA results, A_{ad} was affected by the degree of brand schema incongruity ($F(2,50)=6.48$, $p<0.01$) without being significantly influenced by prior brand attitude ($F(1,50)=1.12$, *NS*). As predicted, the non-monotonic relationship was supported (quadratic effect significant at the 0.001 level), with participants' advert evaluations being the most favorable under moderate schema incongruity. Finally, as expected, it was found that participants' prior brand affect significantly influences their post-exposure A_b ($F(1,50)=69.28$, $p<0.001$). After statistically controlling for the effects of the covariate, a significant main effect of schema incongruity on brand attitude was detected $F(2,50)=8.58$, $p<0.01$). As with advert evaluations, A_b followed an inverted-U

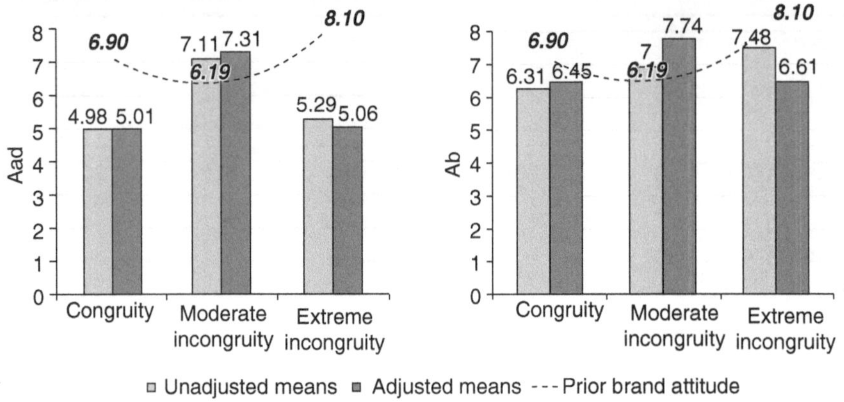

Figure 9.1 Adjusted and unadjusted means for A_{ad} and A_b using prior brand affect as a covariate.

pattern across the degrees of incongruity (quadratic effect significant at the 0.001 level). Pairwise comparisons (adjusted for the effect of the covariate) showed that moderate schema incongruity results in more favorable brand attitude, compared to congruity and extreme incongruity. ANCOVA results are illustrated in Figure 9.1.

Discussion and implications

The results provide full support for the hypothesized relationships, indicating that Mandler's (1982) schema incongruity theory can be applied in persuasive communications to explain consumers' reactions to brand information that deviates from established beliefs and expectations. Moderate incongruity between an advertisement and consumers' schema for the advertised brand is found to most positively influence both cognitive and affective responses. In more detail, incompatible and unexpected brand information seems to attract consumer attention to the point that they contribute to making sense of the intended communication. Otherwise, if a consumer cannot successfully restore understanding, they are led to assume some failure of communication (McQuarrie and Mick 1996). That being said, as information becomes extremely discrepant attention to the message declines, following a quadratic trend across the degrees of incongruity. Resolution of extreme incongruity is a very effort-demanding and doubtful process. As such, it discourages consumers, who seem to abandon the processing of the incoming information, overwhelmed by a feeling of frustration, as they cannot derive coherent meaning from the stimulus content.

The same non-monotonic pattern was reproduced in the results for memory performance. As anticipated, consumers' retrieval and recognition processes were significantly enhanced under moderate schema incongruity. Resolution of incongruity implies that discrepant stimulus information is successfully linked to the knowledge that is already stored in memory. To that end, consumers invest additional cognitive resources to revise schematic knowledge and try to develop new associations and nodes that will update the configuration of the relevant schema. As a result, under moderate schema incongruity a more elaborate and efficient network of associations between stimulus and memory information is developed that consequently facilitates recall of the advert's content. In addition, increased attention to the moderately incongruent stimulus implies deeper encoding of its content, which is rehearsed more times during the exposure. Having the advertisement more finely represented in working memory, consumers are significantly more efficient in recognizing specific features of its content.

Consistent with Mandler's (1982) proposition, moderate schema incongruity significantly enhanced consumer attitudes. The moderately incongruent advert was probably perceived to be more interesting and intriguing by consumers who formed more favorable evaluations, regardless of their prior brand attitudes. Not surprisingly, attitude toward the brand after the exposure was found to be significantly related to the affect already stored in the brand schema. After controlling for individual differences in prior brand affect the positive effect of moderate incongruity was supported. Accommodating discrepant advertising information can be thought of as solving a mental puzzle in which individual pieces or cues are assembled in some sort of logical pattern to finally reveal the answer. Successfully resolving incongruity seems to provide consumers with some sort of metacognitive experience of satisfaction and fulfillment that is intuitively transferred to their evaluations (Meyers-Levy and Tybout 1989). The findings indicate that consumer attitudes generated through more effortful and intellectually challenging processes are more favorable.

From a managerial perspective, the present findings challenge the normative recommendations put forward by traditional models of persuasive communication. Developing messages that conform to consumers' perceptions may not always be the most effective strategy. Marketing practitioners may use incongruity-based tactics to enhance their communication programs. Schema-incongruent messages can stimulate consumers' interest, make them actively participate in the communication process, and increase the memorability of the advert. Moreover, they can be used as a brand rejuvenation and brand repositioning tool by introducing additional or novel brand features. Yet, great caution is required in manipulating incongruity, since discrepancies that cannot be resolved may result in feelings of frustration and confusion, make consumers ignore the incoming information, and dilute the brand image. A careful consideration of the context in which brand communication appears is required. To avoid negative consequences, managers should make sure that consumers will have the ability and the opportunity to devote the necessary cognitive resources to process a message of this kind.

The evidence above provides considerable insight into how people deal with information that is incompatible with existing knowledge in a persuasive communication context. The hypothesized cognitive stimulation produced in response to incongruent stimuli has found support in various studies employing traditional social experimentation (Meyers-Levy 1988; Meyers-Levy and Tybout 1989; Goodstein 1993). Yet, even though the behavioral consequences have been investigated, very little is actually known about the physiological processes behind a specific behavioral pattern. Relevant literature would greatly benefit by the use of neuroscientific techniques and measurement methods, such as eye-tracking, EEG, or fMRI, which may capture more closely consumers' response mechanisms. For instance, using such methods researchers will be more able to distinguish between the extent and the depth of processing, since more attention to a stimulus in terms of longer viewing time does not necessarily mean deeper processing. Significant differences in mental activity may be detected among equivalent time periods. In the same sense, memory performance could be more properly attributed to some more sophisticated mental process adopted as people try to resolve incongruity, or merely to a longer exposure time. In addition, research in neuroscience may attempt to take into account the brain's complex interactions between information encoding, storage, and retrieval, thereby modeling the effects of prior knowledge in relation to new learning instances. Most importantly, the exact processes followed to resolve incongruity still remain a mystery. Different alternatives are hypothesized, including assimilation of discrepancies within existing knowledge, subtyping, or complete restructuring of schematic knowledge (Lee and Schumman 2004; Mandler 1982; Meyers-Levy and Tybout 1989). Presumably, these incongruity resolution processes are associated with increasing requirements in cognitive resources. Neuroscientific consumer research can shed light on the different processes utilized to deal with incongruent information and contribute significantly to research on schema incongruity.

Acknowledgments

This research has been co-financed by the European Union (European Social Fund – ESF) and Greek national funds through the Operational Program "Education and Lifelong Learning" of the National Strategic Reference Framework (NSRF) – Research Funding Program: "Heracleitus II: Investing in knowledge society through the European Social Fund."

References

Aaker, D.A. (1991) *Managing Brand Equity: Capitalizing on the Value of a Brand Name*, New York: The Free Press.

Aaker, D.A. and Keller, K.L. (1990) "Consumer evaluations of brand extensions," *Journal of Marketing*, 54 (1): 27–41.

Areni, C.S. and Cox, K.C. (1994) "The persuasive effects of evaluation, expectancy and relevancy dimensions of incongruent visual and verbal information," *Advances in Consumer Research*, 21: 337–342.

Boush, D.M. and Loken, B. (1991) "A process-tracing study of brand extension evaluation," *Journal of Marketing Research*, 28 (1): 16–28.

Brannon, L.A. and Brock, T.C. (1994) "Test of schema correspondence theory of persuasion: effects of matching an appeal to actual, ideal, and product selves," in E.M. Clark, T.C. Brock, and D.W. Stewart (eds.), *Attention, Attitude and Affect in Response to Advertising*, Mahwah, NJ: Lawrence Erlbaum Associates.

Brannon, L.A. and Brock, T.C. (2006) "Measuring the prototypicality of product categories and exemplars: implications of schema correspondence theory," in L.R. Kahle and C.-H. Kim (eds.), *Creating Images and the Psychology of Marketing Communication*, Mahwah, NJ: Lawrence Erlbraum Associates.

Braun, K.A. (1999) "Postexperience advertising effects on consumer memory," *Journal of Consumer Research*, 25: 319–334.

Crockett, W.H. (1988) "Schemas, affect, and communication," in L. Donohew, H.E. Sypher, and E.T. Higgins (eds.), *Communication, Social Cognition, and Affect*, Hillsdale, NJ: Lawrence Erlbaum Associates.

Dahlén, M., Lange, F., Sjödin, H., and Törn, F. (2005) "Effects of ad–brand incongruency," *Journal of Current Issues and Research in Advertising*, 27 (2): 1–12.

Fiske, S.T. (1982) "Schema-triggered affect: applications to social perception," in M.S. Clark and S.T. Fiske (eds.), *Affect and Cognition: The Seventeenth Annual Carnegie Symposium on Cognition*, Hillsdale, NJ: Lawrence Erlbaum Associates.

Fiske, S.T. and Linville, P.W. (1980) "What does the schema concept buy us?," *Personality and Social Psychological Bulletin*, 6 (4): 543–557.

Fiske, S.T. and Pavelchak, M.A. (1986) "Category-based versus piecemeal-based affective responses: developments in schema-triggered affect," in R.M. Sorrentino and E. Tory (eds.), *Handbook of Motivation and Cognition: Foundations of Social Behavior*, Higgins, NY: Guilford Press.

Fiske, S.T. and Taylor, S.E. (1991) *Social Cognition*, New York: McGraw-Hill.

Fiske, S.T., Neuberg, S.L., Beattie, A.E., and Milberg, S.J. (1987) "Category-based and attribute-based reactions to others: some informational conditions of stereotyping and individuating processes," *Journal of Experimental Social Psychology*, 23: 399–427.

Friedman, A. (1979) "Framing pictures: the role of knowledge in automated encoding and memory for gist," *Journal of Experimental Psychology: General*, 108 (3): 316–355.

Goodman, G.S. (1980) "Picture memory: how the action schema affects retention," *Cognitive Psychology*, 12 (4): 473–495.

Goodstein, R.C. (1993) "Category-based applications and extensions in advertising: motivating more extensive ad processing," *Journal of Consumer Research*, 20 (1): 87–99.

Gutman, J. (1982) "A means–end chain model based on consumer categorization processes," *Journal of Marketing*, 48 (2): 60–72.

Halkias, G. and Kokkinaki, F. (2010) "How schema incongruity influences consumer responses: exploring the degree of incongruity for different sources of discrepancy," in A. Bradshaw, C. Hackley, and P. Maclaran (eds.), *European Advances in Consumer Research*, 9, London: Association for Consumer Research, (in press).

Halkias, G. and Kokkinaki, F. (2011) "Increasing advertising effectiveness through incongruity-based tactics: the moderating role of consumer involvement," *Journal of Marketing Communications*, DOI:10.1080/13527266.2011.592346.

Hastie, R. (1980) "Memory for information which confirms or contradicts a general impression," in R. Hastie, E.B. Ebbesen, R.S. Wyer Jr., D.L. Hamilton, and D.E. Carlston (eds.), *Person Memory: The Cognitive Basis of Social Perception*, Hillsdale, NJ: Lawrence Erlbaum Associates.

Heckler, S.E. and Childers, T.L. (1992) "The role of expectancy and relevancy in memory for verbal and visual information: what is incongruency?," *Journal of Consumer Research*, 18 (4): 475–492.

Houston, M.J., Childers, T.L., and Heckler, S.E. (1987) "Picture–word consistency and the elaborative processing of advertisements," *Journal of Marketing Research*, 24 (4): 359–369.

Keller, K.L. (2003) *Strategic Brand Management: Building, Measuring, and Managing Brand Equity*, Upper Saddle River, NJ: Prentice Hall.

Lange, F. and Dahlén, M. (2003) "Let's be strange: brand familiarity and ad–brand incongruency," *Journal of Product and Brand Management*, 12 (7): 449–461.

Lee, E.-J. and Schumann, D. (2004) "Explaining the special case of incongruity in advertising: combining classic theoretical approaches," *Marketing Theory*, 4 (1–2): 59–90.

Lee, Y.H. and Mason, C. (1999) "Responses to information incongruency in advertising: the role of expectancy, relevancy, and humor," *Journal of Consumer Research*, 26 (2): 156–169.

MacInnis, D.J., Moorman, C., and Jaworski, B.J. (1991) "Enhancing and measuring consumers' motivation, opportunity, and ability to process brand information from ads," *Journal of Marketing*, 55 (4): 32–53.

McQuarrie, E.F. and Mick, D.G. (1996) "Figures of Rhetoric in Advertising Language," *Journal of Consumer Research*, 22 (4): 424–438.

Mandler, G. (1982) "the structure of value: accounting for taste," in M.S. Clark and S.T. Fiske (eds.), *Affect and Cognition: The Seventeenth Annual Carnegie Symposium on Cognition*, Hillsdale, NJ: Lawrence Erlbaum Associates.

Meyers-Levy, J. (1988) "Factors affecting the use of conceptually driven and data driven processing," *Advances in Consumer Research*, 15: 169–173.

Meyers-Levy, J. and Tybout, A.M. (1989) "Schema congruity as a basis for product evaluation," *Journal of Consumer Research*, 16 (1): 39–54.

Meyers-Levy, J., Louie, T.A. and Curren, M.T. (1994) "How does the congruity of brand names affect evaluations of brand name extensions?," *Journal of Applied Psychology*, 79 (1): 46–53.

Mick, D.G. (1992) "Levels of subjective comprehension in advertising processing and their relations to ad perceptions, attitudes, and memory," *Journal of Consumer Research*, 18 (4): 411–424.

Ozzane, J.L., Brucks, M., and Grewal, D. (1992) "A study of information search behavior during the categorization of new products," *Journal of Consumer Research*, 18 (4): 452–463.

Park, C.W., Milberg, S., and Lawson, R. (1991) "Evaluation of brand extensions: the role of product feature similarity and brand concept consistency," *Journal of Consumer Research*, 18 (2): 185–193.

Peracchio, L.A. and Tybout, A.M. (1996) "The moderating role of prior knowledge in schema-based product evaluation," *Journal of Consumer Research*, 23 (3): 177–192.

Percy, L. and Elliott, R. (2005) *Strategic Advertising Management*, New York: Oxford University Press.

Petty, R.E. and Wegener, D.T. (1998) "Attitude change: multiple roles for persuasion variables," in D. Gilbert, S. Fiske, and G. Lindzey (eds.), *The Handbook of Social Psychology*, New York: McGraw-Hill.

Pieters, R., Warlop, L., and Michel, W. (2002) "Breaking through the clutter: benefits of advertisement originality and familiarity for brand attention and memory," *Management Science*, 48 (6): 765–781.

Ratchford, B. (1987) "New insights about the FCB Grid," *Journal of Advertising Research*, 27 (4): 24–38.

Ratneshwar, S. and Shocker, A.D. (1991) "Substitution in use and the role of usage context in product category structures," *Journal of Marketing Research*, 21 (3): 281–295.

Reynolds, T.J. and Gutman, J. (1984) "Advertising is image management," *Journal of Advertising Research*, 24 (1): 27–38.

Rossiter, J.R., Percy, L., and Donovan, R.J. (1991) "A better advertising planning grid," *Journal of Advertising Research*, 31 (5): 11–21.

Sjödin, H. and Törn, F. (2006) "When communication challenges brand associations: a framework for understanding consumer responses to brand image incongruity," *Journal of Consumer Behaviour*, 5 (1): 32–42.

Smith, E.E. and Medin, D.L. (1981) *Categories and Concepts*, Cambridge, MA: Harvard University Press.

Stayman, D.M., Alden, D.L., and Smith, K.H. (1992) "Some effects of schematic processing on consumer expectations and disconfirmation judgments," *Journal of Consumer Research*, 19 (2): 240–255.

Sujan, M. (1985) "Consumer knowledge: effects on evaluation strategies mediating consumer judgments," *Journal of Consumer Research*, 12 (1): 31–46.

Sujan, M. and Bettman, J.R. (1989) "The effects of brand positioning strategies on consumers' brand and category perceptions: some insights from schema research," *Journal of Marketing Research*, 26 (4): 454–467.

Sujan, M., Bettman, J.R., and Sujan, H. (1986) "Effects of consumer expectations on information processing in selling encounters," *Journal of Marketing Research*, 23 (4): 346–353.

Thompson, D.V. and Hamilton, R.W. (2006) "The effects of information processing mode on consumers' responses to comparative advertising," *Journal of Consumer Research*, 32 (4): 530–540.

Törn, F. and Dahlén, M. (2008) "Effects of brand incongruent advertising in competitive settings," *European Advances in Consumer Research*, 8: 234–239.

Wansink, B. and Ray, M.L. (1996) "Advertising strategies to increase usage frequency," *Journal of Marketing*, 60 (1): 31–46.

10 Expert elicitation method selection process and method comparison

Angela Dalton, Alan Brothers, Stephen Walsh, Amanda White, and Paul Whitney

Introduction

Expert judgment is a critical component of forecasting methods and can be implemented by a variety of forecasting tools. Expert judgment has long been employed in computational modeling to develop and structure Bayesian networks (BNs). As the result of advanced computational algorithms that enabled BNs to learn from data, modelers increasingly find expert judgment useful, and even crucial in some cases, in dealing with data limitation problems and calibrating model parameters (Walsh *et al.* 2010; Henrion *et al.* 1991). Due to their technical simplicity and methodological transparency, we focused on four forecasting methods regarding their linkability with Bayes net models: conjoint analysis, probability elicitation, judgmental bootstrapping, and prediction markets. We recognize that different decision-making environments and conditions undergird each of these methods, and their application is largely influenced by the characteristics of the research questions at hand. We do not propose to incorporate all existing judgmental forecasting methods into the integrative framework, or identify the most superior forecasting method, which would be beyond the scope of this project. Our goal is to shed some exploratory light on integrative modeling with the hope of ushering in additional research interests in modeling complex decision-making and risk-assessment problems.

In the following sections we describe the four candidate methods, their theoretical background, areas of application, empirical successes, and limitations. We will then identify the characteristics of decision tasks that are suited to each of the methods. In order to understand the feasibility of linking these methods with computational models, we conducted a small-scale elicitation exercise with a group of researchers. Based on the evaluation results, we developed a methodological comparison matrix to demonstrate each method's strengths and weaknesses. To illustrate the linkability with computational models, we provide an example of applying conjoint analysis to calibrate Bayes net models. This chapter concludes by discussing potential applications of integrating expert elicitation with computational frameworks and our research progress to date.

Methods overview

Conjoint analysis

Conjoint analysis is a form of preference structure measurement (Netzer *et al.* 2008; Kroes and Sheldon 1988; Srinivasan and Park 1997) that estimates the part-worths of multiple attributes of a product, service, or policy option in relation to its overall utility, and uses stated preferences to predict choice behavior (Luce and Tukey 1964). Conjoint analysis can be used when an item being selected can be viewed as a combination of the attributes, the attributes have some intrinsic exchangeability, and the utility of the item is related to the bundle of attributes.

In our modeling approach, scenarios can be constructed and presented as profiles often seen in conjoint analysis. Experts will rank or rate each profile in a pairwise fashion. Through an iterative process, experts will indicate their preferences measured by relative likelihood or probability beliefs for each profile pair. Currently, commercial conjoint analysis tools are widely available and are able to handle complex research designs (Orme 2009). Computer-based conjoint analysis is highly interactive, capable of parsing product part-worths, producing real-time preference calculations, and predicting choice behavior. Researchers recently developed a novel integrative conjoint analysis user interface and algorithms that enable rapid pairwise scenario generation and facilitate the integration of data and expert domain knowledge to calibrate Bayesian network model parameters (Walsh *et al.* 2010). The utilization of this newly developed conjoint analysis tool will help diminish the setup costs of integrated modeling.

In contrast to its major competitor for our considerations (i.e., probability elicitation), computer-based conjoint analysis does *not* require the researcher or facilitator to play an active role in interacting with, motivating, or training domain experts, as model information is provided in the user-friendly web-based interface and the procedural instructions are straightforward. Further, probability elicitation commonly employs an exercise that helps the expert calibrate their opinions and conceptions of a probability. For example, the exercise would help make the distinction between a fairly unlikely event (small probability) vs. an extremely rare event (infinitesimal probability). Conjoint analysis is a clear standout in this regard since relative likelihood is a more natural quantity to conceive for one who is not accustomed to the idea of a probability (cf. Renooij 2001; Gustafsson *et al.* 2007).

With regard to linking conjoint analysis to computational models, the methodology has a long history of being applied to regression-type models. The success of conjoint analysis under commonly used computational methods such as regression has inspired confidence that the methodology could be generalized to elicit a more general probability structure in the form of a Bayes net. Further, the ability to aggregate information across multiple experts, a persistent challenge in probability elicitation, is an inherent trait of conjoint analysis.

Probability elicitation

Probability elicitation is a formal process of obtaining probability estimates in a manner designed to minimize bias and overconfidence. While there are variations in the method (Morgan and Henrion 1990), the basic procedure most commonly in use is the SRI/Stanford protocol developed in Spetzler and Staël von Holstein (1975) and Staël von Holstein and Matheson (1979).

The probability elicitation process typically consists of five or six steps (Hora 2007). The process begins with identifying, recruiting, and motivating domain experts, during which the facilitator establishes rapport with the experts and determines if there are any motivational biases that could influence the results. Then, in the structuring phase, experts will identify relevant state and conditioning variables, and agree on the unit of analysis. Next, the experts are trained to be aware of how heuristics and biases could affect their judgment. During the probability encoding stage, probability assessments are elicited from the experts. The method will vary depending on whether the variables on which the probabilities being elicited are discrete or continuous. Direct elicitation techniques such as fixed probability, fixed value, and the PV method (in which experts provide both probability and value assessments), as well as indirect techniques such as pairwise betting and a lottery, can be used. Probability assessments can be influenced by the elicitation techniques used. For instance, direct probability assessment techniques are more straightforward, efficient, and inexpensive than indirect probability assessment techniques such as betting or lottery (Renooij 2001; Lau and Leong 1999). In the final stage, the facilitator explains and reviews the results with the experts and verifies the consistencies of their assessments. In case of assessment divergence, individual results are shared and discussed with the group to determine if a consensus estimate can be obtained (for a discussion on combining probability elicitation information across experts, see Clemen and Winkler 1999).

Probability elicitation places a considerable emphasis on facilitator-expert interaction, therefore requiring the facilitator to play an active role throughout the elicitation process. For this reason, Spetzler and Staël von Holstein (1975) caution against the use of computer-based probability elicitation applications for the loss of facilitators' "balancing effect" with regard to minimizing experts' biases. Probability elicitation also requires substantial time commitment from domain experts. The time involved in an elicitation process can be even longer for experts who are unfamiliar with the process. Newly developed computer-based applications can enhance the efficiency of elicitation. For example, Lau and Leong (1999) developed an automated system to prompt domain experts to revise their responses in case of inconsistencies in their assessments. The detection of expert judgmental inconsistencies can be performed by automating the calculation of the Inconsistency Index (Lau and Leong 1999; Saaty 1980). In the absence of inconsistencies, the probability responses are directly entered into a theoretic analytic model such as Bayes nets as prior probabilities.

Prediction markets

Prediction markets aggregate diverse opinions and expertise by providing an opportunity to purchase a contract (stock) on a particular outcome tied to real-world events such as sports and elections. Trading in a prediction market is similar to many market exchanges: buyers and sellers discuss, negotiate, and stall until a mutually agreeable price is reached on the outcome. Prediction markets have been extensively practiced with some well-known markets such as the Iowa Election Markets and companies such as INTRADE and the CNN futures market. A wealth of background information and references on the application of prediction markets can be found in Yeh (2006). Empirical successes of these markets in forecasting are documented extensively (Wolfers and Zitzewitz 2004; Hayek 1945). Evidence suggests that prediction markets are among the best-performing predictors of election outcomes. Berg *et al.* (2001) review the performance of the Iowa Electronic Market and point out that it outperformed major polling services in predicting presidential elections. Prediction markets also perform well at the more micro-level analysis, such as cities and districts, where other methods often fail to aggregate information at such levels of analysis (Wolfers and Leigh 2002). In addition, the learning curve required for setting up a prediction market is relatively low. Depending on the contract structure, the price of the contract at any point in time can be interpreted as the expectation or the probability forecast for the occurrence of a future event. Given this interpretation, it is conceivable that the prediction market can be linked to computational models such as Bayes nets. For example, we may consider multiple markets, which represent different scenarios under the model and aggregate the market prices of the scenarios into a Bayes net. Note, however, the application of prediction markets to policy analysis, particularly analysis pertaining to sensitive policy issues such as terrorism, has been subject to harsh media criticism and public scrutiny (Looney 2004; Wolfers and Zitzewitz 2004), thus prompting researchers to give serious consideration to its potential political and ethical consequences.

Judgmental bootstrapping

Judgmental bootstrapping translates experts' assessments into a quantitative model by regressing expert forecasts against the given information. Dawes (1971) accomplished seminal work in this area. More recent development demonstrates its broad applicability. For example, the application of judgmental bootstrapping summarized by Armstrong (2001) spans the disciplines of psychology, education, personnel, marketing, and finance. The rationale behind judgmental bootstrapping is that human judgments are subject to random errors and the model applies expert rules more consistently. Methodological comparative studies suggest judgmental bootstrapping often outperforms individual expert assessment. Dawes (1979), for instance, points out that even quantitative models constructed using "non-optimal" criteria can predict significantly better than expert judgment. Similarly, across those studies reviewed by Armstrong (2001), the bootstrapping forecast was more accurate than individual expert assessment in 8 of 11 of the studies.

The demonstrated forecasting accuracy, technical simplicity, and methodological transparency associated with judgmental bootstrapping warrants its incorporation into this study. It is also worth noting that, even with this technical transparency, the judgmental bootstrapping model can be viewed as a likelihood-based model similar to a dynamic Bayes net (DBN) for summarizing the relationship between the indicators in the narrative and the predictive outputs of interest. We represent this model form generically as $p(\cdot|\theta)$, where θ are model parameters (in this case, the regression model coefficients) and the form of $p(\cdot|\theta)$ is a Gaussian or normal distribution.

Task characteristics and method selection

We argue that no single probability assessment method discussed above is clearly superior to any other methods with regard to eliciting and aggregating expert opinions and that the choice of methods should be the function of the characteristics of the decision tasks and cost–benefit calculations. Method comparison studies also suggest that each judgmental method has its advantages and disadvantages and that method selection should be task-specific. Kadane and Winkler (1988) compared the probabilities elicited from lotteries, scoring rules, and promissory notes under the condition of non-stake and with-stake elicitations, respectively, and their results suggest that the elicited probabilities are congruent with experts' utility functions only if experts have no stake in the elicited subject. Camerer (1981) specifies that although judgmental bootstrapping consistently outperforms raw expert opinion, it is more appropriate for problems for which the criterion information is sparse and the prediction environment vague. Green *et al.* (2007) argue that while prediction markets are more appealing than traditional group decision-making procedures and are more likely to reveal real participant preferences, its predictive accuracy can be influenced by a host of factors such as transaction volume, framing of bets, and ethical considerations. In Table 10.1 we provide an overview of the task characteristics that are suitable for each judgmental method. Within the framework of integrative modeling with BNs, the elicitation task for different nodes in a BN may be most profitably rendered through the method that is most appropriate for attributes of the elicitation tasks and available expertise.

Method evaluation and comparison

When setting up elicitation for parameter estimations, logistical factors such as costs, technological and human resource requirements, and time commitments are all important decision-making considerations. In conjunction with the task characteristics, these considerations will help modelers and experts choose the most cost-effective method that promises the best possible estimations for computational models.

Table 10.1 Task characteristics for method selection

Method	*Task characteristics*	*Limitations*	*Sources*
Conjoint analysis	Appropriate when experts are not comfortable with providing direct probabilistic estimations but are more willing to provide comparative assessments	May not be appropriate if a node's attributes cannot be clearly and reliably identified; does not provide opportunities for exchanging reasoning and justification; difficulty dealing with judgmental inconsistencies	Bradlow (2005)
Probability elicitation	Appropriate when experts are willing to invest considerable time to participate, have some knowledge of statistics, and are comfortable with providing estimates in probabilistic terms	Aggregation of opinions to achieve consensus might be challenging; training sessions might be needed for experts who are not well versed in probabilities and statistics; time consuming and therefore not suitable if decisions need to be reached within a short time frame	Kadane and Wolfson (1998); Dewispelare *et al.* (1995); Renooij (2001)
Prediction markets	When an event can be clearly and specifically defined as contracts; a host of contract formats can be used in prediction markets such as: binary option, index, futures, and spread betting, each of which is designed to provide a different kind of forecast (Green *et al.* 2008: 4).	Not all elicitation problems can be framed as a prediction market contract and even well-defined contracts may still have loopholes. Does not provide opportunity for exchange of reasoning and justification, which can be as important as the outcome itself. Thin markets may not perform well. May be open to manipulation and is subject to ethical limitations	Green *et al.* (2007); Yeh (2006); Wolfer and Zitzewitz (2004)
Judgmental bootstrapping	Suitable when criterion information and prediction environment is vague or limited	Experts must be able to specify properly differential cue weights; cue information may not exist and cue selection can bias prediction; there is limited generalizability across samples; misweighting in judgments can result in bias	Camerer (1981)

To evaluate the advantages and limitations of the methods, the authors conducted a pilot session of method evaluation. We brought a diverse range of expertise to the discussion: mathematics, statistics, computational modeling, psychology, political science, and public policy. The group collectively determined a set of judgmental criteria against which the methods were to be evaluated. Key criteria considerations for elicitation method selection include:

- expert-method interactivity and model representation of experts' feedback;
- setup costs, especially resource requirements;
- potential to link with available and well understood risk analyses;
- consistent with good forecasting practices;
- reusable and updatable as new scenarios become available, new experts' assessments are rolled on, or previous ones updated or removed;
- availability of expertise and technology
- has a demonstrated application track record and the technology is valid and reliable.

We proceeded to rate each method individually using all of the above criteria on a Likert scale of 1 to 5, on which 1 means the least suitable method and 5 the most suitable. After the ratings were completed, we discussed their respective scores in view of each of the criteria and provided a justification and rationale for their scores. We were allowed to revise their scores based on the discussion and feedback. This review and revision process was repeated until a group consensus was reached. After the scores for each of the criteria were collectively evaluated, these scores were summed to generate an overall score for each method. The overall scores provide a quantitative frame of reference for the methods to be compared and assessed in terms of their suitability for integrating with computational modeling methods such as BNs and systems dynamic models. Next, we were asked to reflect on our justification and scores, and to share a final written evaluation of the top two method choices for integrative modeling, in this case BN models. The following are the excerpts from the final written evaluation:

> I vote for Conjoint Analysis and Prediction Markets … I believe conjoint analysis and judgmental bootstrapping are similar in that they require attributes and levels to work and that prediction markets and expert elicitation are also similar in that they provide a probability number for a specific outcome. I also believe that conjoint analysis and judgmental bootstrapping give more information about the specific attributes that could be useful, but they may not apply to all types of stimulus sets (in particular not to sets that don't have well defined parts).
>
> My top two choices are Prediction markets and Conjoint Analysis because they are:

1. Entertaining
2. Excellent empirical record of accomplishment
3. This is a new research area and we can contribute to this line of research through our project
4. Flexibility
5. Can be linked to BN
6. Instant feedback possible
7. Strong theoretical foundation.

I like Prediction Markets (PM) and Conjoint Analysis (CA). Reasons include:

- PM and CA offer "different" output
- Group discussions communicated to me more enthusiasm for CA and PM
- Both seem easily implementable.

Based on the evaluation and feedback, Table 10.2 provides an overview of the method evaluation. Special attention was paid to key factors, such as the degree of interactivity with end users/decision-makers, costs, suitability for tasks, resource requirements, linkage with BN, forecasting success, and political considerations. These characteristics should provide helpful guidance for matching specific decision tasks with appropriate methods. For example, if a problem has a short decision-making time window without substantial resources for building original software, then using commercial conjoint analysis tools would be suitable. If a decision problem involves politically sensitive information, then extra caution should be exercised when considering prediction markets.

Empirical application of conjoint analysis to model calibration

As mentioned previously, calibrating BN models could be challenging due to lack of data or poor data quality, which makes experts' opinion sometimes the sole viable source of information. To benefit from the knowledge and insights from the available experts, we designed an elicitation tool to use conjoint analysis in gathering experts' assessments to calibrate a Bayes net model. In this example, the model focuses on group schism (Sani 2005). The outcome node, schismatic intentions, is said to be influenced by the group members' identification, which is affected by members' perception of group coherence. Group coherence is conditioned on the intensity of intergroup conflict. At the same time, the presence of group identity subversion may weaken group identification and group coherence, and intensify members' expressed feelings of dejection or agitation. These relationships are quantified in accordance with Sani (2005) and are depicted in the Bayes net model. Figure 10.1 shows a fragment of the model.

Table 10.2 Method integration criteria comparison

	Conjoint analysis	*Probability elicitation*	*Prediction markets*	*Judgmental bootstrapping*
Interactivity, level of engagement	Medium–high; interpersonal and computer-expert interaction	High; extensive interaction between facilitators and experts	Medium; user-market instrument interaction	Low–medium
Setup costs/resource	Low–medium; commercial service/tools readily available	Medium–high	Medium–high if markets are created anew	Medium
Linkage with BN	Mathematically feasible	Readily linkable and has been done	Mathematically feasible	Mathematically feasible
Empirical track record – known successes in forecasting	Good performance well documented	Perform well but subject to heuristic biases	Outperforms opinion polls in predicting elections, etc.	Performs better than unaided expert assessment
Political sensitivity or ethical considerations	Minimal	Minimal	Could be controversial	Minimal

As Figure 10.1 shows, the nodes are connected by edges and each node has several states, such as low and high, or present and absent. The nodes and node states are analogous to product attributes and attribute levels in conjoint analysis. By applying this analogy into an elicitation tool, we developed a user interface designed to mimic the format of a classic conjoint analysis with pairwise profiles, and to generate profiles randomly from the associated Bayes net model. Figure 10.2 provides a screen capture of the conjoint analysis elicitation tool.

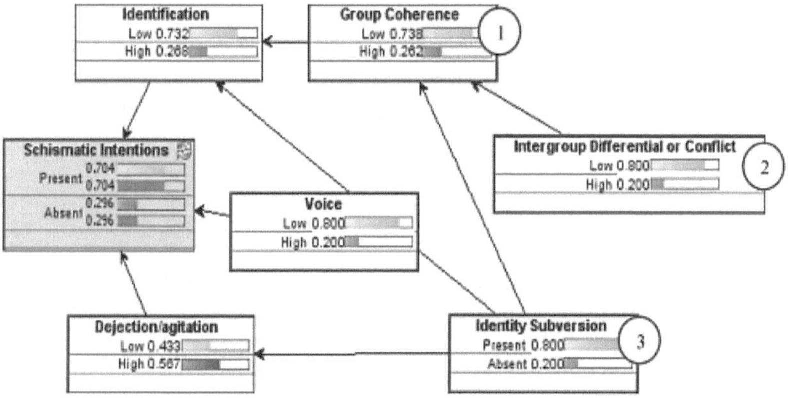

Figure 10.1 Fragment of group schism Bayes net model based on Sani (2005).

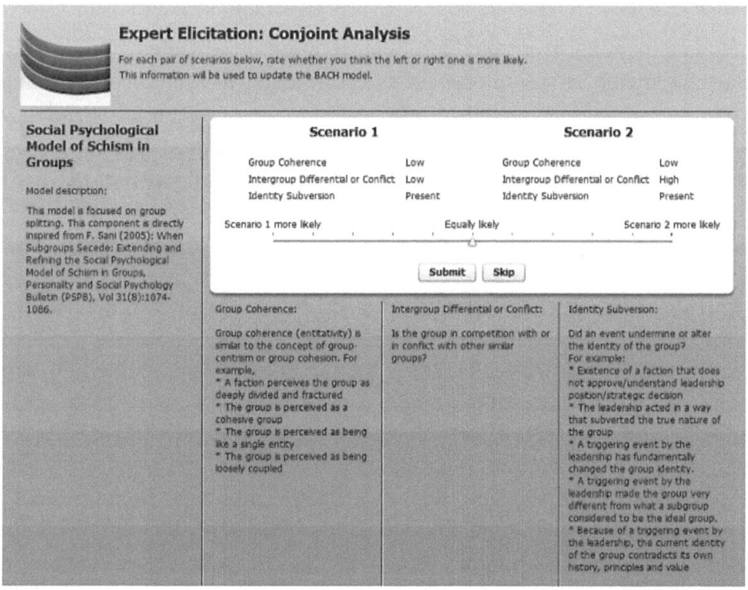

Figure 10.2 Conjoint analysis expert elicitation user interface screen capture with group schism Bayes net model.

Each profile consists of three nodes from the model and the profiles are so designed that the states of at least one of the nodes in the profiles vary. Model description and node definitions are displayed on the screen for easy reference. Experts were recruited to provide feedback in response to the elicitation question. In this case, the question of interest is the relative likelihood of the profile pair. To indicate their assessments, the experts adjust the position of the anchor along the scale accordingly and submit their input, after which a new set of profiles is displayed instantaneously for further elicitation. This process iterates until sufficient information is gathered. The data is then stored in a database for post-elicitation analysis.

To make experts' input suitable for model calibration, mathematical formalism is developed to "translate" the preference judgment into probabilistic assessment needed by the model, expressed as follows:

$$\hat{\theta} = \underset{\theta}{\arg\min}\, g(\theta \mid Y, x_{right}, x_{left})$$

where Y_i represent the ith assessment elicited from the experts; θ denotes the Bayes net model parameters. Let $x_{i,right}$ and $x_{i,left}$ represent the right and left side scenario, respectively, and n the number of elicitations. The heuristic purpose is to compute model parameters so that they are consistent with experts' opinion. The objective function is

$$g(\theta \mid Y, x_{right}, x_{left}) = \sum_{i=1}^{n} \left[Y_i - \Phi_\gamma \left(\frac{\Pr(x_{i,right} \mid \theta)}{\Pr(x_{i,left} \mid \theta)} \right) \right]^2 + \lambda r(\theta)$$

where Φ_γ is a mapping from the likelihood ratio onto the scale of Y, γ represents a scaling parameter, $r(\theta)$ is a regularization function to account for incomplete scenario coverage and for incorporating prior parameterization information, $\lambda > 0$ represents the degree of regularization, and $\Pr(X \mid \theta)$ represents the BN. We have successfully implemented the optimization problem in *R* (Walsh *et al.* 2010). A follow-up experiment using this tool was conducted and related analysis was implemented in C (Walsh *et al.* forthcoming).

Conclusion

As a critical first step toward advancing the integrative social-behavioral modeling framework, we demonstrated a consensus-based decision-making approach to evaluating and selecting expert elicitation methods in view of their suitability for linking with computational modeling methods. We examined the strengths and weaknesses of linking four well-established elicitation methods: conjoint analysis, probability elicitation, prediction markets, and judgmental bootstrapping, with computational models. We identified elicitation task characteristics and limitations for each method. We also conducted an evaluation study to assess methodological and logistical advantages and disadvantages of the four methods to provide a relatively comprehensive view and a better understanding of the feasibility and effectiveness of method integration. As a follow up to this study, a web-based conjoint analysis user interface and algorithms were developed, and successfully incorporated subject matter experts' opinion to calibrate Bayes net models (Walsh *et al.* 2010). Future research will seek to advance the social-behavioral modeling research thrust and expand the integrative modeling endeavor to include additional elicitation methods and apply the current research outcome to a broader range of social-behavioral research inquiries.

References

Armstrong, J.S. (ed.) (2001) *Principles of Forecasting: A Handbook for Researchers and Practitioners*, Norwell, MA: Kluwer Academic Publishers.

Berg, J.E., Forsythe, R., Nelson, F.D., and Rietz, T.A. (2001) *Results from a Dozen Years of Election Futures Markets Research*, Iowa City, IA: University of Iowa School of Business.

Bradlow, E.T. (2005) "Current issues and a 'wish list' for conjoint analysis," *Applied Stochastic Models in Business & Industry*, 21 (4–5): 319–323.

Camerer, C. (1981) "General conditions for the success of bootstrapping models," *Organizational Behavior and Human Performance*, 27: 411–422.

Clemen, R.T. and Winkler, R.L. (1999) "Combining probability distributions from experts in risk analysis," *Risk Analysis*, 19: 187–204.

Dawes, R.M. (1971) "A case study of graduate admissions: applications of three principles of human decision making," *American Psychologist*, 26: 180–188.

Dawes, R.M. (1979) "The robust beauty of improper linear models in decision making," *American Psychologist*, 34: 571–582.

Dewispelare, A.R., Herren, L.T., and Clemen, R.T. (1995) "The use of probability elicitation in the high-level nuclear waste regulation program," *International Journal of Forecasting*, 11 (1): 5–24.

Green, K.C., Armstrong, J.S., and Graefe, A. (2007) "Methods to elicit forecasts from groups: Delphi and prediction markets compared," *International Journal of Applied Forecasting*, 8: 17–20.

Gustafsson, A., Herrmann, A., and Huber, F. (eds.) (2007) *Conjoint Measurement: Methods and Applications*, Berlin: Springer Verlag.

Hayek, F.A. (1945) "The use of knowledge in society," *The American Economic Review*, 35 (4): 519–530.

Henrion, M., Breese, J.S., and Horvitz, E.J. (1991) "Decision analysis and expert systems," *AI Magazine*, 12 (4): 64–91.

Hora, S.C. (2007) "Eliciting probabilities from experts," in W. Edwards, R.F. Miles, and D. v. Winterfeldt (eds.), *Advances in Decision Analysis: From Foundations to Applications*, Cambridge: Cambridge University Press.

Kadane, J. and Wolfson, L.J. (1998) "Experiences in elicitation," *Journal of the Royal Statistical Society: Series D (The Statistician)*, 47 (1): 3–19.

Kadane, J. and Winkler, R.L. (1988) "Separating probability elicitation from utilities," *Journal of the American Statistical Association*, 83 (402): 357–363.

Kroes, E.P. and Sheldon, R.J. (1988) "Stated preference methods: an introduction," *Journal of Transport Economics and Policy*, 22 (1): 11–25.

Lau, A.-H. and Leong, T.Y. (1999) *PROBES: A Framework for Probability Elicitation from Experts*, American Medical Informatics Association Annual Fall Symposium.

Looney, R. (2004) "DARPA's policy analysis market for intelligence: outside the box or off the wall?," *International Journal of Intelligence and Counterintelligence*, 17 (3): 405–419.

Luce, R.D. and Tukey, J.W. (1964) "Simultaneous conjoint measurement: a new type of fundamental measurement," *Journal of Mathematical Psychology*, 1: 1–27.

Morgan, M.G. and Henrion, M. (1990) *Uncertainty: A Guide to Dealing with Uncertainty in Quantitative Risk and Policy Analysis*, Cambridge: Cambridge University Press.

Netzer, O., Toubia, O., Bradlow, E., Dahan, E., Evgeniou, T., Feinberg, F., Feit, E., Hui, S., Johnson, J., Liechty, J., Orlin, J., and Rao, V. (2008) "Beyond conjoint analysis: advances in preference measurement," *Marketing Letters*, 19 (3–4): 337–354.

Orme, B.K. (2009) "Which conjoint method should I use?," *Sawtooth Software Research Paper Series*. Sequim, WA: Sawtooth Software Inc., available at www.sawtoothsoftware.com/download/techpap/whichmth.pdf.

Renooij, S. (2001) "Probability elicitation for belief networks: issues to consider," *Knowledge Engineering Review*, 16 (3): 255–269.

Saaty, T.L. (1980) *The Analytic Hierarchy Process: Planning, Priority Setting, Resource Allocation*, New York and London: McGraw-Hill.

Sani, F. (2005) "When subgroups secede: extending and refining the social psychological model of schism in groups," *Personality and Social Psychology Bulletin*, 31 (8): 1074–1086.

Spetzler, C.S. and Staël von Holstein, C.-A.S. (1975) "Probability encoding in decision analysis," *Management Science*, 22 (3): 340–358.

Srinivasan, V. and Park, C.S. (1997) "Surprising robustness of the self-explicated approach to customer preference structure measurement," *Journal of Marketing Research*, 34 (2): 286–291.

Staël von Holstein, C.-A.S. and Matheson, J. (1979) *A Manual for Encoding Probability Distribution*, Menlo Park, CA: SRI International.

Walsh, S., Dalton, A., White, A., and Whitney, P. (2010) "Parameterizing Bayesian network representations of social-behavioral models by expert elicitation: a novel application of conjoint analysis," Paper read at *Workshop on Current Issues in Predictive Approaches to Intelligent and Security Analytics (PAISA)*, 2010 IEEE International Conference on Intelligence and Security Informatics at Vancouver, BC.

Walsh, S., Shippert, T., Dalton, A., White, A., and Whitney, P. (forthcoming), *Parameterizing Bayesian Networks through Elicitation by Conjoint Analysis: Application to a Model for Assessing States' Nuclear Proliferation Propensity*, mimeo.

Wolfers, J. and Leigh, A. (2002) "Three tools for forecasting federal elections: lessons from 2001," *Australian Journal of Political Science*, 37 (2): 223–240.

Wolfers, J. and Zitzewitz, E. (2004) "Prediction markets," *Journal of Economic Perspectives*, 18 (2): 107–126.

Yeh, P.F. (2006) "Using prediction markets to enhance US intelligence capabilities: a 'Standard & Poor's 500 Index' for intelligence," *Studies in Intelligence*, 4, available at: https://www.cia.gov/library/center-for-the-study-of-intelligence/csi-publications/csi-studies/studies/vol50no4/using-prediction-markets-to-enhance-us-intelligence-capabilities.html.

Part V

Decision-making in social interaction

11 Does sharing payoffs affect gender differences in accountability?

Jordi Brandts and Orsola Garofalo

Introduction

Recent studies argue that when a decision-maker expects to have to justify *ex post* her[1] choices in front of an audience, the likelihood that she will make the right decision is significantly higher (Lerner and Tetlock 1999; Vieider 2011a).

An important issue in these studies is whether the degree of individual accountability, measured as the level of effort the participants provide during the resolution of the task, depends on the characteristics of decision-makers and members of the audience. Gender is, in our opinion, one of the most potentially interesting variables. For example, in relation to the presence of women both in CEO positions and on the board of directors of corporations, it is crucial to understand whether e.g., a monitoring committee spurs accountability differently depending on the gender of decision-makers and committee members.

In a recent study (Brandts and Garofalo 2011) we conduct an experiment to study the behavior of males and females in front of male and female audiences. We found differences in the effects of accountability on men and women, depending on the gender of the audience. On the one hand, this study finds that women's accountability, as measured by the number of correct answers in a decision task, is not influenced by the audience's gender. On the other hand, men's accountability turns out to be strongly affected by the audience's gender and increases when they are paired with a male audience. Vieider (2011b) provides supplementary evidence about this issue. In his study the comparison is between decision-making without an audience and accountability in front of an all-male audience. With respect to gender he finds that "males and females perform approximately equally when they are unaccountable, male participants accountable in front of a male audience perform significantly better."

Both Vieider (2011a, 2011b), and Brandts and Garofalo (2011) study accountability in an environment in which the payoffs of both decision-maker and audience do not depend on the performance in the decision task.

In the present study we extend Brandts and Garofalo's (2011) experiment to a context in which individuals make incentivized decisions and share payoffs with the audience members. Thus, the goal of our experiment is to shed light on whether the effects of accountability on men and women respond differently to monetary incentives and distributional concerns.

The advantage of this new context is that it appears better suited to describe real-world situations, such as the above-mentioned example of CEOs and boards of directors, in which accountable or unaccountable decisions have consequences not only for the decision-maker but also for the committee that asks for an explanation of each choice made.

What are our research hypotheses for the new study? The most basic economic intuition would suggest that incentives should tend to equalize the performance of men and women. In other words, in the absence of incentives it may be natural for various factors to influence behavior, but with incentives men and women will behave like *homo oeconomicus*.

Brandts and Garofalo (2011) found no differences in female behavior depending on the audience's gender, and important differences in men's behavior. The above intuition would imply that the introduction of incentives should eliminate any differences in behavior.[2] One also has to consider the second new element of our experimental environment, the fact that the audience earns exactly the same amount as the decision-maker. Purely selfish individuals will not be affected by this fact, and individuals who are positively affected by others' payoffs can be expected to be additionally motivated by the audience payoff. Hence, overall we expect no gender differences in the average number of correct answers in the decision task.

Contrary to this expectation, our results show that females' level of accountability in an incentivized context is influenced by the audience's gender, and that male participants in this new context do not behave differently depending on the audience's gender. Below we discuss possible explanations of this result.

The chapter is organized as follows. In the second section we present the experimental design. In the third section we present the data and the results. In the fourth section, we conclude.

Design of the experiment

Participants were recruited by email using a database (ORSEE) of students at Universitat Autònoma de Barcelona, who voluntarily registered in the database to participate in previous experiments. We collected data for 66 participants, of whom 32 are women (13 of them participate at the experiment with a female audience and 19 with a male audience) and 34 are men (17 of them participate with a female audience and 17 with a male audience).

Each subject could participate only in one session and was randomly allocated to a male or female audience. As reported in Table 11.1, the average age of participants was around 24, and 29 for the audience members; the percentages of students in social sciences, sciences, and humanities refer only to the participants, they do not include individuals in the audience. The audience is composed of three people (either three women or three men) recruited from the PhD students at Universitat Autònoma de Barcelona. In the instructions we specify that

Table 11.1 Summary statistics

Individual characteristics	*Male*	*Female*
Age participant (average)	22.26	24.88
Age audience (average)	27.28	30.68
Degree/Master in social science (%)	51.52	61.29
Degree/Master in science (%)	36.36	16.13
Degree/Master in humanities (%)	12.12	22.58

Note
Degree/Master indicates participants' type of study.

the audience is composed of three experts in that specific kind of task, so that each participant is aware of that before starting the resolution of the task.[3]

On average, each session takes about 30 minutes. Participants are free to arrive during a period of time of three hours. All subjects (both players and audience members) were paid a variable amount plus a show-up fee of €5 only for the participants. Participants are paid a variable amount based on the number of correct answers they choose in order to incentivize the effort in the resolution of the task. This is explained in more detail below. The average amount earned by the participants was €10.

The experiment involves the analysis of a treatment represented by pairing individuals with an audience of the opposite gender. Overall, there are four gender pairs: female participant–male audience; female participant–female audience; male participant–female audience; male participant–male audience.

Each session takes place in two rooms: the Audience's Room and the Resolution Room. The Audience's Room is a *semi-empty* room containing only a big table in which the participant sits on one side and the audience on the opposite side. The audience stays in the room for the duration of the experiment, waiting for the arrival of each participant. Each meeting with the participant is held in private. The Resolution Room is a big room in which there are ten desks for the resolution of the task.

The session is divided into several parts. In the first part, the experimenter hands to the participant the first part of the instructions (see Appendix) in which the more general conditions of the experiment are explained, and then the experimenter accompanies the participant to the Audience's Room for the first meeting with the audience. The task of the audience during the meeting is to hand to the participant the second part of the instructions, a document to be filled in with personal information, the task sheets, and to explain in detail the rules of the experiment (in particular, how the payoffs are shared between them and the participant). During this meeting, the participant can observe the audience members for the first time, and thereby she creates her own impression about them.

The main part of the experiment consists of solving the task and justifying the options chosen in front of the audience. The audience and the participant earn the same variable amount depending on the participant's choices (e.g., if a participant earns €10 the audience earns €10 as well, which is eventually divided equally among the audience members).

Before the participant leaves the Audience's Room, she is supposed to answer a couple of comprehensive questions about the sharing payoffs rules. These questions are important in order to make sure the participant carefully understands that she will share the overall amount earned with the audience. Afterwards, the experimenter accompanies the participant to the Resolution Room (a room used only for the resolution of the task), where she has to solve the task.

Once the participant has solved all six problems, she raises her hand and the experimenter then accompanies the participant to the Audience's Room for the explanation in front of the audience. The last part of the experiment starts: the participant justifies the decisions made.[4] At the end of the explanation, the audience communicates to the participant the number of correct answers she chose and the overall amount earned. Then the participant leaves the room and goes to the check-in desk to sign the receipt for the payment.

In the experiment, the audience plays an *active* role even if the members of the audience are not asked to interact with the participant during the resolution of the task. The *active* role is given by the sharing rules of the payoffs. They earn as much as the participant gains with the correct resolution of the task. However, the audience is asked to exhibit a neutral behavior and to only pay attention to the participant during the explanation. We asked the members of the audience to be serious during the first meeting and the explanation, but not to *directly* stress or pressure the participant.

The task consists of six problems in which the participant has to choose between simple and compound prospects (as in Bar-Hillel 1973; Holtgraves and Skeel 1992; Vieider 2011a; Brandts and Garofalo 2011). Bar-Hillel (1973) reported an example in which subjects were asked to choose between one of two events. Three types of events were used: (1) simple events, such as drawing a red ball from an urn containing 50 red balls and 50 black balls; (2) conjunctive events, such as drawing a red ball seven times in succession, with replacement, from a bag containing 90 red balls and 10 black balls; and (3) disjunctive events, such as drawing a red ball at least once in seven successive tries, with replacement, from a bag containing 10 red balls and 90 black balls. A significant majority of subjects chose the conjunctive event (probability of 0.48) rather than the simple event (probability of 0.50); they also preferred the simple event rather than the disjunctive event (probability of 0.52). These biases can be explained as effects of an anchoring and adjustment process (Holtgraves and Skeel 1992; Tversky and Kahneman 1974b; Kruglanski and Freund 1983). The stated probability of the elementary event (successful at any stage) provides a natural starting point for the estimation of the probabilities of both conjunctive and disjunctive events. Since the adjustment from the starting point is typically insufficient, the final estimates remain too close to the probability of the elementary events in both cases (Tversky and Kahneman 1974a).[5]

The problems are all of the same type but with different levels of analytic difficulty. Lower numbers of extractions in the compound event makes the calculation easier and should thus increase the choice of the superior event. In the problems chosen, the compound probability to draw the winning balls is always lower than the simple prospect probability (see Appendix).

Data and results

Our dataset contains general details about each subject and each member of the audience. In particular, for each participant we have the gender, age, name of the degree or Master she is currently attending, and the name of the faculty. In addition, we record the time each subject spends on the resolution of the task.

The choices made by the participants are encoded as dummy variables, with 1 indicating the choice of the normatively superior event (simple event), and with 0 the compound event. These dummies are summed for all six choice pairs to obtain a general index ranging from 0 to 6.

Descriptive statistics

Figure 11.1 shows the average index values in the unpaired cases, first by male and female audience, and second by male and female participants. Panel A shows that the mean number of superior simple event choices in the whole sample is 2.4 with the male audience and 2.0 with the female audience. Panel B reports that, independently of the audience's gender, men choose on average 2.8 simple event choices, and women about 1.5 out of six. We find a statistically significant difference only in the group considering the participant's gender.

Figure 11.2 shows the average index values once we take into account gender pairings. The left (right) part of the graph reports the values referring to male (female) participants when they justify their choices in front of the male or female audience. Female participants in the male audience treatment choose, on average, 2.0 superior choices out of 6; yet, with a female audience the number of superior choices goes down to 0.8 out of 6. The difference between the two averages is statistically significant at the conventional level ($p=0.02$). This result indicates that female participants in front of the male audience pay more attention in the resolution of the task; in contrast, in front of a female audience the level of accountability strongly decreases.

Turning to male participants, we do not find any significant difference between the two audience treatments ($p=0.87$). The level of accountability in the male sample is not affected by the audience's gender; they applied the same level of effort during the resolution of the task.

Controlling for the time spent to solve the task, we do not find any significant difference comparing female and male participants nor comparing by the audience's gender.[6]

Finally, we run a significance test to compare the average number of superior choices taken by female participants paired with the male audience (mean value

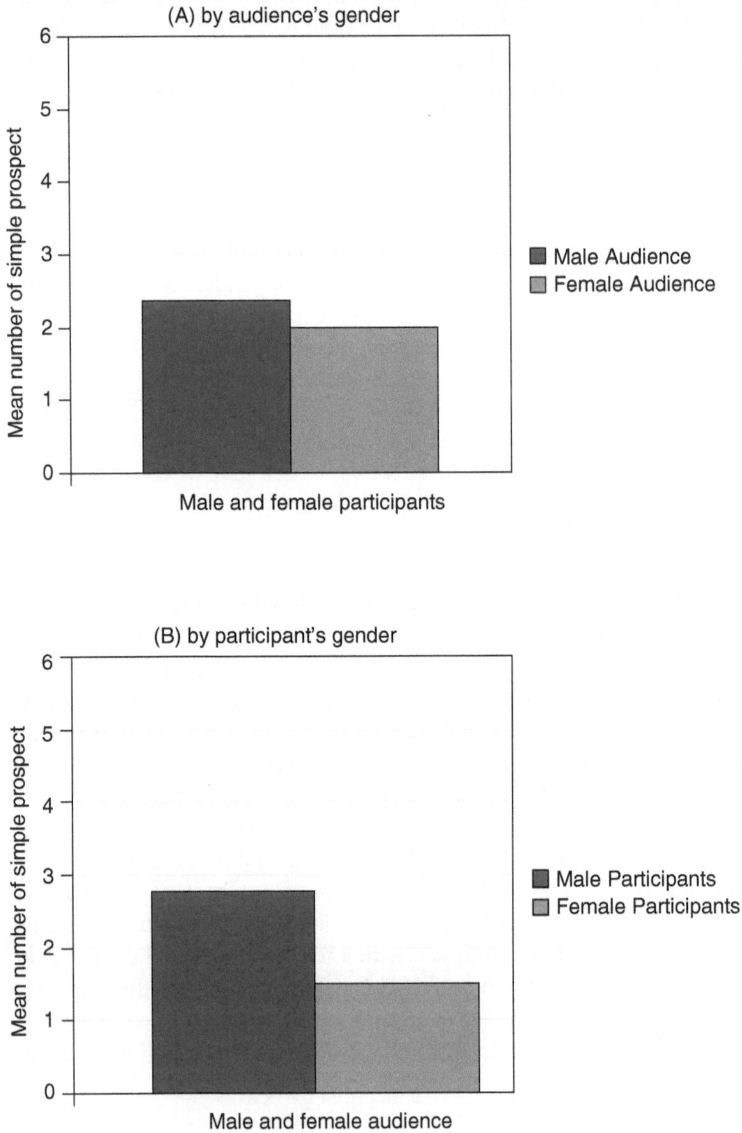

Figure 11.1 Mean number of choices of the simple prospect event.

2.0) to the mean number of superior choices taken by male participants paired with both male and female audience (respectively, mean value 2.76 and 2.88). We do not find any statistical significance between the average number of superior choices taken by female and male participants. Therefore, it is the behavior of women in front of women that is special.

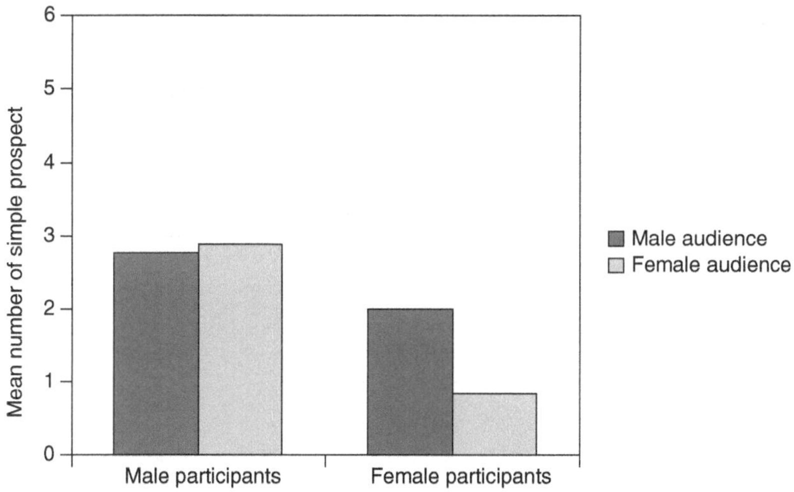

Figure 11.2 Mean number of choices of simple prospect event, by gender pairings.

Regression analysis

Table 11.2 shows the results of OLS regressions, separately for men (columns 1 and 2) and women (columns 3 and 4), in which the dependent variable is the sum of the superior simple event choices – i.e., the number of correct decisions. The main explanatory variable is a treatment equal to one in which audience and participant's gender is the opposite; in addition, we control for the player's age and her field of study (three categories are considered: social science, science, and humanities; humanities is used as a reference group).

Our results show that being paired with the opposite gender has a positive and statistically significant effect for women. By contrast, the effect is quantitatively small and statistically insignificant for men.

We test the robustness of the findings above as in Brandts and Garofalo (2011). Specifically, we estimate an Ordered Probit (see Table 11.2, Panel B) to take into account the ordered structure of our dependent variable. We explore the validity of our results within a smaller range of the dependent variable, excluding participants that choose all right or all wrong answers. Finally, we compute bootstrapped standard errors (using 500 replications) to deal with the limited sample size. Our results (unreported to save space) are in all cases qualitatively unchanged. Females' level of accountability is strongly affected by the gender of the audience; on the other hand the level of accountability in the decision process of the male participants is not affected by the gender of the audience.

Table 11.2 Regression results: dependent variable: sum of simple superior prospect choices

	Male participants		*Female participants*	
	(1)	(2)	(3)	(4)
Panel A: OLS				
Treatment	0.118 (0.725)	–0.120 (0.760)	1.154** (0.436)	1.154** (0.445)
Age of participant		0.027 (0.175)		–0.014 (0.039)
Panel B: Ordered Probit				
Treatment	0.053 (0.367)	–0.079 (0.375)	0.875** (0.371)	0.940** (0.401)
Age of participant		0.017 (0.088)		–0.021 (0.035)
Education dummies	No	Yes	No	Yes
Number of participants	34	33	32	31

Notes

Panel A and B report respectively the results of the OLS and the Ordered Probit regressions. In both panels, columns 1 and 2 report the results using the sample of male participants; columns 3 and 4 report the results using the sample of female participants. The dependent variable in columns 1–4 is an index built as a sum of the number of the superior simple prospect choices; the index ranges from 0 to 6 (each simple event choice is counted as 1, and each participant answers to six questions). The treatment represents the group in which the participant's gender is the opposite of the audience's. Columns 1 and 3 report the regressions using as an explanatory variable the gender of the audience; columns 2 and 4 report the regressions using, in addition to the gender of the audience, the participants' age and the education dummies. Robust standard errors are reported in parenthesis. *, ** and *** denote significance at 10%, 5%, and 1%, respectively.

Concluding remarks

We have conducted an experiment to further examine the relationships between gender and accountability. We use a context-based accountability situation in which decision-makers are paid depending on their performance and have to share their payoffs with the audience members (either all men or all women) that call for an explanation of each decision made. We found that the audience's gender influences females' level of accountability during the decision; by contrast, males' accountability is not affected by the audience's gender. Our results are unexpected since they reject our intuitive working hypothesis that in the presence of monetary incentives the gender pairings of decision-maker and audience would have no effect on performance. At the same time we can say that the differences we find (and the absence thereof) are in line with some of our original ideas on the interaction between gender pairings and accountability. The main initial motivation for studying this topic stems from thinking about situations where top female executives have to justify themselves in front of all-male boards. Our initial hypothesis was that women would be affected by the gender of the audience while men would not, as we find in the data reported above.

However, what is puzzling is the comparison between the gender pairing effects on men's behavior that we found in Brandts and Garofalo (2011) and the effect for women found in the present study. One possibly relevant factor is that, in our previous study, we measured blood pressure and heart rate for each participant involved in the experiment. We did this to detect potential gender differences in stress during the resolution of the task. We then found that blood pressure and heart beat variations only had minor effects on behavior and, therefore, decided to exclude these measurements from the experiment for this chapter. However, the fact that the blood pressure was taken and the heart beat was measured could itself have altered participants' alertness and have lead to differences in the behavior of men.

In the defense of the design used in this chapter we can say that both the presence of the incentives and the absence of the blood pressure and heart beat measurements seem to us to be the most natural environment. At any rate, what the results of our studies suggest is that the interaction between gender pairings and accountability may need to be studied in more depth, perhaps with larger datasets and also using different tasks.

Appendix

Date ________ Name and Surname______________________________ Code _1_

Choice between Simple and Compound Prospects

In the following pages you find 6 problems. In each problem you are asked to choose between two options. One option allows you to extract only one ball from a bag; the other one allows a "multiple extraction" from a different bag. In the multiple extraction option, the ball you have extracted will be placed back in the bag and the balls in the bag will be mixed before you extract again, so as to keep the composition of the bag constant.
These rules are valid for all the problems below. Please pay attention to the composition of the bags and the number of extractions because both vary across problems.
Please, mark one of the two options for <u>each</u> problem. Choose the option you prefer in this way:

__X__Option # (extract ## time from a bag with ## red and ## green balls, win if red)
______Option # (extract ## time from a bag with ## red and ## green balls, win if red)

or

______Option # (extract ## time from a bag with ## red and ## green balls, win if red)
__X__Option # (extract ## time from a bag with ## red and ## green balls, win if red)

Please, take into account that the amount of money you will win (additional to the 5€ show-up fee) depends only on your choices.

For each amount you win the audience will receive the same amount. For example:

-if after solving all the problems you win 0 €: 0€ will be for the audience and 0€ for you.
-if after solving all the problems you win 4 €: 2€ will be for the audience and 2€ for you.
-if after solving all the problems you win 8 €: 4€ will be for the audience and 4€ for you.
-if after solving all the problems you win 12€: 6€ will be for the audience and 6€ for you.
-if after solving all the problems you win 16€: 8€ will be for the audience and 8€ for you.
-if after solving all the problems you win 20€: 10€ will be for the audience and 10€ for you.
-if after solving all the problems you win 24€: 12€ will be for the audience and 12€ for you.

Figure 11.3 Task and instructions.

Code _1_

Comprehension questionnaire

Please mark the correct answer.

1. If you answer correctly to one question and obtain 4 €, the audience gain:
   a. 0 € and you gain 4 €
   b. 4 € and you gain 4 €
   c. 2 € and you gain 2 €

2. If you answer correctly to two questions and obtain 8 €, the audience gain:
   a. 4 euros y tú ganas 4 euros
   b. 8 euros y tú ganas 4 euros
   c. 6 euros y tu ganas 2 euros

Problem 1

You were given a choice between two options to win 4€.
Option A allows you to extract one ball from a bag containing 10 red and 10 green balls. If you extract a red ball, you win 4€; if you extract a green ball, you win nothing.
Option B allows you to extract 7 balls in sequence with replacement from a bag containing 18 red balls and 2 green balls. If all 7 balls extracted are red you win 4€; if one or more of the balls extracted are green, you win nothing.

What would you choose?

_____Option A (extract 1 time from a bag with 10 red and 10 green balls, win if red)
_____Option B (extract 7 times from a bag with 18 red and 2 green balls, win if 7 times red)

Problem 2

You were given a choice between two options to win 4€.
Option A allows you to extract 5 balls in sequence with replacement from a bag containing 15 red balls and 5 green balls. If all 5 balls extracted are red you win 4€; if one or more of the balls extracted are green, you win nothing.
Option B allows you to extract one ball from a bag containing 5 red and 15 green balls. If you extract a red ball, you win 4€; if you extract a green ball, you win nothing.

What would you choose?

_____Option A (extract 5 times from a bag with 15 red and 5 green balls, win if 5 times red)
_____Option B (extract 1 time from a bag with 5 red and 15 green balls, win if red)

Figure 11.3 Task and instructions (*continued*).

Code _1_

Problem 3

You were given a choice between two options to win 4€.
Option A allows you to extract 7 balls in sequence with replacement from a bag containing 16 red balls and 4 green balls. If all 7 balls extracted are red you win 4€; if one or more of the balls extracted are green, you win nothing.
Option B allows you to extract one ball from a bag containing 5 red and 15 green balls. If you extract a red ball you win 4€; if you extract a green ball, you win nothing.

What would you choose?

_____Option A (extract 7 times from a bag with 16 red and 4 green balls, win if 7 times red)
_____Option B (extract 1 time from a bag with 5 red and 15 green balls, win if red)

Problem 4

You were given a choice between two options to win 4€.
Option A allows you to extract one ball from a bag containing 2 red and 18 green balls. If you extract a red ball, you win 4€; if you extract a green ball, you win nothing.
Option B allows you to extract 4 balls in sequence with replacement from a bag containing 10 red balls and 10 green balls. If all 4 balls extracted are red you win 4€; if one or more of the

Figure 11.3 Task and instructions (*continued*).

Code _1_

Problem 5

You were given a choice between two options to win 4€
Option A allows you to extract 6 balls in sequence with replacement from a bag containing 15 red balls and 5 green balls. If all 6 balls extracted are red you win 4€; if one or more of the balls extracted are green, you win nothing.
Option B allows you to extract one ball from a bag containing 4 red and 16 green balls. If you extract a red ball, you win 4€; if you extract a green ball, you win nothing.

What would you choose?

_____Option A (extract 6 times from a bag with 15 red and 5 green balls, win if 6 times red)
_____Option B (extract 1 time from a bag with 4 red and 16 green balls, win if red)

Problem 6

You were given a choice between two options to win 4€.
Option A allows you to extract one ball from a bag containing 6 red and 14 green balls. If you extract a red ball, you win 4€; if you extract a green ball, you win nothing.
Option B allows you to extract 2 balls in sequence with replacement from a bag containing 10 red balls and 10 green balls. If all 2 balls extracted are red you win 4€; if one or more of the balls extracted are green, you win nothing.

What would you choose?

_____Option A (extract 1 time from a bag with 6 red and 14 green balls, win if red)
_____Option B (extract 2 times from a bag with 10 red and 10 green balls, win if 2 times red)

Figure 11.3 Task and instructions (*continued*).

INSTRUCTIONS

Part 1

We thank you for coming to the experiment. The purpose of the experiment is to study how people make decisions in a particular situation.

The experiment will take place in two rooms: one in which you will make the decisions (Room A) and the other one in which you will have to justify your choices in front of an audience composed of three experts in this kind of problem (Room B).

What is the meaning of the number?

The experimenter will give you a number that indicates where you have to sit in Room A. As soon as you finish making your decision, you have to give the number to the audience, which you will find in Room B.

Now what do you have to do?

As soon as you finish registering for the experiment, you have to go to Room B where you will receive the questions you have to answer.

At the end of the experiment we will pay you as follows:

5 euros (show-up fee) + a variable amount that will depend on your choices

Figure 11.3 Task and instructions (*continued*).

INSTRUCTIONS

Part 2

In few seconds we will give you 6 decision problems and you have to take a decision for **each** problem. You can take your time in making the decisions, **there are no time limits.**

After you have made the decision you have to raise your hand and the experimenter in the room will accompany you to the room where you have to justify your decisions.

At the end of the experiment we will pay you as follows:
5 euros (show-up fee) + a variable amount that will depend on your choices

The variable amount you gain will be divided equally between you and the audience. In the text of the decision task you will find a more detailed explanation about the sharing of your earnings.

Figure 11.3 Task and instructions (*continued*).

Acknowledgments

We are grateful to Mario Daniele Amore, Christina Rott, Carles Solà and Alessandro Innocenti (editor). We also thank the Generalitat de Catalunya through an SGR-grant and the Antoni Serra Ramoneda, UAB – Caixa Catalunya Research Chair for providing financial support. Finally, we are grateful to all the researchers that participated in the experiment as audience members. All errors remain our own.

Notes

1 In our experiments we will look at both male and female decision-makers. However, in the text we will for simplicity always use the female pronoun when referring to decision-makers.

2 As such, this result might be consistent with Niederle and Vesterlund (2007), who examine whether men and women of the same ability differ in their selection into a competitive environment. As pre-treatment they run some sessions in which both male and female participants are paid with a piece-rate scheme in a non-competitive setting; their results indicate that there are no gender differences in performance.

3 For the composition of the audience we chose people older than the participants in order to make it credible to students that the audience had expertise in the decision task. The audience comprised PhD students, but they were not really experts in this kind of problem.

4 We did not record the explanations because we are not interested in the reasons given to justify the choices; we focus the attention only on the effect that the presence of the audience has on the decisions made before the explanation.

5 Given these findings, making the simple lottery the correct choice allows for a better detection of the effort exerted in making the decision.

6 The average time spent for the resolution of the task by female participants with male and female audience is, respectively, 16.30 and 15.20 minutes, and the difference is not significant ($p=0.77$). Male participants spend on average 21.58 and 18.41 minutes for the resolution of the task in front of a male and female audience, respectively, and the difference is not significant ($p=0.47$).

References

Bar-Hillel, M. (1973) "On the subjective probability of compound events," *Organizational Behavior and Human Preferences*, 9: 396–408.

Brandts, J. and Garofalo, O. (2011) "Gender pairings and accountability effects," *Journal of Economic Behavior and Organization*, in press.

Holtgraves, T. and Skeel, J. (1992) "Cognitive biases in playing lottery: estimating the odds and choosing the numbers," *Journal of Applied Social Psychology*, 22: 934–952.

Kruglanski, A.W. and Freund, T. (1983) "The freezing and unfreezing of lay-inferences: effects on impressional primacy, ethnic stereotyping, and numerical anchoring," *Journal of Experimental Social Psychology*, 19: 448–468.

Lerner, J.S. and Tetlock, P.E. (1999), "Accounting for the effects of accountability," *Psychological Bulletin*, 125: 255–275.

Niederle, M. and Vesterlund, L. (2007) "Do women shy away from competition? Do men compete too much?," *Quarterly Journal of Economics*, 122: 1067–1101.

Tversky, A. and Kahneman, D. (1974a) "The framing of decisions and the psychology of choices," *Science*, 211: 453–458.

Tversky, A. and Kahneman, D. (1974b) "Judgment under uncertainty: heuristics and biases," *Science*, 185: 1124–1130.

Vieider, F.M. (2011a) "Separating real incentives and accountability," *Experimental Economics*, in press.

Vieider, F.M. (2011b) "Gender pairings and accountability effects: a comment," Working Paper, Ludwig-Maximilians Univsität München.

12 Social learning and rational choice

Stefano Di Piazza, Letizia Vaccarella, Antonio Dell'Ava, Simona Conti and Antonio Rizzo

Introduction

Decision-making is often presented as a matter of rational choice in an uncertain world (to quote the title of a well-known textbook on the subject). One of the main assumptions associated with this vision is that decision-making is a skill, a crucial skill not only for our survival but for the success of our species (Hastie and Dawes 2010).

We dominate this planet today because of our distinctive capacity for good decision-making: 'Our success as a species arouse not thanks to distinctively acute senses or especially powerful physical capacities but thanks to an exceptional ability to choose appropriate means to achieve our ends' (Hastie and Dawes 2010: 1). Rationality itself is defined as the individual skill in making choices that display a coherence of desired ends and the use of appropriate means for attaining them.

In this picture social relationships barely play a role and this is even truer in neoclassical economics, where agents' preferences, aims and beliefs are privately determined. This state of affairs brings about that rational decision-making is mostly a matter of individual choice even though it is well acknowledged that human 'transaction is the basic unit of analysis' (Williamson 1996: 6).

However, today in the literature of experimental economics, mostly under the influence of Game theorists, the need to differentiate between individual and collective rationality is a growing concern (Innocenti 2004).

The collective and commonly cooperative behaviour humans exhibit, while constituting an issue for economic theories of rationality, are one of the more salient features that distinguish human cognitive abilities from the abilities of other primates. Within the mainstream of cultural psychology (Vygotsky, Bruner, Cole), Michael Tomasello has proposed a theory, corroborated by growing empirical and experimental data, that sees the phenomena of shared intentionality and cooperation as the root of human cognition (Tomasello 1999, 2003; Tomasello *et al.* 2005). According to this position it would be this ability in sharing intention that would have leveraged the special human skill in making successful choices, but the implications of this theory for human rational choice are quite different from what is the current mainstream vision about human decision-making. In the following we will present a brief overview of Tomasello's theory of human cognition and human communication focused around the process of social learning. Following this we will present some empirical evidence to exemplify the implication of this theoretical position for psychology and economics. In closing we claim an increasing attention to the emerging phenomena of we-rationality.

Social learning in apes and humans

In Tomasello's theory, social learning is the key aspect of the cultural origins of human cognition and cultural evolution. Resting on a significant amount of experimental evidence he suggests that apes are not capable of the type of learning from others that makes human cultural evolution possible. Tomasello's

> hypothesis is that the uniquely human ability to understand external events in terms of mediating intentional/causal forces emerged first in human evolution to allow individuals to predict and explain the behaviour of co-specifics and has been transported to deal with the behaviour of inert objects.
>
> (Tomasello 1999: 24–25)

This ability allows 'humans to solve problems in especially creative, flexible, and foresightful ways … powerful transforming role in the process of social learning' (Tomasello 1999: 25). Although chimpanzees learn to use simple tools – such as sticks for fishing for termites and rocks for cracking nuts – and thus may have a simple form of culture, they learn their culture in a very different way from humans, even humans as young as nine months old.

Chimpanzees are good at learning to manipulate their environment to acquire rewards by watching others, but they are not very skilful at learning from others a new behavioural strategy per se. For example, if a mother rolls a log and eats the insect underneath, her child will very likely follow suit. This is simply because the child learned from the mother's act that there are insects under the log – a fact she did not know and very likely would not have discovered on her own. But she did not learn from her mother how to roll a log or to eat insects; these are things she already knew how to do or could have learned on her own. (Thus, the youngster would have learned the same thing if the wind, rather than her mother, had caused the log to roll over and expose the ants.) This has been called emulation learning because it is learning that focuses on the environmental events involved – not on a co-specific's behaviour or behavioural strategy (Tomasello 1999: 29).

In 2005 Tomasello revised his position, arguing that though some non-human primates understand their co-specifics as intentional, they do not possess the ability to share attention and intentions – abilities possessed by human children by, on average, nine months of age. The proposition is 'that human beings, and only human beings, are biologically adapted for participating in collaborative activities involving shared goals and socially coordinated action plans (joint intentions)' (Tomasello *et al.* 2005: 2). Furthermore, young human children can understand that an adult will intentionally instruct them, and will focus on the behaviour of the adult as well as on what the adult's attention is focused on. Chimps focus on the manipulation of the environment to secure a reward; human children focus on and copy the behaviour and intentions of adults without the necessity of an immediate reward. Children can accurately copy a process demonstrated by an adult, such as the use of a rake to secure an out-of-reach object, whereas young apes do not closely copy the technique of the instructor when learning the similar use of a rake (Tomasello 1999: 30). The fact that human children are able to focus on the processes or strategies demonstrated by an instructor and, in general, accurately copy them, is important for the process of cultural transmission and evolution. Imitation learning implies a shift from a dyadic interaction (agent to object; agent to agent) to a triadic interaction (agent, object, agent). For instance, young children share attention with a parent by following the parent's gaze to nearby objects, understanding that they and the parent are jointly attending to the object, and they also interpret parental comments or actions as referring to the object.

The capacity to participate in the intersubjective triangle at a very early age is what makes it possible for young children to learn their language and culture. And the intersubjective triangle not only facilitates language and cultural learning, it is necessary for all human cooperative activity. When engaging in mutual activity involving all forms of cooperation, including cultural learning, there is mutual knowledge of a shared attention focused on an object or goal. Each individual understands that the other has plans involving the shared goal and 'each interactant has goals with respect to each other's goals.... The second important aspect of this [collaborative effort] is the fact that the cognitive representation also contains the self and the other – it is thus a joint intention' (Tomasello *et al.* 2005: 11). The intersubjective triangle is key to social and cultural interaction, cooperation and iterative learning by imitation, and it forms the basis of the ontogenetic contribution to the solution of the learnability problem. The capacity for collective intentionality and the intersubjective triangle allows for the creation of social facts which facilitates the efficient use of widely dispersed private knowledge in society by making possible the construction of social institutions.

Emulation and imitation in chimpanzees and humans

One of the more interesting evidences of the different kind of social learning between humans and chimpanzees centres around the distinction between imitation and emulation, produced by a seminal work of Christina Horner and Andrew Whithen (2005). The question that Horner and Whiten asked was straightforward: what effect, if any, would the availability of causal information have on participants' imitation strategy?

Horner and Whiten (2005) presented children and chimpanzees with a tool-using task that was presented both in a transparent form ('clear box') and also in an opaque form ('opaque box'). The human model initially demonstrated irrelevant actions with a tool and then used the tool to perform a relevant action to retrieve the reward from the box. That the first action was irrelevant to gaining the reward was only apparent with the clear box, but not so with the opaque box (see also McGuigan *et al.* 2007).

Both boxes and demonstrations were presented to the subjects in succession, with a response period directly after. The boxes were presented in one of two conditions: (1) the clear then the opaque box; or (2) the opaque then the clear box. It was predicted that when the clear box was presented first the subject would learn that the first action was irrelevant and so would not replicate it in their response period. However, when the opaque task was presented first no such information could be learned and so it was expected that the subjects would copy both the irrelevant and relevant actions. An observer who adopted an imitative approach would be reproducing all of these modelled actions, whereas an observer who reproduced only the relevant actions would be demonstrating a more emulative approach.

Since it has been shown that children's imitation is modulated by an assessment of an observed action's rationality – for example, they copy a demonstrator's action when that action is freely chosen, but less when it is forced by some constraint (Gergely *et al.* 2002; Schwier *et al.* 2006) – we could expect the children in the transparent box condition to omit the experimenter's unnecessary steps. To phrase the prediction more formally, one would expect children to imitate when no causal information is available, but to emulate – to reproduce the adult's goal via more efficient means – when some of the observed actions are visibly unnecessary.

Surprisingly, the chimpanzees conformed exactly to this prediction. Whereas chimpanzees in the opaque condition copied all of the experimenter's actions approximately 60 per cent of the time, in the clear condition they virtually never reproduced the visibly unnecessary steps. In other words, the chimpanzees switched between imitation and emulation in a rationally optimal manner. The children's pattern of responding was a puzzlingly different story. In the opaque condition children showed a strong tendency to imitate all of the adult's actions, just as the chimps had done. In the clear condition, however, children failed to omit the now visibly unnecessary steps; they continued to copy all of the adult's actions, despite the fact that two-thirds of the action sequence was obviously superfluous. There was in fact no statistically significant difference between children's responses in the opaque and clear conditions. Rather than imitating in a rational and selective way, children appeared to blindly copy all of the adult's actions without any regard for their causal necessity. This result was replicated in other studies and there is also some evidence that when aged between 2–3 years and 4–5 years the imitation of superfluous actions does not decrease, but rather increases (McGuigan *et al.* 2007).

In the following we present two pilot studies devoted to exploring the hypothesis that together with an I-rationality we should consider a we-rationality. That is, a coherence of desired ends and the use of appropriate means for attaining them, that springs right away from the shared intentionality process, which can be considered one of the basic processes of the cultural-historical approach to human cognition, and more precisely the process that would allow the *genetic law of cultural development:*

> Every function in the child's cultural development appears twice: first, on the social level, and later, on the individual level; first, between people (interpsychological) and then inside the child (intrapsychological). This applies equally to voluntary attention, to logical memory, and to the formation of concepts. All the higher functions originate as actual relationships between individuals.
>
> (Vygotsky 1978: 57)

In the first study, which is a reply to Horner and Whiten (2005), we tested if the presence/absence of the experimenter would make any difference in emulating or imitating his performance. Moreover, we included in the sample of participants people ranging from 4 to 24 years old, to see what could be the potential trend. In the second study we explored if the opportunity to carry out a joint activity would be sufficient to prevent a direct access to a potential reward.

In other words, we posed the following research questions:

> Would the phenomenon of imitation be exhibited even when the first performer is not even present? This would suggest that a triadic interaction is the kind of interaction we should consider in humans even though we can only observe dyadic pattern.
>
> Facing the choice of getting a potential individual reward (a candy), or performing a joint activity that could even lead to missing the candy, which alternative will children select?

Experiment 1

In this first pilot study we wanted to explore how important the presence of an adult demonstrator while the participants perform their action could be. Would they imitate the demonstrator even when he leaves the scene? Following Horner and Whiten this would be the case, but they did not test this hypothesis directly.

Moreover, since it is controversial whether imitation increases (Whiten 2000) or decreases (Tomasello 1999) with age, we selected a sample of participants ranging from 4 to 24 years old, just to explore potential trends.

Method

- Participants: 20 people between the ages of 4 and 24 years (average age: 10.4) took part in the pilot (Rachele 4; Alessandro 5; Biancamaria 5; Camilla 6; Alessio 6; Giulio 7; Isabel 7; Tommaso 7; Filippo 8; Giada 8;

Martina 9; Marta 9; Lucrezia 13; Adele 13; Giovanni 14; Adrian 14; Gabriello 15; Anna 15; Marta 19; Emanuele 24).

- Apparatus: the apparatus was similar to the one used in seminal works by Victoria Horner and Andrew Whiten (Horner and Withen 2005; McGuigan *et al.* 2007). The apparatus consisted of two boxes (30 × 20 × 20), one in (a) blue wood and one in (b) transparent Plexiglas. Each box had four knobs that the participant could move up and down along vertical guides. Each of the two boxes had a 4 × 6 hole located in the bottom of the front, covered by a 'door' with a horizontal pivot. This simplification of the Horner and Whiten boxes is to simplify the sensory-motor pattern and reduce the amount of causal information.

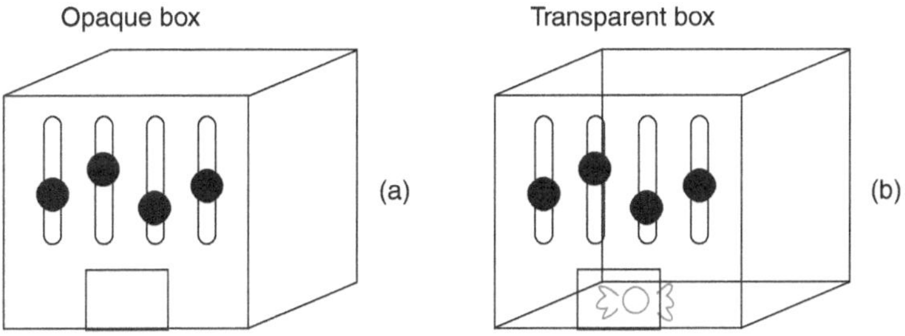

Figure 12.1 Transparent and opaque boxes.

- Design: subjects were assigned randomly to either of two experimental conditions: presence or absence of the experimenter. In each condition half of the group followed the first opaque then transparent box testing and the other half followed the first transparent then opaque box testing. Thus we had a two (presence vs absence) by two (opaque vs transparent) contingency table

- Procedure: subjects were tested individually. When each participant entered the room, he or she was asked to sit on the right-hand side of the experimenter at a small table. From this position, the subject directly faced the box (the opaque one). Once the subject appeared to be comfortable, the demonstrator showed the subject how the boxes 'worked' (Figure 12.2). The demonstrator repeated the motor patterns twice to take the reward then asked the subject to take the reward on her own. Next, the demonstrator took the transparent box and put it in front of the subject, repeated the task demonstration twice and then left the room, instructing the subject to take the reward.
- Coding: the activity was video-recorded (Figure 12.3) and the video-tape of each participant was analysed by recording the occurrence of the sensory-motor patterns in the interaction with each box. We coded as imitation only the participant's activity that reproduced the proper sequence exhibited by

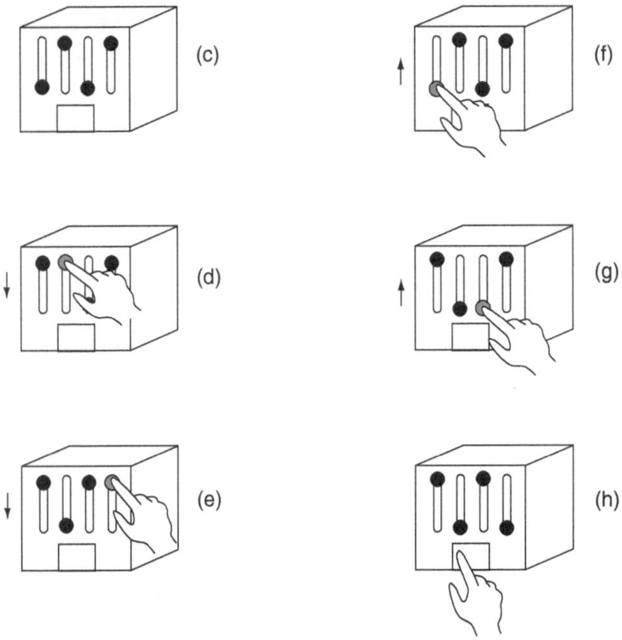

Figure 12.2 The sequence performed by the experimenter.

Note: c = earlier state; d = first movement, bring up the lever; e = second movement, draw down the lever; f = third movement, bring up the lever; g = fourth movement, draw down the lever; h = open door to take the reward.

Figure 12.3 Two shots drawn from the video-recording of the participant performance (experiment 1).

the experimenter. Both the direct access to the reward and other explorative behaviours that included also partial reproduction of the experimenter original pattern was considered emulation.

Results

Table 12.1 reports the distribution of coded behaviour exhibited by the 20 subjects.

Table 12.1 Distribution of coded behaviour exhibited by the 20 subjects

	Presence	*Absence*
Opaque	Imitation 8, emulation 2	Imitation 7, emulation 3
Transparent	Imitation 8, emulation 2	Imitation 8, emulation 2

A contingency table two (presence, absence) by two (opaque, transparent) test carried out on the imitation occurrences showed no significant differences (df = 1, Chi-square = 0.03444, 1; p=0.8528); while overall there was a clear advantage of imitation over emulation (imitation 31 vs emulation 9; df = 1, Chi-square = 12.1; $p \leq 0.01$).

The first experiment suggests that human choice is based on a social interaction contest. That contest plays a fundamental role in circumstances in which these social interactions are not immediately evident. Somehow the social interaction is embodied in the action plans of each subject and emerges in their choice. Therefore, as in economics, the transaction is the basic unit of analysis, so in psychology the fundamental element to understanding the principles that regulate the individuals choices consist of the social interaction. Human social interaction is based on 'joint attention', a process by which two subjects show interest towards the same object and, at the same time, monitor the other's attentive focus. The joint attention is the basis of our capacity to understand ourselves and the others as agents (Tomasello 1999: 97). The joint attention invokes a more sophisticated level of intentional understanding, the shared intentionality.

Experiment 2

Introduction

In a comparative study between chimpanzees and children, Warneken *et al.* (2006) provided experimental evidence that children seem to be motivated not just by the goal but by the cooperation itself. They engaged in social games whose primary goal was the interaction itself, whereas the chimpanzees had little interest in social games without a concrete goal. In this second pilot we tested if the we-intentionality could represent a regard by itself. We built a task in which a demonstrator asks the subject to take a candy, but the setting provides two different possible actions to achieve the goal: take the candy directly or play a game to achieve it.

Method

- Participants: 46 people between the ages of 5 and 55 years participated in this experiment, divided in 23 pairs.
- Apparatus: the apparatus consisted of a vessel on a table that contain eight transparent plastic balls. In each ball was fixed a magnet; in two of the eight balls there were also two rewards. There were two simple 'fishing-rods' made with a stick (1.5 m) and a yarn with an attached magnet.
- Design: the subjects were divided in pairs; most pairs contained subjects of the same age, but in four pairs they had different ages (from 4 to 30 years of difference).
- Procedure: each couple entered the experimental room with a demonstrator. In the room they found two people playing with the fishing rod to obtain the reward. After 30–40 seconds of silent observation, the two players left the rod near the vessel and then left the room. The demonstrator invited the subjects to take the reward and leave the room (Figure 12.5).
- Coding: the video-tape of each pair was analysed by coding how they behaved, specifically, if they:
    - played the game;
    - took the candy immediately.

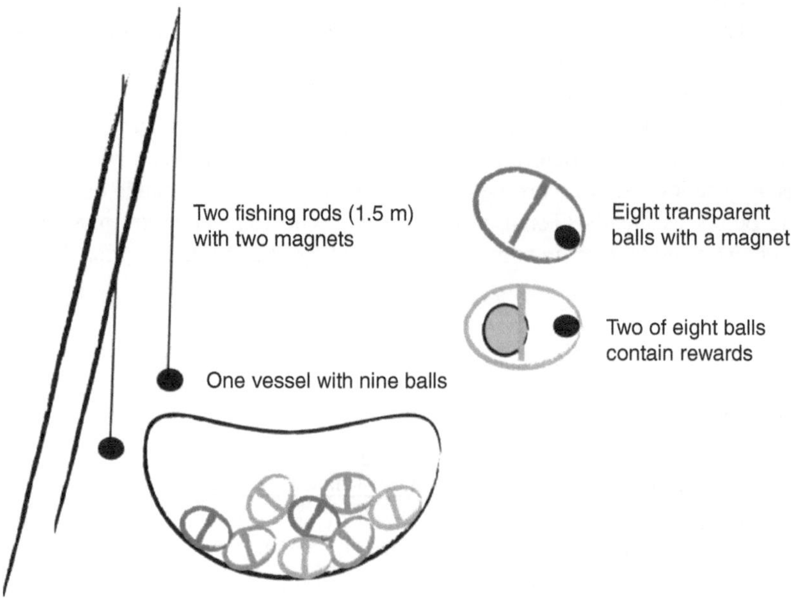

Figure 12.4 The essential components of the experimental apparatus.

(a)

(b)

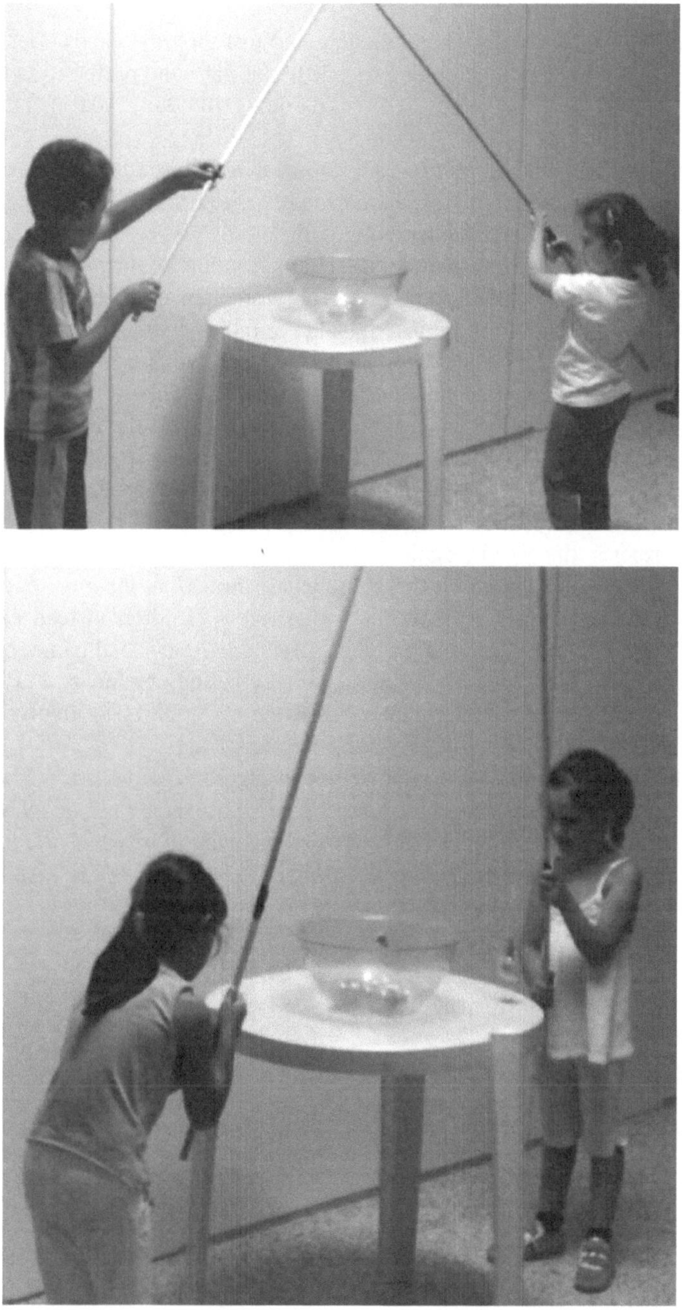

Figure 12.5 Two shots drawn from the video-recording of the participant performance (experiment 2).

Results

Only one pair out of 23 did not play the game and just took the candy. Besides this pair there was one person belonging to a different pair who preferred to take the candy first, then play the game (df=1, Chi-square=34.78; $p \leq 0.01$) (Figure 12.6).

This second experiment, as the first one, shows that children had a particular predisposition to create moments of shared intention towards a common goal. Children try to achieve a goal by interacting with 'others' even when they could achieve the same result with an individual action. Another confirmation of this hypothesis came from a seminal experiment of Warneken *et al.* (2006). They proposed four collaborative activities to some monkeys and some children (18–24 months): two problem-solving activities and two social games that require the presence of an adult female as a partner. The monkeys did not show any interest in the social game, where the collaboration with the experimenter had only entertainment as its purpose, but had success in the problem-solving activities. Moreover, when the human partner stopped acting her role, the monkeys continued to try to achieve their goal alone; they did not even try to involve the partner in the activity again.

Tomasello *et al.* (2005) interpret this result as affirming that the monkeys did not reach a real shared goal with the human partner. Children instead enjoy themselves in the activities, both the problem-solving and the social game; often they turn the problem-solving activity into a game, creating new goals. Furthermore, when the human partner stops interacting, the children try to involve her again in the activity, showing her the role that she 'must' act.

The results of our second experiment point in the same direction; it shows that the children have a motivation to create shared goals, regardless of achievement of an individual gain. Children in some contexts tend to privilege the game

Yes	No	Total	Pair
43	3	46	23

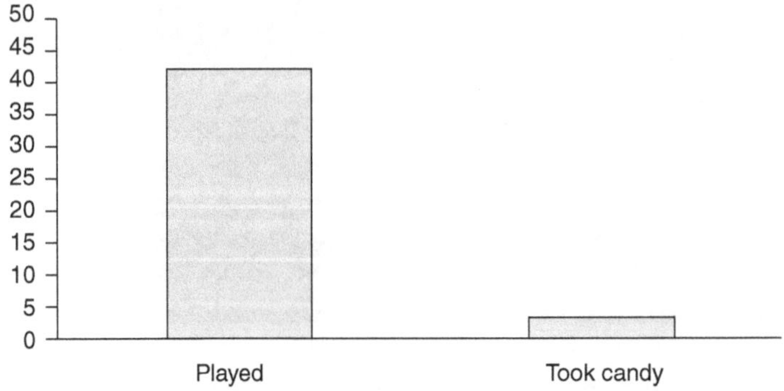

Figure 12.6 Results (experiment 2).

and the collaboration, even in the case that this implicates a postponement of the individual reward.

Conclusion

Many economic theories can hardly address issues that they consider fundamental for properly understanding human transactions. As stressed by De Vecchi (2003: 153), two very basic issues Hayek felt were fundamental to his theory of social spontaneous order were:

> (1) How does an individual classify other people's actions and give them meaning in order to decide what action to take? (2) What makes it possible to coordinate the actions of many individuals who have a partial and personal knowledge of the actual circumstances in which they act?

Both economics and cognitive psychology have mostly considered human interaction with the world as a private matter of a subject facing objects and people as if there was not an immediate perceivable ontological difference among them. But it is important to understand: (1) that we are natural-born dualists and relate with objects and people in very different ways; (2) that transactional relationships are not dyadic but rather triadic. At a minimum, a transaction does not just involve two individuals or an individual and an object, it involves two individuals and the object of the transaction. Culture as a social construct owes its existence, evolution, learnability, and usability to this intersubjective triangle (Gifford 2009).

The important ability of *Homo sapiens* to share intentionality and to participate in the intersubjective triangle cannot be overstated. This triangle, and the capacity for collective intentionality upon which it relies, not only facilitates individual transactions, it makes possible the scaling up of individual interaction into complex spontaneous orders, it makes possible the very existence of most of the components of culture – including all institutions and organizations (Searle 2005) – and, first of all, it makes possible complex human cooperation. The implicit and explicit cultural knowledge that individuals share facilitates the complex social orders, which make possible the efficient decentralized use of both the public and private knowledge of individuals, including various skills, abilities and talents, production technologies and preferences.

The two pilot studies described above support the idea that together with an I-rationality we should consider a we-rationality. The idea is that rationality, defined as coherence of desired ends and the use of appropriate means for attaining them, is not just a matter of individualist choice, since agents' preferences, aims and beliefs are also jointly determined through a we-vision of the world that spring out along the same process that allow the production of human knowledge.

The we-rationality hypothesis suggests a reappraisal of trust and reciprocity; it goes in the direction of 'a theory of trust which can make it rational to repay trust, even when this is contrary to self-interest' (Bruni and Sugden 2000: 26). However, introducing relationships and reciprocity while rethinking the classic model of rationality does not imply substitution of personal with altruistic concern. It is more a matter of taking into account that there are more often than not situations in which people build collective aims. In such situations the rationality of human activity can by understood only by taking into consideration the intentionality shared among the individuals of a given group. The key issues related to the coherence of means and ends is not called into question, but trusting and rewarding the others becomes an intimate component of the collective aims. For example, the Nash equilibrium in the Bach-Stravinsky dilemma represents a formal description of such a situation even though the way in which the dilemma is presented is not psychologically sound and does not allow a proper definition of the shared intentionality process.

The I-rationality model proposed by most of the economic theories seems to describe accurately non-human primate more than human behaviour (Lakshminarayanan *et al.* 2011). The species-unique model of rationality of human beings seems to reflect the social nature of the human cognition: the agent's identity turns out instrinsically relational. In other words, when we analyse the subject's behaviour, we have to consider that there are different paradigms of rationality and that some of them imply a distribution of the 'responsibility' of action. In a sense, the action does not 'belong' exclusively to the agent that performs it, but to the wider social context in which human actions are constituted and take place. Our results support the Vygotskian intelligence hypothesis proposed by Michael Tomasello, and in particular his statement that 'when children internalize generalized collective conventions and norms and use them to regulate their own behavior, this provides for a new kind of social rationality'. The individual rationality that we share with our cousins, chimpanzees, in humans becomes at least associated with a 'shared rationality of interdependence with the other', a social rationality that does not allow us to be alone, for the good, but also for the bad.

References

Bruni, L. and Sudgen, R. (2000) 'Moral canal: trust and social capital in the work of Hume, Smith and Genovesi', *Economics and Philosophy*, 16: 21–45.

De Vecchi, N. (2003) 'The place of gestalt psychology in the making of Hayek's thought', *History of Political Economy*, 35: 135–162.

Gergely, G., Bekkering, H. and Király, I. (2002) 'Rational imitation in preverbal infants', *Nature*, 415: 755.

Gifford, A. (2009) 'Cultural, cognition and human action', *The Journal of Socio-Economics*, 38: 13–24.

Hastie, R. and Dawes, R.M. (2010) *Rational Choice in an Uncertain World: The Psychology of Judgment and Decision Making*, Thousand Oaks, CA: Sage Publications.

Horner, V. and Whiten, A. (2005) 'Causal knowledge and imitation/emulation switching in chimpanzees (*Pan troglodytes*) and children (*Homo sapiens*)', *Animal Cognition*, 8: 164–181.

Innocenti, A. (2004) 'Paradoxes versus formalism in economics: evidence from the early years of game theory and experimental economics', Working paper 433, Quaderni del Dipartimento di Economia Politica, Università di Siena.

Lakshminarayanan, V., Chen, M.K. and Santos, L.R. (2011) 'The evolution of decision-making under risk: framing effects in monkey risk preferences', *Journal of Experimental Social Psychology*, in press.

McGuigan, N., Whiten, A., Flynn, E.F. and Horner, V. (2007) 'Imitation of causally necessary versus unnecessary tool use by 3- and 5-year-old children', *Cognitive Development*, 22: 356–364.

Schwier, C., van Maanen, C., Carpenter, M. and Tomasello, M. (2006) 'Rational imitation in 12-month-old infants', *Infancy*, 10: 303–311.

Searle, J. (2005) 'What is an institution?', *Journal of Institutional Economics*, 1: 1–22.

Tomasello, M. (1999) *The Cultural Origins of Human Cognition*, Cambridge, MA: Harvard University Press.

Tomasello, M., Carpenter, M., Call, J., Behne, T. and Moll, H. (2005) 'Understanding and sharing intentions: the origins of cultural cognition', *Behavioral and Brain Sciences*, 28: 675–691.

Vygotsky, L. (1978) 'Problems of method', in M. Cole (ed.), *Mind in Society*, Cambridge, MA: Harvard University Press.

Warneken, F., Chen, F. and Tomasello, M. (2006) 'Cooperative activities in young children and chimpanzees', *Child Development*, 77: 640–663.

Whiten, A. (2000) 'Primate culture and social learning', *Cognitive Science*, 24: 477–508.

Williamson, O.E. (1996) *The Mechanisms of Governance*, Oxford: Oxford University Press.

Index

Page numbers in **bold** denote tables, those in *italics* denote figures.